# LOOKING GOOD IN PRINT

# LOOKING GOOD IN PRINT

**Deluxe CD-ROM Edition**

**Roger C. Parker**
With Carrie Beverly

VENTANA

**Looking Good in Print, Deluxe CD-ROM Edition**
Copyright ©1997 by Roger C. Parker

**Library of Congress Cataloging-in-Publication Data**
Roger Parker.
    Looking good in print, deluxe CD-ROM edition — 1st ed.
        p.  cm.
    Includes index.
    ISBN 1-56604-471-5
    1. World Wide Web (Information retrieval system)  2. HTML
(Document markup language)  3. Multimedia systems.  I. Title.
TK5105.888.B48  1996
741.6—dc20

                                        96-31280
                                          CIP


First Edition  9 8 7 6 5 4

Printed in the United States of America

Ventana Communications Group, Inc.
P.O. Box 13964
Research Triangle Park, NC 27709-3964
919.544.9404
FAX 919.544.9472
http://www.vmedia.com

**Chief Executive Officer**
Josef Woodman

**Vice President of
Content Development**
Karen A. Bluestein

**Managing Editor**
Lois J. Principe

**Production Manager**
John Cotterman

**Technology Operations
Manager**
Kerry L. B. Foster

**Product Marketing
Manager**
Jamie Jaeger Fiocco

**Creative Services
Manager**
Diane Lennox

**Art Director**
Marcia Webb

**Acquisitions Editor**
JJ Hohn

**Project Editor**
Beth Snowberger

**Developmental Editor**
Michelle Corbin Nichols

**Copy Editor**
Angela Anderson

**Assistant Editor**
Patrick Bragg

**Technical Director**
Dan Brown

**Technical Reviewer**
Richard Jessup

**Desktop Publisher & Illustrator**
Patrick Berry

**Proofreader**
Chris Riffer

**Indexer**
Richard T. Evans, Infodex

**Cover Illustrator**
Alice Whicker

## About the Authors

Roger C. Parker is author of *Newsletters From the Desktop* and *Desktop Publishing With WordPerfect*, both published by Ventana. He has conducted numerous seminars and workshops on desktop publishing design. He is president of The Write Word, Inc., an advertising and marketing firm based in Dover, New Hampshire.

Carrie Beverly is a technical instructor, writer, and electronic publisher for Onsite Advertisers in El Paso, Texas. Her work has been featured in magazines, journals, training books, and on various sites on the Internet. Carrie can be reached at cbeverly@onsite-info.com and P.O. Box 12933, El Paso, Texas 79913.

## Acknowledgments

The authors and publisher wish to express appreciation to many illustrators, graphic designers, and desktop publishers who assisted in the creation of this book. Of particular note is Patrick Berry, who contributed great skill and enormous amounts of time to the project. The following Ventana staff members also contributed to the book by creating illustrations or assisting with the layout of the book: Mike Benson, John Cotterman, Lance Kozlowski, Gail Pheister, and Jenn Rourke.

Carrie Beverly would like to extend special thanks to Chip Staley, researcher and illustrator; Albert Lozoya, graphic artist; and Gilbert J. Hatala and Sylvian M. Gibson, peer editors.

# Contents

## 4   Building Blocks of Design ..................... 93

## 5   The Art of Illustration ..................... 113

## ⌐ Section Three: Solving Design Problems

## Section Four: Appendices

# Introduction

With today's tools, any of us can create documents that are good enough. Constructed with templates, wizards, and even design-error correction, our information is made available in a richer and more fully developed fashion. Yet there's been a change in the big picture: no publication is an island. At least, it doesn't have to be.

*Looking Good in Print* shows you exactly how to design what you need. Whether you're creating a proposal, a brochure, a CD music label, or a Web page, good design will enhance your message.

## A Brave New World

Publishing technology now takes advantage of the power of the computer. Vast amounts of information are made available on CD-ROMs, Web-based online companions, and searchable, instantly-updated electronic catalogs. Publishing no longer means just putting words to paper. Publishing means putting words to screen, too. Designers must transform printed material into great looking electronic information on a CD or on the Web and they must ensure that information designed specifically for a CD or the Web can look good printed as well.

It's no wonder that for many people this brave new world is daunting. Don't panic, *Looking Good in Print* is the reference source that will save you time, money, and energy-wasting anxiety.

This is a design book for computer users with little or no design background who want to make the most of their publishing investment. This book outlines the skills necessary to create attractive, effective materials no matter where and how they are printed.

## What's Changed in This Edition?

So much has changed about design and desktop publishing in the three years since the third edition of this book was published. Hardware has become more powerful and publishing software has expanded with robust and easy-to-use features. It's true that improved tools for traditional desktop publishing have brought publishing technology to the fingertips of even sixth graders, but with the Internet and its corresponding software we all have a whole new medium to work with.

There are other factors operating besides the Net. Self-publishing has risen 200 percent in the last decade because of desktop publishing advances and market forces, and not because of the Internet. The same forces that brought the Net and desktop publishing advances are the same forces that caused heightened interactivity and broadened participation.

Much more of this book is devoted to creating a well-dressed presence regardless of the publishing task at hand. With this approach you get relevant information about using design to stay on your feet while technology and publishing continually reshape the world around you.

You can flatten your learning curve with just-in-time information by learning only those design skills you need when you need them. The power of design can help you to achieve clear, powerful documents that grab attention and reduce information overload.

You'll find this book filled with sensible, easy-to-apply techniques that enable you to glide through the publishing and design matrix with confidence. Whatever your document needs, *Looking Good in Print* can help make your design task easier.

Finally, we've included the Companion CD-ROM with large collections of useful documents, helpful visual galleries about design elements, and a variety of software that can help you create good design for all kinds of projects. We hope to introduce you to new ways to look at your many publishing needs thus saving you hours of research and many wasted dollars.

## Effective Graphic Design

Today's free flow of communication results in a staggering volume of information produced daily, all competing for attention. As both the amount of information and the ways it is delivered continue to expand, getting through the noise level can be challenging.

The decisions concerning what people pay attention to and what they choose to ignore are some of the most critical ones made. Such decisions are often made automatically, almost instantaneously, with little conscious thought or effort. This information gatekeeper, albeit subconscious, is perpetually filtering everything we encounter. Good design enhances a message both by attracting us to read it in the first place and then presenting the content in a series of planned and logical steps that are easy to follow and difficult to resist.

Far from a luxury, design is an absolute necessity. *Looking Good in Print* can help you use various design elements to create documents that attract rather than repel the gatekeepers in all of us.

## The Myth of One-Size-Fits-All

Everything from an annual report to a jelly jar label can be designed, laid out, and created on your computer. Often, however, it takes more than just an application and a slick template to create performance-driven materials.

For every type of publishing software on the market, the program designers have built in a number of templates that are widely used because of convenience. Good or excellent design is more than filling in the blanks.

The fact is, one size does not fit all. Professionals in design and advertising know this. To generate a concept and implement it effectively takes design sense—the sense of what goes where on a page, and how, when, and why it goes there.

To make the best use of the dazzling array of templates that accompany your publishing program, it helps to understand the underlying structure of their design and how to match or modify a template to highlight the salient aspects of your message.

## Who Should Read *Looking Good in Print*?

*Looking Good in Print* is a practical design guide for anyone discovering the challenges of desktop publishing, including:

- Retailers, entrepreneurs, and other professionals who produce their own materials.

- Managers who need to capture and keep the attention of personnel.

- Writers producing their own finished works.

- Students with a variety of communication and report needs.

- Educators who need to interact in print and online in a variety of situations ranging from one-on-one to groups.

So, this book is for anyone—students, professionals, home or office workers, small business owners, and corporate representatives—who, more than ever, want to know and need to understand how to succeed in a communication-drenched world.

Whether you're a serious or casual desktop publisher, experienced graphic artist, or a first-time publisher, *Looking Good in Print* will show you what works, what doesn't, and why.

# How To Use This Book

*Looking Good in Print* is organized into four sections.

Section One, "Elements of Design," describes the underlying principles of design, as well as the basic graphics tools available in desktop publishing, and the techniques for putting them into action. We'll explore the most effective way to use photographs, illustrations, and color with plenty of examples on the Companion CD-ROM.

Section Two, "Putting Your Knowledge Into Action," features the hands-on side of design. We'll demonstrate how the communicating power of a variety of different projects can be enhanced by arranging and rearranging design elements in more effective ways.

In Section Three, "Solving Design Problems," you'll learn to apply the basic tools of design to specific projects as they exist in today's information climate. We'll show you how to recover from design mistakes and how to choose the right design elements for the job.

Section Four, "Appendices," contains useful information about the Companion CD-ROM as well as listings of clip art, photograph, and font resources.

People new to desktop publishing and design should read the book from beginning to end, with special emphasis on Section One. Intermediate and advanced users can probably skip Section One, but will gain valuable insights from reading the remaining sections.

## How Well Should You Know Desktop Publishing?

This book assumes you're already familiar with your publishing hardware and software. It assumes your computer and printer are up and running, and that you've gone through the tutorials included with your software and know its basic commands.

While it's not a substitute for your software's documentation, *Looking Good in Print* will help you get the most from your desktop publishing program. Techniques you once found intimidating, such as containers for objects or drop shadows, are less formidable if you know when and how to use them.

## Hardware/Software Requirements

*Looking Good in Print* is a generic guide, independent of any particular hardware or software. In other words, this book will be a valuable resource, regardless of whether you use a Macintosh or a PC, a dedicated page layout program like PageMaker or QuarkXPress, a state-of-the-art word processing program like WordPerfect or Microsoft Word for Windows, or any of the other fine software programs available. The elements of good design are constant and are achievable in any system. Yet mastering all the features of your publishing program doesn't guarantee great results.

Please note that throughout this book, the terms publication and document are used to refer to any publishing project regardless of size or content: it may be as small as a business card or as large as a book. So please join me and the best designers in finding new eye-catching reasons to break design rules beautifully, to push beyond aesthetics, and to understand and work with nonstop change.

# SECTION ONE

# Elements
# of Design

# Getting Started

## Overview

- Use design guidelines and occasionally vary them to add interest and excitement.

- Group elements that are related.

- Prioritize parts of your message.

- Hand sketch your plans and experiment.

- Use design concepts: relevance, proportion, balance, constraint, and detail.

If design were governed by a set of hard-and-fast rules, computer programs would replace graphic artists, and every advertisement, book, brochure, newsletter, and poster would look the same. The resulting uniformity would rob the world of the diversity and visual excitement that add so much to magazines, newspapers, and even our daily mail!

Most designers will tell you that there are no rules you can't break. In part, they're right, but only in part. Design experts break the rules beautifully. The rules, however, do have validity. You have to know and understand them to break them to add interest and excitement.

Good design stems from a thorough understanding of the building blocks of graphic design.

Good design stems from a thorough understanding of the building blocks of graphic design. You need to identify and group elements that are related—just as a tool goes in the toolbox and keys go on a key chain. But because tools and techniques you use effectively in one situation will not necessarily work in another, we will avoid the trap of declaring "the rules" as confining concrete bunkers. You would do just as well (or better) to consider these flexible guidelines that help you critique your pages.

For example, framing an advertisement in a generous amount of white space may draw a lot of attention to the message and look striking. On the other hand, a large border of white space on a newsletter page may make the text look like an afterthought and create a sparse, uninviting look.

Or consider typeface choices. A combination of Palatino for text and Helvetica for headlines may look great for an instruction manual, but too bland for a flyer or a Web page announcing a jazz concert in the park.

Successful design also evolves from a flexible mind-set:

- A willingness to experiment.

- Confidence in your perceptions.

- Recognition that effective design is a process, not an event.

- Devotion to detail.

Because good design is often transparent, understanding the fundamentals of design—those building blocks that transform a scribbled note into a professional, attractive print communication—will give you the tools you need to use your publishing system to full advantage.

First, let's examine some general principles and preliminary steps that will help you gain solid footing in designing your projects.

# Understanding Your Message

*The design process is simply an extension of the organizing process that began as you developed the concept for your project. Good design makes order out of clutter.*

To the extent that you can define your project's purpose and prioritize the different parts of your message, you can create effective, good-looking print communications. You need a basic sense of logic and order.

If, however, you're unclear about the purpose and are undecided about the sequence and relative importance of the information you want to communicate, you're in muddy and dangerous waters. Your potential audience will sense this.

Let's say you're designing a layout for a newsletter article that includes a series of photographs. Unless you've thought through the role of the photographs in the article, you won't know how to position them. You'll be left with casual reasoning: "I think this photograph looks good here," and so on. But if you know how they relate to the story and each other, you can easily decide on the proper order and size for them.

In this sense, desktop publishing and the tools of graphic design are an extension of your communication skills. They make it easier for you to give visual logic and emphasis to your message. They cannot compensate for a lack of initial planning or organization, which is why the success of your project hinges on this initial stage.

Before starting a project, ask yourself these questions:

- Who is the intended audience?

- What is the basic message you're trying to communicate?

- In what format will readers encounter your message: computer screen, slide presentation, or paper copy?

The tools of graphic design are an extension of your communication skills. They make it easier for you to give visual logic and emphasis to your message.

- What similar messages have your readers encountered from other sources or competitors?

- How does this publication relate to your other publications?

The more you define your project's purpose and environment, the stronger your design will be.

# Planning & Experimenting

*Turn off your computer to plan and experiment.*

Planning typically accounts for 25 to 35 percent of the entire project.

The tools of any trade ultimately impact design. The most sophisticated tools used for planning are paper and pencil—the old technology—to sketch your page ideas. Planning typically accounts for 25 to 35 percent of the entire project. Shocked? Expect your project to take twice as long if you insist on using your computer for planning or decide to design-on-the-fly.

## First Things First

If you were to win the lottery and decide to build a house, you'd likely hire an architect to design your dream home. Your architect, if worth any salt at all, isn't likely to pick a hammer and saw to tackle such a project. Well thought-out plans in the form of blueprints and designs can make big differences in the success, efficiency, quality, and enjoyment of the finished project. First things first.

Although desktop publishing lets you produce graphics on your computer, it's often best to loosely sketch initial ideas and trial layouts with pencil and paper. The most powerful computer system won't teach you how to make effective design decisions. The human mind thinks with ideas and your ideas are unique to you and the moment at hand.

Try out a variety of ideas. When you finish one sketch, begin another. Let speed become a stimulant. You'll need a minimum of three sketches. With two sketches, you can see differences; with three or more, you begin to see patterns and rhythms.

Don't bother with detail for now. Think big: use thin lines for text, thick lines or block lettering for headlines, and happy faces for art or photographs.

You'll find your ideas flow much faster and you'll arrive at a design solution much quicker if you sketch out by hand alternative ways of arranging text and graphics. Good or excellent design solutions don't appear like magic in a burst of creative energy or like a light bulb illuminating over the head of a cartoon character. Successful graphic design emerges from disciplined planning and from playful experimentation.

## Why Not Plan at the Computer?

Even with a 10 zillion–megahertz system, it will take much longer to plan and experiment at your computer. Let's say you can conceptualize the finished page very quickly in your mind. Then, you look up the proper commands in your "mental manual" and translate them into keystrokes or mouse clicks. Once you've finished your document onscreen, the results appear on your monitor—you stop and verify that what you see is what you wanted. If not, you make a change. Or two. Or three or four. This means you've just spent two-thirds of your time processing content and one-third designing!

This effect is called *creeping elegance* and you will find yourself constantly tweaking small elements on the page. As you change one, the next could use some improvement and pretty soon you have a cascading effect (and endless loop) of moving, sizing, placing, and replacing what content is there without adding to or improving the actual content itself or the design.

You'll find yourself working six hours on a simple page and wonder where the time went. The deadline clock won't wait for you and the only remaining option is to dump whatever you've completed and start again.

Hand-sketching helps you focus on the presentation and placement of page elements and appropriate styles. Planning in this context means making decisions about layout, grid, number of page elements, and so on. Experimenting is trying on a few different decisions.

Drawing out your plans first gives you a concrete guideline to follow. And having all your pages planned and in front of you at the same time allows you to check for continuity and a logical flow between pages. This is a fast and efficient method of creating your documents.

## TIP

Don't misinterpret the message here; you can plan using your computer, but it can take up to two or three times as long to complete.

## Seek Inspiration

*Train yourself to analyze the work of others. You can learn a lot from design mistakes.*

Sensitize yourself to examples of effective and ineffective design. If a direct-mail piece you like appears in your mailbox, examine it and determine why it appeals to you. If you see an advertisement in the newspaper that's confusing or too busy, dissect it and identify why it doesn't work.

Sensitize yourself to examples of effective and ineffective design.

## Maintain a Swipe File

Most experienced graphic artists maintain a *swipe file* containing samples they like. A swipe file is simply a collection of materials that are attractive and have especially effective designs. These could be ads, brochures, technical training documents, or just fun pieces.

Make a note to indicate what you like—and dislike—about the pages. Add to your swipe file whenever you see an example of good design, even if it has no immediate bearing on your current project.

The goal here is not to copy the works of others, but to pick up an idea here, an idea there, and combine them into your own projects. Your swipe file can become an idea-generator that will come in handy when you're starting a new project or need some fresh ideas.

When you get stuck on a project, spend a few moments reviewing your favorite designs on file. Chances are, they'll serve as catalysts for your design decisions.

If your projects will be printed in two-, three-, or four-color, you may want to collect samples of color projects that you feel are particularly eye-catching.

## Adopt a New Perspective

*It's easy to become so involved with desktop publishing and so focused on design that you lose sight of the fact that your real purpose is communicating your message.*

Once you understand something, you cannot conceive of what it was like to not have understood it. You lose some ability to identify with others who don't understand.

The moment we know something, we forget what it was like to not know it. Can you remember what it was like to not be able to read? While we cannot completely escape this dilemma, we can at least try to put ourselves in the place of someone who knows nothing or little about what we want to convey. This practice can help you approach your project with a fresher perspective.

When you get stuck on a project, spend a few moments reviewing your favorite designs on file. Chances are, they'll serve as catalysts for your design decisions.

At the same time, you'll need to convey the notable parts and not the whole history of your product or service. It's probably not a good idea to describe the theater when you only want to announce a movie.

### Look Beyond Your Desktop

Join a local advertising group, art directors club, or communications forum. Even if you're not involved in the advertising or public relations fields, you, as a desktop publisher, share a common goal of informing, motivating, and persuading others. You're likely to return from these meetings with a fresh perspective on your communication and design efforts.

## Using Design Concepts

Good design practice follows basic concepts that go with the publishing process from start to finish. These qualities—relevance, proportion, direction, consistency, contrast, the total picture, restraint, and detail—ensure the performance and appeal of your materials. They apply to all kinds of information from hard-copy documents to electronic and online pages.

### Relevance

*Group elements that relate to each other by their communication function and their environment.*

In music, there's nothing right or wrong about notes such as middle C or B-flat; similarly, there are no good or bad design elements—only appropriate or inappropriate ones. Far from a random choice of notes, music composition follows time-honored principles and mathematical formulas. Yet music-making frequently yields to serendipity and surprise. Design also has standards that support your creativity. By attending to design standards, you'll discover new ways to add interest and logic to your documents. Simple basics applied in design (as in music) add integrity. It helps ensure that your design remains transparent and your message visible.

It's best to cluster related elements into grouped units. For example:

- Your company name, logo, and phone number can be a single unit.

- Several related photographs grouped together can work best as a single visual unit.

- A cartoon and its caption can be a separate unit, a part of a headline, or wrapped in a block of text.

Successful graphic design is relevant. Each design is judged on its ability to help the reader quickly and easily understand your message. Think of graphic design as a means of communication rather than mere decoration. Ensure that your message is appropriate for its intended audience.

A letterhead for a healthcare agency needs to be easily distinguishable from a letterhead for a rock music promoter.

Think of graphic design as a means of communication rather than mere decoration. Ensure that your message is appropriate for its intended audience.

A financial newsletter requires a totally different design than a gardening newsletter with lots of pictures and short articles.

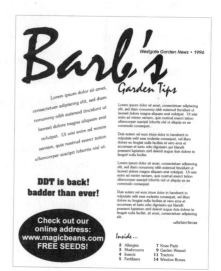

An image-building magazine ad requires a different design approach than a priced-based newspaper ad.

## TIP

With more and more features being added to your computer toolbox, it's easy to get carried away. Don't let your publishing system get in the way of clear communication. Your message is the heart of your document.

Clarity, organization, and simplicity are as critical to design as they are to writing.

Clarity, organization, and simplicity are as critical to design as they are to writing.

Make sure your message is cohesive. Find an appropriate balance between appearance and content. Important ideas, for example, are made visually more prominent than secondary ideas or supporting facts and figures. Emphasizing everything makes it difficult for your audience to determine which part of your message is most important. If everything is highlighted then nothing stands out.

## Proportion

*The size of all graphic elements is determined by their relative importance and environment.*

Because there are no absolutes in graphic design, success is determined by how well each piece of the puzzle relates to the pieces around it.

Because there are no absolutes in graphic design, success is determined by how well each piece of the puzzle relates to the pieces around it.

For example, proper headline size is determined partly by its importance and partly by the amount of space that separates it from adjacent borders, text, and artwork. A large headline in a small space looks cramped.

## HIGH ROLLS ROCKS

Den se perpetuo Tempus as revolubile gyro Iam
revocat Zephyros, vere tepente, novos.
Induiturque brev Tellus reparata iuventam,
Iamque soluta gelu dulce virescit b_____ Fallor?
an et nobis redeunt in carmi_____
Ingeniumque mihi munere_____
veris adest, iterumque vi_____
atque aliquod iam sib_____

Likewise, a small headline in a large space looks lost.

### HOME HEALTH FAIR

Den se perpetuo Tempus as revolubile gyro Iam
revocat Zephyros, vere tepente, novos.
Induiturque brev Tellus reparata iuventam,
Iamque soluta gelu dulce virescit b_____ Fallor?
an et nobis redeunt in carmi_____
Ingeniumque mihi munere_____
veris adest, iterumque vi_____
atque aliquod iam sib_____

The proper thickness of lines—called rules—is determined by
the size of the type and the surrounding white space. Rules that
are too thick can interfere with legibility.

### Who's important here?

Rules that are too thin can lack effectiveness.

# FREE TICKETS

When working with groups of photographs or illustrations on a page, also consider proportion. When one photograph is larger, it enhances interest and sends the reader a nonverbal message about the relative importance of the photographs.

Type size and the distance between lines need to properly relate to the column widths that organize the type. As you'll see later, wide columns are generally preferable for large type. And narrow columns are appropriate for small type.

## TIP

Type the lowercase alphabet one and a half times in the typeface and type size you use for body text. Measure the line with a pica ruler.

**abcdefghijklmnopqrstuvwxyzabcdefghijklm**

The measurement is a good guideline for the column width for that particular typeface and type size. See Chapter 3, "The Architecture of Type," for more.

## Direction

*Effective graphic design guides the reader through your publication.*

Readers want to encounter a logical sequence of events as they read through your advertisement or publication. Graphic design is the road map that steers your readers from point to point.

The design of that map generally follows the readers' natural tendency to read an advertisement or publication from upper left to lower right.

Graphic design is the road map that steers your readers from point to point.

Reading a printed publication is a linear process that occurs through a series of steps over a period of time. Your map needs to support this type of process so your readers are not surprised or confused.

## Consistency

*Consistency leads to an integrated style.*

Style reflects the way you handle elements that come up again and again. Part of a document's style is decided from the beginning. The rest emerges as the document develops visually.

Consistency is a matter of detail. It involves using restraint in choosing typefaces and type sizes and using the same spacing throughout your document.

One of your biggest challenges as a desktop designer is to reconcile the continuing conflict between consistency and variety. Your goal is to create documents that are consistent within themselves, without being boring. Boredom occurs when predictability and symmetry dominate a document. Too little consistency and your readers will have to work to find the information they need.

Check that your publications are consistent within themselves and with your organization's other print communications. For example, if you use 1-inch margins in the first chapter of a book, you need to use 1-inch margins in all chapters.

You can provide page-to-page consistency in any of the following ways:

- Consistent top, bottom, and side margins.

- Consistent typeface, type size, and spacing specifications for text, headlines, subheads, and captions.

- Uniform paragraph indents and spaces between columns and around photographs.

- Repeating graphic elements, such as vertical lines, columns, or borders on each page.

Your goal is to create documents that are consistent within themselves, without being boring.

For example, you can create an "artificial horizon" by repeating a strong line or graphic on each page in your publication.

## Contrast

*Contrast provides dynamic interest.*

Contrast gives "color" to your publication by balancing the space devoted to text, artwork, and white space. When analyzing an attractive publication, compare "dark" areas—such as large, bold headlines, dark photographs, or blocks of text—and notice how they're offset by lighter areas with little type.

High-impact publications tend to have a lot of contrast. Each page or two-page spread has definite light and dark areas, with lots of white space and illustrations.

Contrast gives "color" to your publication by balancing the space devoted to text, artwork, and white space.

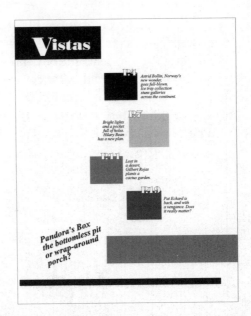

You can create publications low in contrast, where all pages and parts of pages are a uniform shade of gray. You'll find that formal reports, policy statements, and press releases often have low contrast.

Contrasting sizes create visual tension that can keep the reader interested.

Contrast can be observed by turning the publication upside down. Viewed from that perspective, your eyes aren't misled by the tendency to read individual words. Instead, you concentrate on the overall "tonal balance" of the publication.

Contrasting sizes create visual tension that can keep the reader interested. For example, you might have a headline set in a large size above a subhead set in the same typeface at a much smaller size.

> We hold these truths to be self-evident, that all People are created equal, that they are endowed by their Creator with certain unalienable rights, that among these are Life, Liberty, and the Pursuit of Happiness.
>
> # VISUAL TENSION
> ## THE CAUSE AND THE CURE
>
> that all People are created equal, that they are endowed by their Creator with certain unalienable rights, that among these are Life, Liberty, and the

Effective graphic design is based on balancing contrast and consistency. Your designs must be dynamic enough to keep the reader interested, yet consistent enough so that your advertisement or publication emerges with a strong identity.

## TIP

Consistency and contrast are two design elements that can rightly be considered a single tool. Your design needs to provide consistency for the reader's comfort with enough contrast to maintain interest.

## The Total Picture

*Think of graphic design as the visual equivalent of a jigsaw puzzle.*

Your job is to assemble a total picture from a series of parts. No piece of the puzzle should be isolated from the others. The various parts need to fit together harmoniously.

Your job is to assemble a total picture from a series of parts. No piece of the puzzle should be isolated from the others.

The total picture includes consideration of the environment in which your advertisement or publication will be distributed. For example, when designing a newspaper advertisement, consider how it will look when surrounded by news items and other ads.

When planning a newsletter or direct-mail piece, imagine how it will look when it arrives in the recipient's mailbox. When designing a Web page, consider how it will be viewed and printed. When creating product literature, visualize it displayed in a brochure rack.

In a printed publication, the most important part of the total picture is the two-page spread. When designing multipage publications, such as newsletters, brochures, or books, focus on two-page spreads instead of individual pages. If you concentrate on designing each page as though it were a self-contained entity, you might end up creating two pages that look good individually, but don't work side by side.

This left-hand page is visually attractive and self-contained.

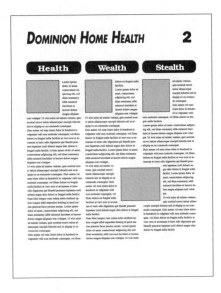

This right-hand page also works well on its own.

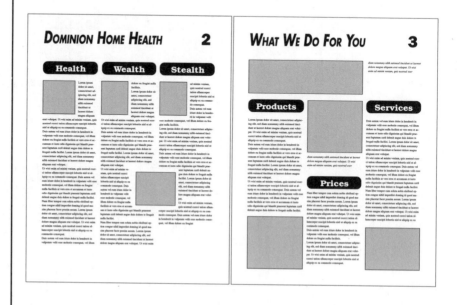

When viewed side by side, however, they fight each other and present a disorganized, difficult-to-read image.

Remember that readers see left- and right-hand pages together as one large piece.

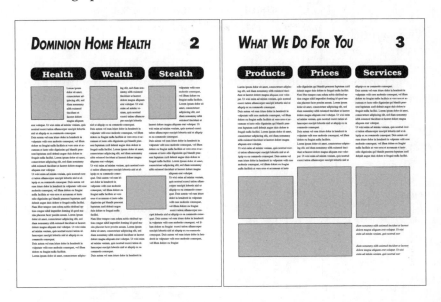

Don't isolate Web pages from one another. While it isn't impossible to view two Web pages side-by-side (with two browsers open), it rarely occurs. Your readers generally "flip" between pages with hypertext. Still, the pages need to look visually similar to create the sense of a unified Web site. You need to design each Web page at a single site with common headers, footers, and similar graphics.

## Restraint

*Strive for simplicity in design.*

Restraint is probably the most difficult design principle to apply in a consistent manner. That's because desktop publishing presents you with tremendous design power. New designers often forget to use restraint or have too much fun showing off their talents and overlook the importance of communicating their message.

With so much power at your fingertips, it's easy to forget that straightforwardness is a virtue and that graphic design needs to be invisible to the reader. Most people will quickly examine the overall appearance of a document or article to get an idea of what it involves. Generally they are unaware of design structures, but can certainly make judgments about what looks difficult and tedious to read and what's inviting and easy to read.

When designing Web pages and other electronic and online media, you'll need to resist those urges to add every graphic trick and slick add-on at your disposal. It's easy to get carried away and lose sight of your message. Your design structure needs to be transparent and your content highly visible. Also keep in mind that the more flashy graphics, the slower your Web page will load and the more impatient your Internet audience is likely to become.

> With so much power at your fingertips, it's easy to forget that straightforwardness is a virtue and that graphic design needs to be invisible to the reader.

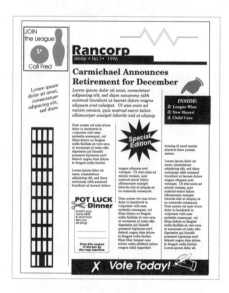

> In making design decisions, consider the degree to which design enhances the basic message you want to communicate.

Restraint is exemplified by sticking to a few carefully chosen typefaces, styles, and sizes.

In making design decisions, consider the degree to which design enhances the basic message you want to communicate.

Keep in mind that emphasis can be effective when used strategically. Avoid excessive use of emphasis—it weakens your publication to the point where it loses all impact.

## Detail

*Successful design is based on attention to detail.*

Design is detail. Often, the smallest offending details can sabotage the appearance of an otherwise attractive project.

Extra spaces after periods, for example, can create annoying rivers of white space in a text block. This can also be true of justified columns of text in which all lines are the same length. Some lines are very sparse, with huge gaps created between words. These can be distracting and cause the reader's eyes to drag diagonally through a column.

### *Rivers of white space…*

Lorem ipsum dolor sit amet, consectetuer adipis cing elit, sed diam nonum nibh euismod tinc idunt laoreet ut dolore magna aliquam erat volutpat. Ut wisi enim minim veniam, quis nostrud exerci tation ullamcorper suscipit lob ortis nisl ut aliquip ex ea commodo consequat.

Duis autem vel eum iriure dolor in hendrerit vulputate velit esse molestie conseq vel illum dolore eu feugiat nulla facilisis at vero eros et accumsan et iusto odio dignissim qui blandit praesent luptatum zzril delenit augue duisdolore feugait nulla facilisi. Lor ipsum dolor sit amet, conse ctetuer adipiselit, sed diam nonum mynibh euism tincidunt ut laoreet dolore magna aliquam erat volutpat.

Ut wisi enim ad minim veniam, quis nostrud exerci tation ullam corper susci pit lobortis nisl ut aliquip

vulputate velit es molestie consequat, vel illum dolore eu feugiat nulla facilisis at vero amet.

Eros et accumsan et iusto odio dignissim qui blandit praesent luptatum zzril delenit augue duis dolore te feugait nulla facilisi.

Nam liber tempor cum soluta nobis eleifend option congue nihil imperdiet doming id quod mazim placerat facer possim assum. Lorem ipsum dolor sit amet, consectetuer adipiscing elit, sed diam nonummy nibh euismod tincidunt laoreet dolore magna aliquam erat volutpat. Ut wisi enim ad minim veniam, quis nostrud exerci tation ullamcorper suscipit lobortis nisl ut aliquip ex ea com modo consequat.

Duis autem vel eum iriure dolor in hendrerit in vulp utate velit molestie con sequat, vel illum dolore eu feugiat nulla facilisis.

Headlines and subheads placed at the bottom of columns or pages set the readers up for disappointment when the promised topic doesn't appear until the start of the next column or page.

Text placed in boxes should be indented on both sides. Otherwise, it may bump into the borders of the boxes.

Editorial tasks such as proofreading also require a lot of attention to detail. For example, correctly spelled, misused words sneak by spell-checking programs, which often can't differentiate spelling from usage. Be careful not to let these and other errors go unnoticed until the presses are running.

## Examining Proofs

*Analyze reduced-size copies of your pages.*

Most desktop publishing programs let you print out *thumbnail proofs*, or a number of pages at a reduced size on a single sheet of paper. These programs typically organize facing pages next to each other, so you can see how spreads will look.

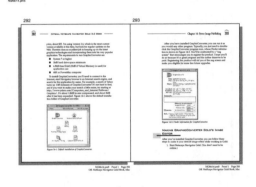

Thumbnail proofs let you see where good design has been sacrificed for expediency.

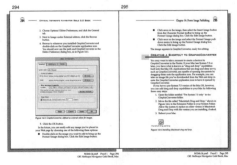

Thumbnail proofs let you see where good design has been sacrificed for expediency. Too much symmetry or too much contrast also becomes obvious.

Many desktop presentation programs that let you create slides and overhead transparencies offer a *handouts* feature. This lets you print the visual for six or more slides or overheads in a reduced size on one page so that each audience member can take one along to use for future reference. Handouts are also good for analyzing your work.

## Moving On

Practicing restraint, concentrating on proportion, achieving a balance between consistency and contrast, and paying attention to detail are a part of a disciplined approach to design. A structured approach will train you to avoid common design errors and make your publications a reading pleasure.

Now let's get to the actual page makeup by exploring important organizational tools you'll use in creating your published projects.

# 2

# Tools of Organization

## Overview

- Grid-based design encourages a logical plan for what goes where on a page.

- Column widths can vary while the grid stays the same.

- Styles keep track of all the page format specifications and save you time.

- Headlines help readers decide whether to read a document—keep them short, concise, and attention-grabbing.

Effective graphic design is based on organization as much as it is on inventiveness.

If you want to be successful—and sane—you'll want to get organized. Effective graphic design is based on organization as much as it is on inventiveness. Document organization guides your readers' eyes from one point to another in a document and alerts them to what's of primary importance. It helps readers locate information quickly.

The two primary page elements—graphics and type—are given form by applying various organizing tools. In part, this is how the function of the document itself is defined.

All of the design organization decisions you make now relate to the tone and image you want to present. Plus, a well-organized page is perceived by readers as having a higher quality of content and information.

## Page Organizers

Fundamental to the overall page layout are page organizing tools. Different desktop publishing programs offer different ways of implementing these essential tools.

### Grids

*You can establish the overall structure of a page by specifying the placement of text, display type, and artwork through a grid.*

Grids become the underlying framework that you use to shape, format, and present the content of your document.

Made of nonprinted lines, grids show up on your computer screen but not on the finished publication. Grids determine the number of columns, margin size, placement of headlines, sub-heads, pull-quotes, and other page elements.

They're valuable for a number of reasons: they set page-to-page or project-to-project consistency and they help you avoid reinventing the wheel each time you create another ad or news-letter issue. In other words, once you determine layout, you can reuse it by making only slight variations.

Desktop publishing programs differ in their ability to create grids. Some programs provide you with ready-made grids you can modify.

A well-organized page is perceived by readers as having a higher quality of content and information.

Many programs use a series of horizontal and vertical lines that define columns and page margins.

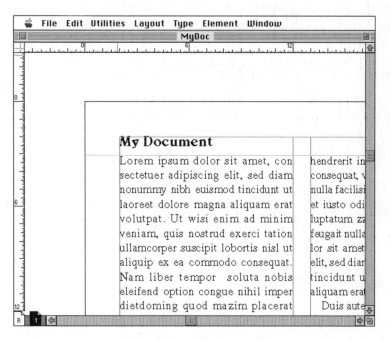

Other page-layout programs are based on setting text into boxes or frames.

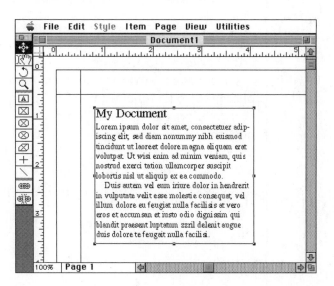

Many word processing programs also let you format pages by setting parameters that define column placement and margins, even though the column boundaries aren't always visible onscreen.

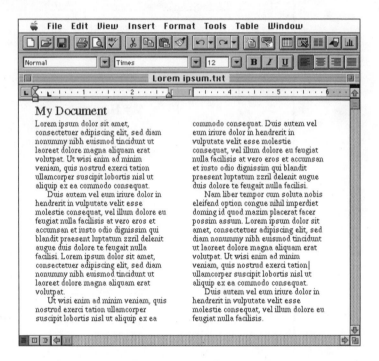

One way or another, all programs let you establish formats that are automatically maintained from page to page or through-out a series of documents.

Grid design works for both the reader and the designer. Most people have an inherent need for predictability and orderliness. Your readers expect some indication as to where they start and how they proceed—what's first, second, and third.

With grids, you can establish a content pattern that creates a comfortable, uninterrupted flow of information (continuity) for readers. Grids present a fast and easy way to provide order and eliminate guesswork. Not only will using grids save you time, it will also help provide identity and add recognition value to your project.

Whether your design is printed on paper or displayed on a monitor, the creative possibilities in applying a grid structure are nearly endless.

Charts, graphs, photos, and illustrations can be sized and shaped to work with the invisible guidelines of a grid. Using your common sense, everything has a logical placement that can be aligned within your grid. You can position text to fit within your structure by:

- Centering between two column guides.

- Justifying between two column guides.

- Applying flush right or left against a guideline.

- Aligning against a horizontal guideline at the top or bottom of a page.

Some elements can be placed at angles so they break the neat confines of the grid. Elements that don't align to the grid or other elements in the layout catch the reader by surprise—unaligned elements stand out.

## A Kinder, Gentler Nation

Lorem ipsum dolor sit amet, consectetuer adipiscing elit, sed diam nonummy nibh euismod tincidunt ut laoreet dolore magna aliquam erat volutpat. Ut wisi enim ad minim veniam, quis nostrud exerci tation ullamcorper suscipit lobortis nisl ut aliquip ex ea commodo consequat.

Duis autem vel eum iriure dolor in hendrerit in vulputate velit esse molestie consequat, vel illum dolore eu feugiat nulla facilisis at vero eros et accumsan et iusto odio dignissim qui blandit praesent luptatum zzril delenit augue duis dolore te feugait nulla facilisi. Lorem ipsum dolor sit amet, consectetuer adipiscing elit, sed diam nonummy nibh euismod tincidunt ut laoreet dolore magna aliquam erat volutpat.

Ut wisi enim ad minim veniam, quis nostrud exerci tation ullamcorper suscipit lobortis nisl ut aliquip ex ea commodo consequat. Duis autem vel eum iriure dolor in hendrerit in vulputate velit esse molestie consequat, vel illum dolore eu feugiat nulla facilisis at vero eros et accumsan et iusto odio dignissim qui blandit praesent luptatum zzril delenit augue duis dolore te feugait nulla facilisi et iusto.

Nam liber tempor cum soluta nobis eleifend option congue nihil imperdiet doming id quod mazim placerat facer possim assum. Lorem ipsum dolor sit amet, consectetuer adipiscing elit, sed diam nonummy nibh euismod tincidunt ut laoreet dolore

magna aliquam erat volutpat. Ut wisi enim ad minim veniam, quis nostrud exerci tation ullamcorper suscipit lobortis nisl ut aliquip ex ea commodo consequat.

Duis autem vel eum iriure dolor in hendrerit in vulputate velit esse molestie consequat, vel illum dolore eu feugiat nulla facilisis. Ut wisi enim ad minim veniam, quis nostrud exerci tation ullamcorper suscipit lobortis.

You can break from the grid for a planned effect, but first you need a well-established grid.

## Avoiding Gridlock

While grids are nearly universally applied, especially for multipage documents, there are times when you'll want to avoid them. Any single-page document with little text, such as simple flyers or ads, or those documents having only illustrations or photographs, perform better without grids. You'll notice this approach used successfully in advertising where ads need to stand out from surrounding copy.

## Columns

*Columns are fundamental parts of a grid—they organize text and visuals on a page.*

Text and visuals rarely extend in an unbroken line from the left side of the page to the right. They're usually arranged in columns or vertical blocks. For most documents, column formats range from single-column to seven-column page layout. As the number of columns increases, so do the possibilities for creative layout.

THERE'S NOT A LOT OF FLEXIBILITY in a one-column format. Lorem ipsum dolor sit amet, con sectetuer adipiscing elit, sed diam nonummy nibh euismod tincidunt ut laoreet dolore magna aliquam erat volutpat. Ut wisi enim ad minim veniam, quis nostrud exerci tation ullamcorper suscipit lobortis nisl ut aliquip ex ea commodo consequat. Nam liber tempor soluta nobis eleifend option congue nihil imper dietdoming quod mazim placerat possim assum. Lorem ipsum dolor sit amet, consec tetuer elit, sed diam nonummy nibh euismod.

Duis autem vel eum dolor in hendrerit in vulputate velit molestie consequat, vel illum dolore eu feugiat nulla facilisi at vero eros et accumsan et iusto odio dignissim qui praesent luptatum zzril augue duis dolore te feugait nulla facilisi. Lorem ipsum dolor sit amet, consectetuer adipiscing elit, sed diam nonummy nibh euismod tincidunt ut laoreet dolore magna aliquam erat volutpat.

Cuismod tincidunt ut laoreet dolore magna aliquam erat volutpat. Ut wisi enim ad minim veniam, quis nostrud exerci tation ullamcorper suscipit lobortis nisl ut aliquip ex ea commodo conse. Nam liber tempor soluta nobis eleifend option congue nihil imper dietdoming quod mazim placerat possim assum. Lorem ipsum dolor sit amet, consec tetuer elit, sed diam nonummy nibh euismod tincidunt ut laor dolore magna aliquam erat volutpat. Ut wisi enim ad minim veniam, nostrud exerci tation ullamcorper suscipit lobortis nisl ut aliquip ex ea commodo consequat ex ea commodo. Duis autem vel eum dolor in hendrerit in vulputate velit molestie consequat, vel illum dolore eu feugiat nulla facilisi at vero eros et accumsan et iusto odio dignissim qui praesent luptatum zzril augue duis dolore te feugait nulla facilisi. Lorem ipsum dolor sit amet, consectetuer adipiscing elit, sed diam nonummy nibh euismod tincidunt ut laoreet dolore magna aliquam erat volutpat.

Duis autem vel eum iriure dolor in hendrerit in vulputate velit esse molestie consequat, vel illum dolore eu feugiat nulla facilisi. Nam liber tempor soluta nobis eleifend option congue nihil imper. Lorem ipsum dolor sit amet, con sectetuer adipiscing elit, sed diam nonummy nibh euismod tincidunt ut laoreet dolore magna aliquam erat volutpat. Ut wisi enim ad minim veniam, quis nostrud exerci tation ullamcorper suscipit lobortis nisl ut aliquip ex ea commodo consequat.

THERE'S A GREAT DEAL OF FLEXIBILITY in a multi-column format. Lorem ipsum dolor sit amet, con sectetuer adipiscing elit, sed diam nonummy nibh euismod tincidunt ut laoreet dolore magna aliquam erat volutpat. Ut wisi enim ad minim veniam, quis nostrud exerci tation ullamcorper suscipit lobortis nisl Nam liber tempor soluta nobis eleifend option congue nihil imper diet do quodlib mazim place possim assum.

Lorem ipsum dolor sit amet, consec tetuer elit, sed diam nommy nibh euismod. Duis autem vel eum dolor in hendrerit in vulp tate velit molestie consequat, vel illum dolore eu

**More columns provide more flexibility.**

feugiat facilisis at vero eros et accumsan et iusto odio dignissim qui praesent luptatum zzril augue duis dolore feugait. Lorem ipsum do lor consectetuer adipiscing elit, sed diam nommy nibh euismod tin cidunt ut laoreet dolore ut magna erat volutpat.

Cuism laoreet dolore aliquam volutpat. Ut wisi enim ad minim veniam, quis exercitation ullam suscipitus

*Caption for the picture above.*

lobortis nisl ut aliquip ex ea commodo conse. Nam liber tempor soluta nobis eleifend option congue nihil imper dietdoming quod mazim placerat

possim assum. Lorem ipsum dolor sit amet, consec tetuer elit, sed diam nonummy nibh euismod tincidunt ut laor dolore magna aliquam erat volutpat. Ut wisi enim ad minim veniam, nostrud exerci tation ullamcorper suscipit lobortis nisl ut aliquip ex ea commodo consequat ex ea commodo. Duis autem vel eum do lor in hendrerit in vulputate velit molestie consequat, vel illum dolore eu feugiat nulla facilisi at vero eros et accumsan iusto odio dignissim qui praesent luptatum zzril augue dolore te feugait facilisi. Lorem noummy nibh vel iriure dolor hendrerit vulputate velit esse molestiess consequat, vel illum dolore eu feugiat nulla facilisis. Nam liber tempor soluta nobis eleifend option congue nihil imper. Lorem ipsum dolor sit amet, con sectetuer elit, sed nonummy nibh euismod tincidunt ut laoreet dolore magna aliquam erat volutpat. Ut wisi enim ad minim veniam, quis nostrud exerci tation ullamcorper suscipit lobortis nisl ut aliquip ex ea commodo consequat. Lorem ipsum dolor sit amet, con sectetuer elit, sed nonummy nibh euismod tincidunt ut laoreet dolore magna aliquam erat volutpat. Ut wisi enim ad minim veniam, quis exercitation ullam suscipitus lobortis nisl ut aliquip ex ea commodo consequat. Ut wisi enim ad minim veniam, quis nostrud exerci tation ullamcorper suscipit lobortis nisl ut aliquip ex ea commodo consequat. Lorem ipsum dolor sit amet, con sectetuer elit, sed nonummy nibh euismod tincidunt ut laoreet dolore magna aliquam erat volutpat. Ut wisi enim ad minim veniam, quis exercitation ullam suscipitus lobortis nisl ut aliquip ex ea commodo consequat. Ut wisi ea commodo consequat. Nam liber tempor soluta nobis.

Column width has a profound influence on a publication's readability. The greater the number of columns on a page, the narrower each of the columns, the shorter the line length, and the smaller the typeface. As readers, we scan groups of words rather than individual letters. Narrow columns can be difficult to read because our eyes have to shift to the next line more often than with longer line lengths.

**Column width has a profound influence on a publication's readability.**

Still, narrow columns are popular because wide columns have limitations too. Wider columns make it more difficult for a reader's eyes to make a smooth transition from the end of one line to the beginning of the next without getting lost; lines over 60 characters long will generally intimidate any reader.

> 8-point text placed on a 23-pica column is very difficult to read. 8-point text placed on a 23-pica column is very difficult to read. 8-point text placed on a 23-pica column is very difficult to read. 8-point text placed on a 23-pica column is very difficult to read. 8-point text placed on a 23-pica column is very difficult to read. 8-point text placed on a 23-pica column is very difficult to read. 8-point text placed on a 23-pica column is very difficult to read. 8-point text placed on a 23-pica column is very difficult to read. 8-point text placed on a 23-pica column is very difficult to read.

Column width affects the type size of the text. Narrow columns work best with small type sizes.

> But 8-point text in a 12-pica column is readable. But 8-point text in a 12-pica column is readable. But 8-point text in a 12-pica column is readable. But 8-point text in a 12-pica column is readable.

Wider columns usually require larger type sizes.

> 12-point type looks good when placed in 23-pica columns. 12-point type looks good when placed in 23-pica columns. 12-point type looks good when placed in 23-pica columns. 12-point type looks good when placed in 23-pica columns.

Don't forget, not all columns on a page have to be the same width! Good-looking publications can be created by varying column widths based on an established multicolumn grid.

For example, the five-column grid lends itself to a variety of arrangements.

In a five-column format, subheads and illustrations can be laid out side by side in a narrow column adjacent to one or two wide columns of text.

Variations on the above are permissible within a document, but should always conform to the overall column scheme. A two-column photo, "A," on a five-column grid looks good when its edges are aligned with column guides.

Likewise, a three-column photograph, "B," on a five-column grid works well when the edges of the photograph are lined up with the column guides.

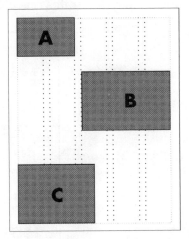

However, a two-and-a-half-column photograph, "C," on a five-column grid creates unsightly half-columns of white space or short columns of type.

Just as establishing the number of columns influences the color and the feel of a publication, so does the space between columns.

Just as establishing the number of columns influences the color and the feel of a publication, so does the space between columns.

Closely spaced columns "darken" a document and often make it more difficult to read—the reader's eye tends to jump the gap between columns.

Extra space between columns "lightens" or opens up a page and clearly separates one column from another.

See the Column Gallery on the Companion CD-ROM for examples of the many ways to set up column formats.

# Style

*Styles provide the memory bank for desktop publishing, giving you instant access to the design specifications on a project.*

Keeping track of all these organizers—column specifications, headline font and size, caption placement and size, the picas between a subhead and the text—is too daunting for those of us not blessed with a photographic memory. Fortunately, desktop publishing programs offer the ultimate organizer—styles.

Each specification concerning type or format in your document can be defined as part of your document's styles. Once defined, the style can be conveniently applied as you create your document.

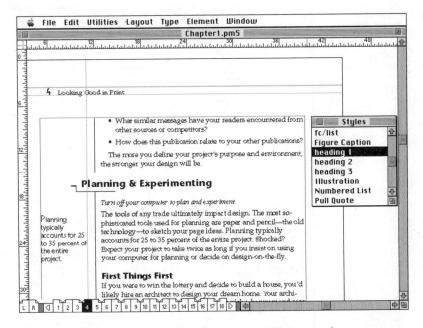

Styles are critical if you're creating a multipage document or a standard format that will be repeated frequently on future projects. After you've finalized your document design, setting up styles is probably the most important part of production planning.

## Gutters

*In designing multipage documents, pay particular attention to the gutter, or inner space, of facing pages.*

Gutter size depends primarily on the type of binding you plan to use. For example, perfect binding, a method in which all pages are glued together, (used in this and most books) will reduce the size of the inner margin. It's usually a safe bet to leave a traditional gutter margin of ½ inch to accommodate this type of binding.

|←— X —→|

For ring binding, reserve a ⅝- to ¾-inch gutter. Most plastic spiral bindings don't require such wide gutters, but it's best to choose a particular binding first and design your gutter width around it.

## Margins

*Margins determine the space between columns and the borders and edges of a page.*

Effective design allows breathing room between the live area and the physical boundaries of a page, referred to as *trim size*. Wide margins can make a page more inviting.

Wide margins can make a page more inviting.

The larger the margin, the lighter the publication. Thinner margins result in darker publications. By increasing the left and right margins, you can achieve an attractive vertical look. With a widetop margin, you can achieve a horizontal appearance.

## Text Organizers

Text organizers include headlines, subheads, and captions. Often referred to as *display type*, these organizing tools highlight your message and help readers understand it quickly and easily.

### Headlines

*Use headlines to invite readers to become involved in your advertisements or articles in your publication.*

Headlines, the most basic text-organizing tool, help readers decide whether to read a document. They should be as concise as possible so they can be quickly read and understood.

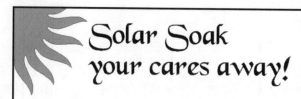

To be effective, clearly differentiate your headlines from text. In addition to setting them in a large type size, you can add emphasis to headlines and give contrast to your page by setting them in a different typeface than the one used for the text.

For example, headlines set in sans-serif type are often used with text set in a serif typeface—a popular font combination for documents such as advertisements, books, brochures, and newsletters.

**TIP**

When a letter has little flared-out tops and bases it's called *Serif*. When it's squared, rounded, or even, it's *Sans Serif*. See Chapter 3, "The Architecture of Type," for more about typefaces and their appropriate uses.

Alternately, you can emphasize headlines by setting them in the text typeface, but in a larger size or heavier weight (or both).

21    Tools of Organization

Use headlines to invite readers to become involved in your advertisement or articles in your publication.

The most basic text organizing tool, headlines help readers decide whether to read a document. They should be as short and concise as possible so they can be read and understood quickly.

To be effective, headlines should be clearly differentiated from text, which can be done in two ways.

In addition to setting headlines in a large type size, you can add emphasis to them and give contrast to your page by setting headlines in a different typeface than the one used for the text.

For example, headlines set in sans-serif type are often used with text set in a serif typeface—a popular technique for documents such as advertisements, brochures and newsletters.

**GREATER CONTRAST MEANS EASIER READING**

To be effective, headlines should be clearly differentiated from text, which can be done in two ways.

In addition to setting headlines in a large type size, you can add emphasis to them and give contrast to your page by setting headlines in a different typeface than the one used for the text.

For example, headlines set in sans-serif type are often used with text set in a serif typeface—a popular technique for documents such as advertisements, brochures and newsletters.

Alternately, you can emphasize headlines by setting them in the same typeface as text, but in a larger size and/or heavier weight. Use headlines to invite readers to become involved in your advertisement or articles in your publication.

The most basic text organizing tool, headlines help readers decide whether to read a document. They should be as short and concise as possible so they can be read and understood quickly.

To be effective, headlines should be clearly differentiated from text, which can be done in two ways.

The greater the size difference between headline and text, the easier it is for readers to identify and read your headline.

Even though headlines are designed for impact, make them as readable as possible. For example, avoid setting long headlines in uppercase type. Not only do long, uppercase headlines occupy more space, they slow readers down because they're difficult to read.

Even though headlines are designed for impact, make them as readable as possible.

It's best to limit uppercase headlines to a few words. This adds impact without slowing down the reader.

The most readable type scheme for headlines is to use uppercase only for the first letter of each word (except for articles and short prepositions).

The most readable type scheme for headlines is to use uppercase only for the first letter of each word (except for articles and short preposi- tions).

### Set Your Headlines With Initial Caps

Use headlines to invite readers to become involved in your advertise- ment or articles in your publication.

The most basic text organizing tool, headlines help readers decide whether to read a document. They should be as short and concise as possible so they can be read and under- stood quickly.

To be effective, headlines should be clearly differentiated from text, which can be done in two ways.

In addition to setting headlines in a large type size, you can add empha- sis to them and give contrast to your page by setting headlines in a different typeface than the one used for the body copy.

For example, headlines set in sans-serif type are often used with text set in a serif typeface—a popular tech- nique for documents such as adver- tisements, books, brochures and news- letters.

To be effective, headlines should be clearly differentiated from text, which can be done in two ways.

In addition to setting headlines in a large type size, you can add empha- sis to them and give contrast to your page by setting headlines in a different typeface than the one used for the text.

For example, headlines set in sans- serif type are often used with text set in a serif typeface—a popular technique for documents such as advertisements, books, brochures and newsletters.

Alternately, you can emphasize headlines by setting them in the same typeface as text, but in a larger size and/ or heavier weight. Use headlines to in- vite readers to become involved in your advertisement or articles in your publi- cation.

The most basic text organizing tool, headlines help readers decide whether to read a document. They should be as short and concise as possible so they can be read and understood. Use head- lines to invite readers to become in- volved in your advertisement or ar- ticles in your publication.

The most basic text organizing tool, headlines help readers decide whether to read a document. They should be as short and concise as possible so they can be read and understood quickly.

To be effective, headlines should be clearly differentiated from text, which can be done in two ways. ▪

For long headlines, limit them to a maximum of three lines. Long headlines of four or more lines can look too wordy and complex to read at a glance. Also, avoid centering headlines that contain more than two lines. Long, centered headlines slow readers down because they have to search for the beginning of each line.

### Sleet and Snow Storms Predicted to Occur Over the Next Several Days in the Midwest

Use headlines to invite readers to become involved in your advertise- ment or articles in your publication.

The most basic text organizing tool, headlines help readers decide whether to read a document. They should be as short and concise as possible so they can be read and understood quickly.

To be effective, headlines should be clearly differentiated from text, which can be done in two ways.

In addition to setting headlines in a large type size, you can add emphasis to them and give contrast to your page by setting headlines in a different type- face than the one used for the text.

For example, headlines set in sans- serif type are often used with text set in a serif typeface—a popular technique for documents such as advertisements, books, brochures and newsletters.

To be effective, headlines should be clearly differentiated from text, which can be done in two ways.

In addition to setting headlines in a large type size, you can add emphasis to them and give contrast to your page by setting headlines in a different type- face than the one used for the text.

For example, headlines set in sans- serif type are often used with text set in a serif typeface—a popular technique for documents such as advertisements, books, brochures and newsletters.

Alternately, you can emphasize headlines by setting them in the same typeface as text, but in a larger size and/ or heavier weight. Use headlines to in- vite readers to become involved in your articles in your publication.

The most basic text organizing tool, headlines help readers decide whether to read a document. They should be as short and concise as possible so they can be read and understood. Use head- lines to invite readers to become in- volved in your advertisement or articles in your publication.

The most basic text organizing tool, headlines help readers decide whether

Flush-left headlines, on the other hand, let readers move directly down to the first words of the following paragraph.

## Kickers

*Lead into your headline with a kicker—a short summary phrase.*

Kickers can introduce the headline by relating it to other articles or existing information. Kickers also can categorize an article.

You'll see kickers used to provide meaning and add interest to a headline. Let's say your headline reads: "Fireman Risks Life to Save Cat." Your kicker can read "Profile of a Modern Hero."

*Profile of a Modern Hero:*

### Fireman Risks Life to Save Cat

We hold these truths to be self-evident, that all People are created equal, that they are endowed by their Creator with certain unalienable rights, that among these are Life, Liberty, and the Pursuit of Happiness. That to secure these rights, governments are instituted among Men and Women. We hold these truths to be

to be self-evident, that all People are created equal, that they are endowed by their Creator with certain unalienable rights, that among these are Life, Liberty, and the Pursuit of Happiness. That to secure these rights, governments are instituted among Men and Women. We hold these truths to be self-evident,

unalienable rights, that among these are Life, Liberty, and the Pursuit of Happiness. That to secure these rights, governments are instituted among Men and Women. We hold these truths to be self-evident, that all People are created equal, that they are endowed by their Creator with certain unalienable rights, that among these are Life, Liberty, and the Pursuit of Happiness. That to secure these rights, governments are instituted among Men and Women. We hold these truths to be self-evident,

## Subheads

*Subheads clue readers in to the organizational setup of the content within an article.*

Subheads placed between the head and the text improve the appearance of a page by providing a transition between headlines and text. They give visual contrast and offer readers more detailed information about the text.

Subheads placed within a document, instead of following the headline, let readers quickly locate information and break text into manageable bite-sized chunks or segments.

Compare these two examples: In the left-hand example, you're faced with a long expanse of type. Because the page is so dark and you don't have a clue to its contents, reading it is a chore.

## Don't Make Reading A Chore

Subheads clue readers into the content organization within an article. Subheads break text into manageable segments, improve the appearance of a page and enhance readership by providing a transition between headlines and text. They also provide visual contrast and identify the subject of the text. They let readers locate information.

Subheads clue readers into the content organization within an article. Subheads break text into manageable segments, improve the appearance of a page and enhance readership by providing a transition between headlines and text. They also provide visual contrast and identify the subject of the text. They let readers locate information.

Subheads can be set apart from text by using various techniques. For example, they can be placed inside or next to the text. Subheads should always be closely associated with the text they introduce. There should be more space above the subhead than below it to link it with the text. Like headlines, subheads tend to stand out when set in a larger type size than the text and in a typeface that contrasts with the text. Subheads can be set centered, flush-left or flush-right.

As with other organizing tools, uniformity is important. Subheads should be treated consistently. Subheads clue readers into the content organization within an article. Subheads break text into manageable segments, improve the appearance of a page and enhance readership by providing a transition between headlines and text. They also provide visual contrast and identify the subject of the text. They let readers locate information. Subheads can be set apart from text by using various techniques. Subheads should always be closely associated with the text they introduce. There should be more space above the subhead than below it to link it with the text.

## Don't Make Reading a Chore

**Open up Your Pages**

Subheads clue readers into the content organization within an article. Subheads break text into manageable segments, improve the appearance of a page and enhance readership by providing a transition between headlines and text. They also provide visual contrast and identify the subject of the text. They let readers locate information.

Subheads can be set apart from text by using various techniques. For example, they can be placed inside or next to the text. Subheads should always be closely associated with the text they introduce. There should be more space above the subhead than below it to link it with the text.

Like headlines, subheads tend to stand out when set in a larger type size than the text and in a typeface that contrasts with the text. Subheads can be set centered, flush-left or flush-right. Subheads clue readers into the content organization within an article. Subheads can be placed inside text.

**Add Subheads Frequently**

Subheads can be set apart from text by using various techniques. For example, they can be placed inside or next to the text. Subheads should always be closely associated with the text they introduce. There should be more space above the subhead than below it to link it with the text. Subheads should contrast with text. Subheads should be closely associated with the text they introduce.

**Use Various Subhead Techniques**

Subheads can be set centered, flush-left or flush-right.

As with other organizing tools, uniformity is important. subheads should be treated consistently throughout your document.

Subheads clue readers into the content organization within an article. Subheads break text into manageable segments, improve the appearance of a page and enhance readership by providing a transition between headlines and text. They also provide visual contrast and identify the subject of the text. They let readers locate information. Subheads can be set apart from text by using various techniques.

The right-hand example is more inviting because the page is more "open" and you can easily decide whether the text relates to your interests.

There are various ways to set subheads apart from text. For example, they can be placed inside or next to the text.

## Don't Make Reading a Chore

**Open up Your Pages**

Subheads clue readers into the content organization within an article. Subheads break text into manageable segments, improve the appearance of a page and enhance readership by providing a transition between headlines and text. They also provide visual contrast and identify the subject of the text. They let readers quickly locate information.

Subheads can be set apart from text by using various techniques. For example, they can be placed inside or next to the text. Subheads should always be closely associated with the text they introduce. There should be more space above the subhead than below it to link it with the text. Subheads should always be closely associated with the text Subheads can be set apart from text by using various techniques. For example, they can be placed inside or next to the text. Subheads should be closely associated with the text they introduce.

**Use Various Subhead Techniques**

Subheads can be set centered, flush-left or flush-right. As with other organizing tools, uniformity is important. subheads should be treated consistently.

Subheads clue readers into the content organization within an article. Subheads break text into manageable segments, improve the appearance of a page and enhance readership by providing a transition between headlines and text. They also provide visual contrast and identify the subject of the text. Subheads can be set apart from text by using various techniques.

## Don't Make Reading a Chore

**Open up Your Pages**

Subheads clue readers into the content organization within an article. Subheads break text into manageable segments, improve the appearance of a page and enhance readership by providing a transition between headlines and text. They also provide visual contrast and identify the subject of the text.

**Add Subheads Frequently**

They let readers locate information. Subheads can be set apart from text by using various techniques. For example, they can be placed inside or next to the text. Subheads should always be closely associated with the text they introduce. There should be more space above the subhead than below it to link it with the text.

Like headlines, subheads tend to stand out when set in a larger type size than the text and in a typeface that contrasts with the text. Subheads can be set centered, flush-left or flush-right. Subheads break text into manageable segments, improve the appearance of a page and enhance readership by providing a transition between headlines and text.

**Use Various Subhead Techniques**

They also provide visual contrast and identify the subject of the text. They let readers quickly locate information. Subheads can be set apart from text by using various techniques. For example, they can be placed inside or next to the text. Subheads should always be closely associated with the text they introduce. There should be more space above the subhead than below it to link it with the text. Subheads should contrast with the body copy.

You'll need to position subheads so they are closely associated with the text they introduce. Leave more space above the subhead than below it to link it with the text.

You'll need to position subheads so they are closely associated with the text they introduce.

Subheads clue readers into the content organization within an article. Subheads break text into manageable segments, improve the appearance of a page and enhance readership by providing a transition between headlines and text.

**Subhead Linked to Text Mystery**

Subheads can be set apart from text by using various techniques. For example, they can be placed inside or next to the text. Subheads should always be closely associ-

Incorrect

Subheads clue readers into the content organization within an article. Subheads break text into manageable segments, improve the appearance of a page and enhance readership by providing a transition between headlines and text.

**Subhead Linked to Text Mystery**

Subheads can be set apart from text by using various techniques. For example, they can be placed inside or next to the text. Subheads should always be closely associ-

Correct

Like headlines, subheads tend to stand out when set in a larger type size and a different typeface than the text.

Subheads clue readers into the content organization within an article. Subheads break text into manageable segments, improve the appearance of a page and enhance readership by providing a transition between headlines and text.

**Missing Contrast Is Suspected**

Subheads can be set apart from text by using various techniques. For example, they can be placed inside or next to the text. Subheads should always be closely associated with the text they introduce. There should contrast between the subhead

Subheads clue readers into the content organization within an article. Subheads break text into manageable segments, improve the appearance of a page and enhance readership by providing a transition between headlines and text.

**Correct Contrast Has Been Located**

Subheads can be set apart from text by using various techniques. For example, they can be placed inside or next to the text. Subheads should always be closely associated with the text they introduce. There

Subheads can be set centered, flush-left, or flush-right.

Subheads clue readers into the content organization within an article. Subheads break text into manageable segments, improve the appearance of a page and enhance readership by providing a transition between headlines and text.

### Subheads Offer Great Variety

Subheads can be set apart from text by using various techniques. For example, they can be placed inside or next to the text. Subheads

Subheads clue readers into the content organization within an article. Subheads break text into manageable segments, improve the appearance of a page and enhance readership by providing a transition between headlines and text.

### Subheads Offer Great Variety

Subheads can be set apart from text by using various techniques. For example, they can be placed inside or next to the text. Subheads should always be closely associated with the

Subheads clue readers into the content organization within an article. Subheads break text into manageable segments, improve the appearance of a page and enhance readership by providing a transition between headlines and text.

### Subheads Offer Great Variety

Subheads can be set apart from text by using various techniques. For example, they can be placed inside or next to the text. Subheads should always be closely associated with the

Horizontal rules above or below subheads can add emphasis.

Subheads clue readers into the content organization within an article. Subheads break text into manageable segments, improve the appearance of a page and enhance readership by providing a transition between headlines and text.

### THE RULES OF SUBHEADS

Subheads can be set apart from text by using various techniques. For example, they can be placed inside or next to the text. Subheads should always be closely associated

As with other organizing tools, uniformity is important. Remember to treat subheads consistently throughout your desktop-published document.

## Captions

*Use captions to tie photographs and illustrations into the rest of your publication.*

Headlines and captions are more likely to be read than any other part of a publication. You can take advantage of this by using captions to summarize important points.

Typically, you can write a *tag* (a sentence fragment that names the figure or illustration) or a full sentence. Sometimes, you'll see a tag followed by a full sentence. Whichever writing style you choose, keep your caption style and construction type consistent across all figures and illustrations in a publication.

Captions can be placed in a variety of ways. They can be placed next to the artwork they describe.

Headlines and captions are more likely to be read than any other part of a publication.

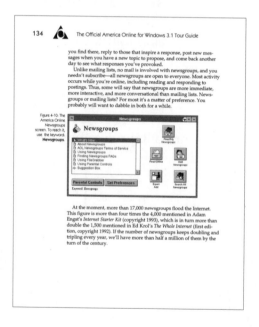

Most often, captions are placed below the artwork.

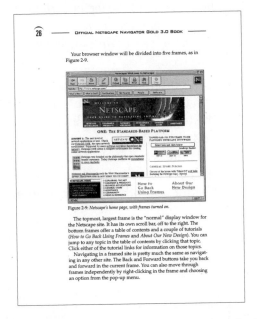

Another alternative is to place the caption inside the artwork.

## Headers & Footers

*Information at the top or bottom of each page in a newsletter, book, or training manual can be used to reinforce the publication's identity as well as serve as a quick reference to help readers locate the information they seek.*

Can you imagine how hard it would be to locate a specific word in a dictionary without the aid of headers? Header information at the top of a page can include publication number, section title and chapter title, chapter number, and page number.

Footers can include the same information as the header but at the bottom of a page. You can place some information in the header and other information in the footer.

Alternately, this space can be used to summarize the contents of each page, helping readers quickly locate information.

## Pull-quotes & Sidebars

*Pull-quotes and sidebars give your pages editorial diversity and add visual interest to your layouts.*

In addition to subheads, you can add graphic interest to your page by using *pull-quotes*—a sentence or two extracted from the text and set in display type within the text column or in a side margin.

Pull-quotes are only a few short lines in length, making it easy for the reader to glance at them quickly. They are typically written in a concise style to invite interest in the related text.

Pull-quotes are typically written in a concise style to invite interest in the related text.

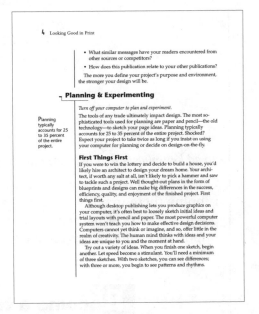

Another page element you may want to use is the sidebar—a block of copy set apart from, but related to, the rest of the text on a page. This is an ideal format for supplemental information, such as a biographical sketch of an individual important to a major article.

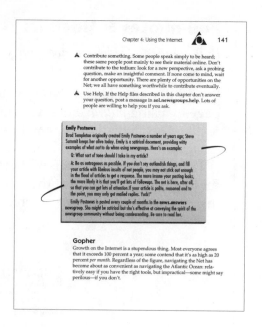

## Bullet Lists

*To add emphasis to a list, use bullets or icons to mark each item.*

Often, you'll want to list items in a long column instead of running them in with the text. By inserting a bullet (usually a boldface dot or square) or other icon, the list takes on a new importance and invites readership. This technique is particularly effective in advertising.

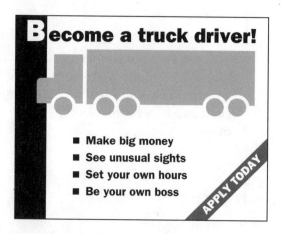

## Jumplines

*Use jumplines to inform readers when articles are continued from one page to another.*

By continuing articles on inside pages, you can offer readers a wider variety of editorial material on the front page of your publication. As the number of articles included on Page 1 increases, so does the likelihood you'll interest the reader.

Continuing articles on other pages also allows for more flexibility in laying out a long story that won't fit on a single page. The jumpline eliminates any confusion readers may have about where to read next.

## Nameplates & Logos

*Establish the identity of your publication with a distinctive and prominent nameplate.*

A nameplate is a distinctive type treatment of your publication's title. As the first item on the first page, its purpose is to be prominent enough to immediately establish a lasting visual identity. A nameplate remains the same from issue to issue.

Nameplates and logos—together referred to as *banners* in online environments—are a long-standing element for providing users their sense of orientation in "virtual space." A home page on the Web is both the starting point for your audience and your all-important introduction. It's your opportunity to welcome your visitors' arrival and invite them to stick around, explore, and learn about you.

Banners are important for both the designer and the reader. Your visitors expect to know clearly "where" they are. You want to quickly establish an identity and also capture and keep their attention.

You'll build consistency by repeating your banner, some variation of it, or a smaller version on every major page as your readers navigate through your page, publication, and site.

Although large and recogniz- able at a glance, a name- plate should not overshadow the headlines on a page.

OCTOBER 1989

A NEWSLETTER FOR PARENTS & KIDS

Although large and recognizable at a glance, a nameplate should not overshadow the headlines on a page.

## Legal Logos

Logos, specially designed typefaces, and associative word phrases are often legally protected under state and federal trademark laws. The blue lines used by IBM enjoy trademark protection and cannot be used by another company.

Both trademark and copyright laws are used in the advertising industry to protect ads. Slogans and product and service names in ads are protected by trademark laws while copyright laws protect specific expressions in the main copy of the ad.

A logo is a graphical device that symbolizes your firm's type of business, particular style, or certain association. Logos can be created using letters, shapes, images, or any combination of them. You'll want to keep logo images simple enough to ensure their legibility over a wide variety of reproduction projects, from business cards to letterheads to nameplates.

**BRIGHT IDEAS**

Most aspects of our lives are replete with symbols, which can compress meaning and represent that meaning in a unified image—just as a national flag symbolizes a country. A carefully crafted logo can express your firm's philosophy, credibility, character, and style. We think and communicate in symbols; even the alphabet is a set of symbols. Their "associative" properties (the ideas they help us connect) can be exciting and enduringly etched in our minds when designed well.

**TIP**

Letterforms—called typefaces—are symbols too, and are frequently modified to create unique nameplates and logos.

Often, a carefully chosen typeface for a logo is more powerful than an image or graphic.

Sometimes letter-spacing is specifically modified to create a distinct effect called logo type.

In other cases, portions of the letters are omitted or exaggerated.

Logos are particularly important in magazine and newspaper advertisements. They provide a visual shorthand for immediate identification and ad-to-ad consistency. They also give the ad a strong finish.

## Moving On

By now you have an understanding of some of the organizational tools that form the foundation of a well-designed document. In the next two chapters, you'll learn about some important building blocks of design that can enhance the communicating power of your printed materials.

# 3

# The Architecture of Type

## Overview

- Use type as a design tool and not just as a wordsmith.

- Apply typefaces and assign roles to the variations of typefaces.

- Limit the number of typefaces to two—three at most—per project.

- Present typefaces effectively by managing the spaces they occupy, and their weight and posture.

*Typography—the design of the characters that make up text and display type (headlines, subheads, captions) and the way they're presented on a page—influences your print communications more than any other single visual element.*

The term *type* describes a printing character regardless of how it is stored—on metal, film, magnetic tape, paper, or as a series of mathematical formulas in a computer. A *typeface* refers to one complete set of characters (or type) of a distinctive design and that is distinguished by its weight (such as bold), posture (such as italic), and size. Technically, *font* also refers to one complete set of type in a given typeface, weight, posture, and size. Helvetica italic 12 is a font (or typeface), and a member of its *font family*. The following list illustrates part of the Helvetica font family:

| | |
|---:|:---|
| Helvetica | AaBbCcDdEeFfGgHh |
| Helvetica Oblique | *AaBbCcDdEeFfGgHh* |
| Helvetica Bold | **AaBbCcDdEeFfGgHh** |
| Helvetica Bold Oblique | ***AaBbCcDdEeFfGgHh*** |

Typography influences your print communications more than any other single visual element.

## A World of Type

You can find true public domain fonts listed at The Internet Font Archive (http://www.ora.com/homepages/comp.fonts/ifa/). It contains information and sample images of many thousands of PostScript Type 1 fonts and linked lists to many more for PCs and Macs.

Each typeface you choose sends an important and unique message to your reader. It conveys mood, communicates attitude, and sets tone. Consequently, type choices can help or hinder your readers' ability to understand your message. Type that grabs attention, but is unreadable, is not a success.

Many other factors must be considered in choosing type: column alignment, width and spacing, font family, size, style, and weight. Plus, your desktop publishing system may give you such options as rotating and distorting type, as well as wrapping type around visuals and composing it to fit the available space.

What's crucial for creating good-looking print is developing a discerning eye for type and knowing how typefaces work for you.

The basic typographic principles in this chapter can also help make your Web pages easier on the eye but there are specific limitations and freedoms for type when used on a computer screen.

# Examining Type & Type Decisions

*The finer characteristics of letter shapes create an overall distinct mood.*

You'll want to pay attention to various type samples and what other designers use for specific projects. Become aware of the type used for a business newsletter, an instruction guide, a tire sale advertisement, and so on. What features create the appropriate mood and tone? How many variations of type are there in each piece? What function does each variation perform? Do they work? Why?

## TIP

Often you'll find body text in a serif typeface and display type (headlines, banners) in sans serif.

One good way to begin to work with type is to architecturally digest it. Examine it and become familiar with the basic parts of letters and notice how they vary in detail from one typeface to another.

- **Ascender**: The part of the letter that extends above the main body of lowercase letters. In uppercase letters, this is called the stem.

- **Descender**: The part that extends below the main body of lowercase letters.

- **Cap Height**: The distance from the baseline to the top of an uppercase character.

- **Bowl** (Counter): The space found within some letters.

- **Serif**: The short cross-strokes at the top and bottom ends of a letter; also a classification for all type with serifs.

- **Sans Serif**: Type without serifs; also a classification for all type without serifs.

Each typeface you choose sends a unique message to your reader. It conveys mood, communicates attitude, and sets tone.

- **X-height**: The part that makes up the main body in lower-case letters.

Each typeface influences the tone of a publication. By combining different characteristics, you can identify general style patterns and establish a tone appropriate to your message. For example:

- **Conventional**: serifs, small x-height, tall ascenders and descenders.

- **Contemporary**: sans serif, high x-height, short ascenders and descenders.

- **Dignified**: serif with slightly pinched bowls and vertical letterforms.

- **Friendly**: rounded bowls and letterforms.

- **Fashionable post-modern**: very squeezed or exaggerated bowls and elongated letterforms.

Typefaces with rounded serifs tend to be friendly (Caslon244):

# Many hands make light work.

Typefaces with squared serifs look official or architectural (Officina Serif):

# Tax Form Enclosed

The simplicity and elegance of sans-serif typefaces make them ideal for large headlines and other display treatments.

# A TOUCH OF CLASS

Serif type, on the other hand, works well in smaller sizes, particularly for a text face, but can look busy and cluttered when set in large sizes for display purposes.

Serifs help the reader recognize the shapes of the letters. Take away the serifs and there's less letter-to-letter differentiation.

# Distinct letters
# Indistinct letters

## Using Type Families & Fonts

*One advantage of working with a type family is that it allows you to assign roles to each variation.*

Each typeface generally comes in several styles such as normal, italic, bold, and bold italic. The most common treatments are based on changing the density or width of letters. A set of characters in one style and one size of one typeface is called a font.

By limiting your type decision to two or three fonts at most, you still have all the variations within the font to contrast emphasis. For example, regular weight for body text and bold for headlines. Bold italics could be assigned to pull quotes or subheads and medium italics reserved for captions.

### Type Style

*Type style refers to variations in weight and stroke that lend flexibility in contrast and emphasis to each type family.*

Characters set in bold type have thicker strokes and add authority or emphasis to a typeface. Bold type is also frequently used for subheads to break up long expanses of text.

## Lend Contrast to Your Publication

Lorem ipsum dolor sit amet, consectetuer adipiscing elit, sed diam nonummy nibh euismod tincidunt ut laoreet dolore magna aliquam erat volutpat. Ut wisi enim ad minim veniam, quis nostrud exerci tation ullamcorper suscipit lobortis nisl ut aliquip ex ea commodo consequat.

Duis autem vel eum iriure dolor in hendrerit in vulputate velit esse molestie consequat, vel illum dolore eu feugiat nulla facilisis at vero eros et iusto odio dignissim qui blandit praesent luptatum zzril delenit augue duis dolore te feugait nulla facilisi. Lorem ipsum dolor sit amet, consectetuer adipiscing elit, sed diam nonummy nibh euismod tincidunt ut laoreet dolore magna aliquam erat volutpat.

### Lorem ipsum dolor sit

Ut wisi enim ad minim veniam, quis nostrud exerci tation ullamcorper suscipit lobortis nisl ut aliquip ex ea commodo consequat. Duis autem vel eum iriure dolor in hendrerit in vulputate velit esse molestie consequat, vel illum dolore eu feugiat nulla facilisis at vero eros et accumsan et iusto odio dignissim qui blandit praesent luptatum

zzril delenit augue duis dolore te feugait nulla facilisi.

Nam liber tempor cum soluta nobis eleifend option congue nihil imperdiet doming id quod mazim placerat facer possim assum. Lorem ipsum dolor sit amet, consectetuer adipiscing elit, sed diam nonummy.

### Ut wisi enim ad minim veniam

Nibh euismod tincidunt ut laoreet dolore magna aliquam erat volutpat. Ut wisi enim ad minim veniam, quis nostrud exerci tation ullamcorper suscipit lobortis nisl ut aliquip ex ea commodo consequat.

Duis autem vel eum iriure dolor in hendrerit in vulputate velit esse molestie consequat, vel illum dolore eu feugiat nulla facilisis.

Lorem ipsum dolor sit amet, consectetuer adipiscing elit, sed diam nonummy nibh euismod tincidunt ut laoreet dolore magna aliquam erat volutpat. Ut wisi enim ad minim veniam, quis nostrud exerci tation ullamcorper suscipit lobortis nisl ut aliquip ex ea commodo consequat.

Duis autem vel eum iriure dolor in hendrerit in vulputate

velit esse molestie consequat, vel illum dolore eu feugiat nulla facilisis at vero eros et accumsan et iusto odio dignissim qui blandit praesent luptatum zzril delenit augue duis dolore te feugait nulla facilisi. Lorem ipsum dolor sit amet, consectetuer adipiscing elit, sed diam nonummy nibh euismod tincidunt ut laoreet dolore magna aliquam erat volutpat.

Ut wisi enim ad minim veniam, quis nostrud exerci tation ullamcorper suscipit lobortis nisl ut aliquip ex ea commodo consequat. Duis autem vel eum iriure dolor in hendrerit in vulputate velit esse molestie consequat, vel illum dolore eu feugiat nulla facilisis at vero eros et accumsan et iusto odio dignissim qui blandit praesent luptatum zzril delenit augue duis dolore te feugait nulla facilisi.

### Duis autem vel eum iriure dolor in hendrerit

Nam liber tempor cum soluta nobis eleifend option congue nihil imperdiet doming id quod mazim placerat facer possim assum. Lorem ipsum dolor sit amet, consectetuer adipiscing elit, sed diam nonummy.

Use bold type carefully and sparingly because a lot of bold type darkens a page, making it look dense and uninviting.

Use boldface type carefully and sparingly because a lot of bold type darkens a page, making it look dense and uninviting.

## Bold Not Always Better

Characters set in boldface type have thicker strokes and add authority or emphasis to a typeface. Bold type is frequently used for subheads that break up long expanses of text.

### Close-Up of Typefaces

Boldface type must be used carefully. In small sizes, the counters-enclosed spaces within letters like e and o - often become filled in on laser printed output. A lot of boldface type also darkens a page.

Setting isolated words in boldface type in the middle of a block of text can draw more attention to a word than it warrants and can also create a "checkerboard" appearance on the page. Characters set in boldface type have thicker strokes and add authority or emphasis to a typeface. Bold type is frequently used for.

### Letters Move In

Setting isolated words in boldface type in the middle of a block of text can draw more attention to a word than it warrants and can also create a "checkerboard" appearance on the page.

Characters set in boldface type have thicker strokes and add authority or emphasis to a typeface. Bold type is frequently used for subheads that break up long expanses of text.

Boldface type must be used carefully. In small sizes, the counters - enclosed spaces within letters like e and o - often become filled in on laser printed output. A lot of boldface type also darkens a page.

Setting isolated words in boldface type in the middle of a block of text can draw more attention to a word than it warrants and can also create a "checkerboard" appearance on the page. Characters set in boldface type

have thicker strokes and add authority or emphasis to a typeface. Bold type is frequently used for subheads that break up long expanses of text. Boldface type must be used carefully. In small sizes, the counters often fill in on laser printed output. Characters set in boldface type have thicker strokes and add authority or emphasis to a typeface. Bold type is frequently used for subheads that break up long expanses of text.

Boldface type must be used carefully. In small sizes, the counters - enclosed spaces within letters like e and o - often become filled in on laser printed output. A lot of boldface type also darkens a page.

Setting isolated words in boldface type in the middle of a block of text can draw more attention to a word than it warrants and can also create a "checkerboard" appearance on the page.

Also, avoid setting isolated words in boldface type in the middle of a block of text. The bold type can draw more attention to a word than it warrants and create a checkerboard look to the page.

> Using **bold** as a means of emphasis can create a **"checkerboard" look** to your page. It's **much** better to use **italic type** for emphasis. Words in italic type are perceived as **spoken words**.

You can use italic type for emphasis or when irony or humor is intended. Italics also implies a conversational tone. You'll find ads that use italics to indicate a quote where no quote exists—as if someone were speaking. Because italics is perceived as spoken words, its emphasis is often more powerful than bold lettering alone.

> Using *bold* as a means of emphasis can create a *"checkerboard" look* to your page. It's *much* better to use *italic type* for emphasis. Words in italic type are perceived as *spoken words*.

Shadow, outline, and underline are also offered as styles for some typefaces. Exercise restraint when using these kinds of styles because they're more difficult to read. In the following example, shadow and outline seriously hinder legibility.

## Outline and **shadow text** should be used **sparingly.**

Likewise, underlining interferes with the reader's ability to recognize letterforms by obscuring descenders.

<u>Lines of emphasis quickly</u>
<u>become lines of annoyance.</u>

Small caps type is approximately 20 percent smaller than regular uppercase type. Small caps lets you emphasize words without darkening the page with bold type or drawing attention with large caps.

You can use large or small caps together to indicate acronyms or abbreviations.

He's a VIP in the CIA.
He's a VIP in the CIA.

## Type Weight

*Weight—letter width and stroke thickness—gives you further flexibility in lightening or darkening your page.*

For example, in the Helvetica family, Helvetica Black has more impact than Helvetica Bold. Helvetica Black is an ideal choice for short, high-impact headlines.

**BLACK WINS**

**BOLD IS OKAY**

Helvetica Light gives headlines a gentler look, lightening the page in comparison to the heavier Helvetica Black.

Lighten up and live longer.

Condensed weights offer a narrower *footprint*. This increases the number of letters that can fit on a line. Univers Condensed, for example, preserves the essential attributes of Univers, but the letters are narrower. Narrow footprints are ideal where space is a premium.

Combinations are also available. Univers Condensed, for example, is available in both Light and Bold variations.

The maximum horizontal distance that a single letter occupies is called the letter's footprint.

# Univers Condensed Light

# Univers Condensed Regular

# **Univers Condensed Bold**

Typeface variations offer you extra flexibility in giving your publication a voice without having to introduce entirely different typefaces.

## Presenting Type Effectively

*Experienced designers evaluate how well type choices can be presented or configured in a layout. Attention to such detail provides the appeal and communication power you want for your documents.*

The design potential of type—from the ordinary to the ornate—includes applying them effectively. Once you've made your choice of letter types, you need to evaluate how well they'll work in a given layout and environment.

Your attention needs to shift to type sizes, word and line spacing, line endings, spacing and position for headlines, and column widths. You're looking for details that enhance your message. You want to avoid those items that may distract—misaligned elements, mismatched proportions—anything that disrupts the flow of information and the ease of reading.

Luckily, you don't need to know every nuance about type-setting to achieve good presentation. A little vocabulary and a sense of measurement work wonders.

Points and picas are part of the vocabulary of typesetting. Type is measured in point size (72 points to the inch). Most desktop programs let you adjust type size in half-point increments. Line spacing is measured in points. Line lengths are measured in picas.

## TIP

6 picas = 1 inch
12 points = 1 pica
72 points = 1 inch

Measuring type is an inexact science because of design differences. Stroke, ascenders and descenders, and footprints vary. Still you may find the printable pica ruler on the Companion CD-ROM handy for examining print materials and obtaining an apparent size. Print it on a sheet of transparency film used to make overheads. Then carefully cut it out, keeping the edges as straight as possible.

The environment and position your type occupies need to behealthy ones. Type needs breathing room. Too much room, though, and your message gets lost, too little and it gets cramped. This breathing room is called white space. While white space is generally perceived as the absence of something (space that doesn't contain text or graphics), it is actually the basis of a well-dressed presence and a strategic way to draw attention to important text and graphics.

# Type Size

*Type size is determined by balancing proportionately both the impor-tance of the message and its surroundings.*

When choosing type size, consider the amount of white space available. Keep in mind the width and the number of columns because they also impact size and space decisions.

Strive for the balance that calls attention to the message by both applying the appropriate type size and giving it sufficient breathing room.

## Body Text Choices

The best measure for setting text type size is achieving a comfort level that makes the material easy and inviting to read. If you're new to design, stick with safe body text types. As your confidence builds, you'll naturally explore more creative and artistic styles.

Safe text choices include both serif and sans-serif type. Most readers are familiar with serif type for text. Use simple serif letterforms that:

- Don't call attention to themselves.
- Have rounded and oval characteristics.
- Provide some contrast between uppercase and lowercase letters.
- Are of medium weight.

A variety of types fit these qualifications, including Goudy, Baskersville, and others. Which serif type you choose is less important than understanding how it breathes on a page. Consider, for example:

- Small sizes in light or condensed typeface can break apart or blur together.

Type needs breathing room. Too much and your message gets lost, too little and it gets cramped. This breathing room is referred to as white space.

This text is not very easy to read.

- Large type with a narrow column width can cause too many hyphenated line endings (three or more are too many).

> This text is aw-
> fully large in re-
> lation to the col-
> umn width, caus-
> ing hyphen over-
> kill.

- Tight spacing can result in serifs that collide and adjoin letters.

## Letters will run into each other if letter spacing is too tight.

Sans-serif types like Helvetica, Optima, and Futura are also functional, readable, and less risky for body text when they:

- Are of medium weights.
- Show subtle variation of thick and thin strokes.
- Offer contrast with smaller x-height and rounded form.

When setting sans-serif typefaces in their allotted spaces you'll want to pay attention to their particular mannerisms:

- Small sizes with small x-height types can make letters look tiny.
- Line lengths that are outside a range of 35 to 60 characters, including punctuation and word spacing, can make reading difficult. (You'll need to adjust both size and column width.)
- Added line spacing can make text blocks look pallid and washed out.

Some styles of type are not recommended for body text because they are too difficult to read in any significant length. Stay away from script and ornamental typefaces that are meant for display type and brief phrases. The use of all italics and all caps quickly undermines character recognition and becomes tedious when used beyond their emphasis roles.

## Display Text Choices

The safety guidelines for "display text" (headlines, subheads, captions) follow two simple rules:

- Use the opposite type of classification (serif or sans serif) as used in the body text. If you used sans serif in the body, you can use serif in the display text.

- Use the same type family, generally in bold.

You'll need to assess display text for balance in contrast. Is there enough contrast? Is there too much so as to dominate or overwhelm?

### TIP

Generally, headlines are 1.5 times larger in point size than the body text, and one full level greater in boldness. For example, if you select 12-point body text then you'll use 18-point size for headlines.

For display text, remember that spacing mistakes are more apparent. Most large typefaces (18 points and higher) need spacing adjustments between letters, words, and columns.

You don't need to extend display text across the entire length of a column or columns of text. They require more breathing room than body text. Display text attracts more attention if framed in white space.

Display text attracts more attention if framed in white space.

## White Space Comes in Handy

Lorem ipsum dolor sit amet, consec tetuer adipiscing elit, sed nonummy nibh euismod tincidunt ut laoreet dolore magna aliquam erat volutpat. Ut wisi enim ad minim veniam, quis nostrud exerci tation ullamcorper suscipit lobortis nisl ut aliquip ex ea commodo consequat.

Duis autem vel eum iriure dolor in hendrerit in vulputate velit esse

laoreet dolore magna aliquam erat volutpat.

Ut wisi enim ad minim veniam, quis nostrud exerci tation ullamcorper suscipit lobortis nisl ut aliquip ex ea commodo consequat. Duis autem vel eum iriure dolor in hendrerit in vulputate velit esse molestie consequat, vel illum dolore eu feugiat nulla facilisis at vero eros et accumsan et

Large type squeezed into a small area is hard to read and is visually disturbing and claustrophobic.

## White Space is Sorely Needed

Lorem ipsum dolor sit amet, consec tetuer adipiscing elit, sed nonummy nibh euismod tincidunt ut laoreet dolore magna aliquam erat volutpat. Ut wisi enim ad minim veniam, quis nostrud exerci tation ullamcorper suscipit lobortis nisl ut aliquip ex ea commodo consequat.

Duis autem vel eum iriure dolor in hendrerit in vulputate velit esse

laoreet dolore magna aliquam erat volutpat.

Ut wisi enim ad minim veniam, quis nostrud exerci tation ullamcorper suscipit lobortis nisl ut aliquip ex ea commodo consequat. Duis autem vel eum iriure dolor in hendrerit in vulputate velit esse molestie consequat, vel illum dolore eu feugiat nulla facilisis at vero eros et accumsan et

Typically, display type with two or three lines of text or all caps either needs no adjustment between lines or less line space. Rarely will space be added.

If you want to use ornamental letterforms for display text type, check your swipe file for examples similar to your project. Even in all caps, ornamental type can be unruly. Also, all caps in script fonts can be nearly impossible to adjust. Some type families were not designed for capitalization even though today's technology can create them—Old English is one. Generally, ornamental fonts are used for headings and rarely for anything else.

Safe choices are violated regularly by talented and seasoned professionals who know exactly what they're doing. As you work with type, your confidence will grow and you'll soon gravitate to more daring and well-executed decisions.

Most of the daring uses of type include letterforms that have a high x-height, uniform letter weights, unusual letter shapes, or prominent serifs. Such typefaces as Eurostile, Korinna, Avant Garde, and others for body text choices require careful consideration and manipulation for successful results; if applied improperly they can distract or become tedious for readers.

---

### Body text is distracting

Safe choices are violated regularly by talented and seasoned professionals who know exactly what they're doing. As you work with type, your confidence will grow and you'll soon gravitate to more daring and well-executed decisions.

Most of the daring uses of type include letterforms that have a high x-height, uniform letter weights, unusual letter shapes or prominent serifs. Such typefaces as Eurostile, Korinna, Avant Garde, and others for body text choices require careful consideration and manipulation for successful results; if applied improperly they can distract or become tedious for readers.

---

## Tools & Techniques for Presenting Type

Type is a wonderful graphic design tool. Any job is easier to complete and more enjoyable when you have the right tools and understand their purpose. The effective presentation of type includes several elements of fine-tuning that accompany successful results.

### Alignment

*Alignment can alter the amount of space given to type, the tone your message conveys, and the readability of your materials.*

There are four basic alignment options, each with a different impact. Lines of type can be set the following ways:

- Justified (flush-left/flush-right)
- Flush-left with a ragged right margin
- Flush-right with a ragged left margin
- Centered

Readability studies show that many people favor flush-left/ragged-right alignment, meaning the first letters of each line are lined up with each other, but the lines themselves are of irregular length. The irregular line endings create a ragged margin of white space, giving publications a lighter look. In addition, the even word spacing enables readers to easily recognize word groups.

Flush-left/ragged-right type gives a publication an informal, contemporary, "open" feeling. The space between each word is the same. Such lines generally end where words end. Only long words that fall at the end of lines are hyphenated.

> Readability studies show that many people favor flush-left/ragged-right alignment, meaning the first letters of each line are lined up with each other, but the lines them-selves are of irregular length.

> "This country, with its institutions, belongs to the people who inhabit it. Whenever they shall grow weary of the existing government, they can exercise their constitutional right of amending it, or their constitutional right to dismem-ber or overthrow it."
> *Abraham Lincoln*

Justified type produces lines of equal length. Type is aligned on both left and right margins. Word spacing is adjusted automatically to create the even line endings.

Because of the uniform line length, justified columns lack the white space created with ragged alignment, and thus tend to darken a publication. In addition, justified type is sometimes considered more difficult to read because more words are hyphenated and there may be large gaps between words.

Nevertheless, many magazines, newspapers, and books use justified alignment because the word density is higher. As a result, less space is needed to communicate the same amount of information, which can reduce the number of pages in a document and result in cost savings.

> "This country, with its institutions, belongs to the people who inhabit it. Whenever they shall grow weary of the existing government, they can exercise their constitutional right of amending it, or their constitutional right to dismem-ber or overthrow it."
> *Abraham Lincoln*

For display type, centering is another alignment scheme that's useful for short headlines that span more than one column of type. Centering text can lend a formal tone to a document; it's frequently used for wedding invitations and official announcements.

However, avoid centering long blocks of type, particularly for a three- or four-line headline. Because readers have to search for the beginning of each line, centered type is more difficult to read.

## In lengthy center-justified headlines, readers must search for the beginning of each line.

Type also can be set flush-right/ragged-left. Like centered type, flush-right alignment forces the reader to slow down to find the beginning of the next line, and therefore, you'll need to limit its use to concise headings and headlines.

|  |  |
|---|---|
| **Try not to be too wordy when setting subheads flush-right** | **Be concise instead** |
| Lorem ipsum dolor sit amet, consec tetuer adipiscing elit, sed nonummy nibh euismod tincidunt ut laoreet dolore magna aliquam erat volutpat. Ut wisi enim ad minim veniam, quis nostrud exerci tation ullamcorper suscipit lobortis nisl ut aliquip ex ea commodo consequat. | Lorem ipsum dolor sit amet, consec tetuer adipiscing elit, sed nonummy nibh euismod tincidunt ut laoreet dolore magna aliquam erat volutpat. Ut wisi enim ad minim veniam, quis nostrud exerci tation ullamcorper suscipit lobortis nisl ut aliquip ex ea commodo consequat. |
| Duis autem vel eum iriure dolor in hendrerit in vulputate velit esse | Duis autem vel eum iriure dolor in hendrerit in vulputate velit esse dignissim qui blandit praesent veleum iriure dolor in hendrerit in vulputate velit esse dignissim qui blandit |

Setting short headlines flush-right is a way to lock them to text-heavy columns.

## Kerning, Tracking & Letter Spacing

*Most page layout programs provide you with multiple tools to adjust spacing and there's a good reason: designers use them a lot.*

Kerning is the adjustment of space between selected pairs of letters. Tracking automatically governs the amount of space placed between each character throughout a block of text. Letter spacing can be used for special effects.

Certain pairs of letters sometimes appear to be separated by too much space. This effect is particularly apparent in a headline with an uppercase T next to a lowercase o, or an uppercase W next to a lowercase a, and so on.

**Kerning** reduces the space between individual pairs of letters to improve readability.

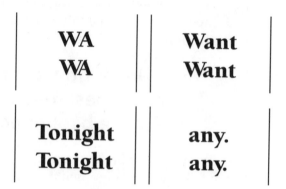

Kerning reduces the space between individual pairs of letters to improve readability. It can also be used to add space between certain letter pairs. This is often done to improve legibility when setting white type against a black background.

Most larger typefaces require less space between letters and between words. Letters such as "O" and letter pairs such as "WA" and "To" carry implied space around them. Some publishing programs provide automatic kerning especially of letter pairs. Some do not, so you may need to manually adjust letter spacing.

Tracking allows you to control the overall spacing within:

- A selected range of text.

- Part of a style.

- Part of a default (a track setting that a program automatically uses unless you specify another numeric value).

By tightening tracking, you increase the density of your text, fitting more words into the same amount of space. This tends to darken a publication.

> **Usually, if you've set reasonable parameters for justification in your program, the very worst offenders in hyphenation will be lines with bad breaks, caused by long single-syllable words or words with**

Conversely, loose tracking lightens a page.

> **Usually, if you've set reasonable parameters for justification in your program, the very worst offenders in hyphenation will be lines with bad breaks, caused by long**

Different software programs allow you to adjust "track" in different ways. Some will let you change tracking by changing the default, by changing the numeric value through a command, or manually by highlighting and "dragging" a selected range or paragraph.

Letter spacing, or stretching a word across a space (such as the top of a column or page), can transform that word into a graphic element. Letter spacing is often used to create department headings and to identify standard recurring features in periodicals.

## Word Spacing

*The amount of space between words affects word density and the readability of a publication.*

When word spacing is tight, more words can be included on each line. In certain situations, this reduces the number of hyphenated words.

When word spacing is tight, more words can be included on each line. In certain situations, this reduces the number of hyphenated words.

You'll need to be careful with word spacing. If you reduce word spacing too much, the text becomes difficult to read and the publication looks too dark.

Tracking and word spacing are often adjusted simultaneously. One common

When word spacing is tight, more words can be included on each line. In certain situations, this reduces the number of hyphenated words.

You'll need to be careful with word spacing. If you reduce word spacing too much, the text becomes difficult to read and the publication looks too dark.

Tracking and word spacing are often adjusted simultaneously. One common

You'll need to be careful with word spacing. If you reduce word spacing too much, the text becomes difficult to read and the publication looks too dark.

Tracking and word spacing are often adjusted simultaneously. One common technique, especially with high x-height typefaces, is to slightly reduce letter spacing and increase word spacing.

When experimenting with tracking and word spacing, be sure to review proofs to ensure you've achieved the right balance.

## Paragraph Spacing, Tabs & Indents

*Use tabs, indents, or extra space between paragraphs to enhance readability. Tabs and indents also can be used to effectively set off lists and quotations.*

Be sure to make the space at the beginning of paragraphs consistent in your documents. Generally, two types of spacing schemes are used: a two- to five-space indent at the beginning of the first line of each paragraph or extra spacing between paragraphs with the first line set flush-left.

Adding space between paragraphs makes each paragraph appear more like a self-contained unit. It also adds an openness to a publication by breaking up the grayness of large expanses of text.

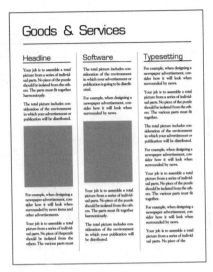

To increase paragraph spacing, always use your desktop publishing program's paragraph-spacing command, rather than using two carriage returns, which can result in far too much space between paragraphs. The paragraph-spacing command lets you add just enough white space between paragraphs to add interest without creating a page filled with distracting parallel bands of white space.

also adds an openess to a publication by breaking up the "grayness" of large expanses of text.

To increase spacing between paragraphs, always use your desktop publishing program's paragraph-spacing command, rather than using two carriage returns, which can result in too much space between paragraphs.

The paragraph-spacing command lets you add just enough white space between paragraphs to add interest without creating a page filled with distracting parallel bands of white space.

Extra space between paragraphs enhances readability. Adding additional space between paragraphs makes each paragraph appear

also adds an openess to a publication by breaking up the "grayness" of large expanses of text.

To increase spacing between paragraphs, always use your desktop publishing program's paragraph-spacing command, rather than using two carriage returns, which can result in too much space between paragraphs.

The paragraph-spacing command lets you add just enough white space between paragraphs to add interest without creating a page filled with distracting parallel bands of white space.

Extra space between paragraphs enhances readability. Adding additional space between paragraphs makes each paragraph appear more like a self-contained unit. It

Tabs can be used in conjunction with extra space between paragraphs to further open up a publication.

Indents can be used to call attention to quotations in a publication by moving a text block in from the left- and right-hand margins. Indents can also set a list off from the body copy.

> According to Dr. Ignatz P. Daley, of the VIrtual Reality Institute in Racida, CA, virtual reailty is only beginning to come into its own.
>
> > "The future remains to be seen through the eyes of virtual reality."
>
> Daily says the Institute, renowned as one of the world's foremost VR research centers, has been struggling with the issue of how to bring virtual reality to the mass market at

Lines of type with no added space at all between them are called set solid—and their appearance is just that—solid, dense, and dark. Generally, body type looks best with one point of space added while display type looks best set solid.

Leading (pronounced "ledding") is the space above and below a line of type. It's a critical factor in determining legibility. Leading, like type size, is measured in points.

**TIP**

For every publishing program on the shelves, software engineers have built in a number of default settings that set a value automatically, unless you specify a different one. Mainly, this is to get you up and running quickly, while keeping your frustration level low. Most programs also allow you to modify certain default values so you can customize to fit your specific needs.

The default (or automatic) line spacing found on most desktop publishing systems is approximately 20 percent greater than the type size being used. Thus, the default leading for 10-point type is 12 points—written as 10/12.

**TIP**

Finding how to change your software's default setting isn't always easy or obvious. Dig, dig, dig. Setting up any program to work the way you work will save time and aggravation later.

Typically, the setting for most display type is changed to subtract line spacing. Headlines often improve in appearance and readability when leading is reduced between lines. Tighter leading integrates the words into a distinct visual unit instead of a series of seemingly unrelated lines.

> **Latest Business Research Provides Explanation for Increase in Log Home Sales**
>
> The most recent issue of *Log Home Digest* published a survey which indicated that more people are buying log homes because "they like the way they look." Industry sources say a drop in log

> **Latest Business Research Provides Explanation for Increase in Log Home Sales**
>
> The most recent issue of *Log Home Digest* published a survey which indicated that more people are buying log homes because "they like the way they look." Industry sources say a drop in log prices may also be contributing to the trend.

On the other hand, extra leading often improves the appearance of text. It opens up the page, making it seem less gray.

Extra leading is usually called for when sans-serif typefaces are used for text.

**Leading should be proportional to line length. In general, use minimal leading for short lines of type. Increase leading as line length increases.**

People are created equal, that they are endowed by their Creator with certain unalienable rights, that among these are Life, Liberty, and the Pursuit of Happiness. ✎

## Women in Multimedia

That to secure these rights, governments are instituted among Men and Women. We hold these truths to be self-evident, that all People are created equal, that they are

People are created equal, that they are endowed by their Creator with certain unalienable rights, that among these are Life, Liberty, and the Pursuit of Happiness. ✎

## Women in Multimedia

That to secure these rights, governments are instituted among Men and Women. We hold these truths to be self-evident, that all People are created equal, that they are

Be careful to avoid leading so generous that readers get lost when their eyes leave the end of one line and try to find the beginning of the next line.

Leading should be proportional to line length. In general, use minimal leading for short lines of type. Increase leading as line length increases.

Leading also can be used as a design tool for special effects. You may sometimes want to tighten leading so that descenders (letter stems such as g and p that drop below the invisible line text rests on) from one line of type touch the ascenders (rising stems of letters such as b and d) from the line below. That lets you create special effects, particularly in designing logos and nameplates.

One of the advantages of using uppercase letters for headlines is that you can substantially reduce leading, because capitals lack descenders.

Happy Birthday to all employees | HAPPY BIRTHDAY TO ALL EMPLOYEES

## Special Type Effects

*Computers offer limitless ways to transform type into special graphic elements.*

Technology and publishing have liberated designers' imaginations, letting them fulfill their most inspired visions of how type can be manipulated. As tempting as a creative type treatment may be, it's most successful when there's a reason for it. Legibility is paramount—if your type can't be read, your message isn't getting across.

## Using Color for Type

*Dynamic execution of color type requires planning its role and purpose. Most designers will tell you that the more colors you have on your palette the more difficult it is to design the job.*

With today's color printers, brilliance in documentation is nearly a given. Even slick ads in magazines frequently use color for emphasis only, rather than entirely banishing black type. High costs in advertising is one reason, but not the only one. The major reason is that color can quickly overwhelm. We'll take a closer look at color in Chapter 8, "Working With Color."

## Reversing & Screening Type

*By reversing and screening type, you can achieve the effect of color and eye-catching contrast.*

Two simple type effects can be easily achieved by reversing type out of a black background or screening it in a lighter shade of gray.

By using these techniques, you can add enough visual contrast to your pages to achieve a "color" effect with only black ink and white paper.

When screening type against a background, be sure to create sufficient contrast to ensure that your type is clearly legible.

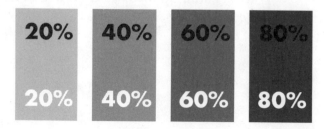

Use light type against dark-gray backgrounds and dark type against light-gray backgrounds; otherwise the type might be obscured.

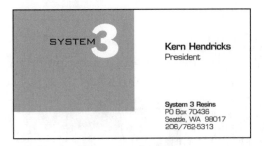

You can also screen type you want to highlight or draw attention to, such as in sidebars or logos.

When using screens, always consider the limitations of your output device. For example, a 300 dpi laser printer produces a coarse, grainy screen. It may be better to use other design techniques if you're limited to 300 dpi. Another option is to send desktop publishing files that contain screens to a service bureau to be output on a high-resolution imagesetter. The results will be much smoother and more professional looking. For more details about the limits of 300 and 600 dpi laser printers, see Chapter 9, "Working With Service Bureaus."

Similar to screened type, reversed type is usually white (or zero percent black) letters reversed out of a solid (or 100 percent black) background. Reversing type is a great way to draw attention to headlines, subheads, and other important display copy.

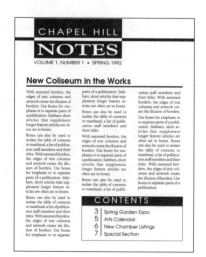

Reversing type is a great way to draw attention to headlines, subheads, and other important display copy.

Reversing works best with large sized single words or small phrases—lots of small reversed copy is difficult to read.

It's also best to use clean, bold, sans-serif typefaces when reversing type. Serif type, particularly ornate scripts, tend to break up when reversed.

More effects can be achieved through screening and reversing colored type. For more details, see Chapter 8, "Working With Color."

### Stretching & Compressing Type

*Distorted type is an option for words that are "recognized" instead of "read."*

Most desktop publishing and graphics software packages let you stretch or compress individual letters, words, and sentences to create interesting designs.

# STRETCH   COMPRESS

As with other special effects, use stretched or compressed type with caution. Too much of it can create a confusing document.

### Rotating Type

*Rotated type can be a real attention-grabber when used strategically.*

Most desktop publishing software packages offer some degree of type rotation capabilities. For example, a program may allow rotation in 45- and 90-degree increments, which is handy for setting photo credits or copyright notices and vertically designed letterhead stationary.

Photo by Lance Kozlowski

Other programs let you rotate type in nearly any fraction of a degree across all 360 degrees. You can achieve some interesting effects with this feature. Make sure the effect is warranted.

### Setting Type Along a Path

*Forcing type to follow a path offers several design options.*

By flowing type along a path, whether it's a geometric shape (circular or diamond path) or a custom-drawn line, you can achieve amazing results without hours of tedious work. This technique works well when combined with simple graphics to create illustrations and logos that draw and hold the reader's interest.

### Filling Type

*Filling letters changes their tone, shape, and impact.*

Another eye-popping effect involves filling letters with a pattern or image. It's best to limit this to easily recognized words; complex messages are not legible under this treatment. Bold, sans-serif typefaces work best for optimum impact.

Never let special effects stand between your message and the reader— legibility is more important than novelty and design for the sake of design.

### Other Effects

*You can achieve a variety of special type effects with most desktop publishing programs.*

You can apply dozens of other custom treatments to type, depending on the software you're using.

As enticing as these effects may be, remember to rely on them only when they are appropriate to the subject and content at hand. Never let special effects stand between your message and the reader—legibility is more important than novelty and design for the sake of design. Yet when used thoughtfully, these typographic enhancements can create compelling graphics.

# Fine Tuning

*Attractive desktop-published documents rely on typographic consistency and restraint.*

The keys to effective typography are based on consistency, restraint, and attention to detail. When choosing typefaces for a project, keep in mind that each font sets a tone or sends a message. Choosing and mixing fonts involves a careful look at the architecture of type and an evaluation of how well your type choices enhance your layout.

In general, stay with two typefaces on a page—three if you include a symbol typeface for lists and end signs. Many great-looking documents are based on a single sans-serif typeface for heads and subheads with a second serif typeface for text and captions.

## Refining Punctuation

*Replace "typewritten" characters with "typeset" punctuation whenever possible.*

For example, replace two hyphens with a single long dash called an em dash:

```
"I am in earnest--I will not
equivocate--I will not excuse--
I will not retreat a single
inch--and I will be heard!"
        Salutatory Address of
        The Liberator
```

"I am in earnest—I will not equivocate—I will not excuse—I will not retreat a single inch—and I will be heard!"
Salutatory Address of
*The Liberator*

Also, be sure to use open and closed quotation marks (often called smart quotes) instead of vertical ones (often called straight quotes). Some programs automatically make the substitution; others rely on you to do it.

## Moving On

Typography is a time-honored craft and an important one for every desktop publisher to learn.

By taking advantage of the wide variety of typeface alternatives available on desktop publishing systems and using the full range of spacing controls at your disposal, you'll quickly earn the label of designer.

In the next chapter, we'll explore some of the most fundamental elements of design essential to creating winning projects.

# 4

# Building Blocks of Design

## Overview

- Combine and balance visual tones to draw attention.
- Use white space to frame important elements.
- Techniques with boxes, rules, shadows, and sinks can isolate and highlight information while unifying page tones.

*A skillful designer uses the basic building blocks of design to examine a project and determine what it needs—or lacks—to capture readers' interest and communicate effectively.*

Many of the guidelines presented so far can help you establish a balance of the visual "tone" of your document. The color and visual tone of your document are important factors that separate good design from dreary, difficult documentation. Now we'll look closer at their meanings and uses.

When a reader looks at information, either printed on a page or displayed on a computer screen, there are three tones of space that represent a mental hierarchy: black space, white space, and gray space. Test this on yourself, it works!

When you open a printed document like this book, your eye is first attracted to black space.

Black space is a photo, graphic, or drawing that is neither a text block nor an empty area.

Black space is a photo, graphic, or drawing that is neither a text block nor an empty area. You will glean as much information from that area as you can to avoid reading the text. If the picture tells the story, why read the story? This natural attraction to black space is one reason why the Web and many Web pages enjoy such popularity.

Next, your eyes are drawn to white space.

White space doesn't contain text or graphics—it's a place for your eyes to rest.

White space doesn't contain text or graphics—it's a place for eyes to rest. The narrow column on this page for example, isn't always filled with text, yet the white space draws your eyes there and, by comparison, the column of text doesn't look so intimidating now. It also makes a great place to scribble notes, doesn't it?

Last and least, and if you can avoid it, you'd rather not look at gray space.

Gray space is text. Big blocks of text signal you—before you even begin reading—that this is work. As easy as reading may be to you, reading a "gray page" requires a lot of mental processing. A cursory glance, maybe a quick scan—and you're outta there! Stock market listings look best in the bottom of a bird cage, don't they?

Gray space is text.

Black space, white space, and gray space—the components of visual tone—and the balancing of these spaces are the basic building blocks of design.

## Balancing Black, Gray & White Tones

*To cultivate acute designer skills, assess tonal variety—the balance of black, gray, and white tones that appear in a project.*

Each of the black, gray, and white tones has its relative value and must be viewed in combination with—and in contrast to—the opposing tones. It's the judging and shuffling of all three that create visual interest.

Too much gray can look boring and turn readers away. Add rules, heavier subheads, and appropriate white space, and the same drab text comes alive and has a much better chance of being read.

Gather related elements from all three tones, and you've got the foundation for a well-designed page. Throw them together without a plan, and your creation is relegated to the bottom of Polly's birdcage or, in the case of a Web page, to the class of a ransom note.

### TIP

Each type of element has a tone. Graphics and photos are black; text blocks are gray; and white space is open or empty and retains a white tone.

In order to wear the official hat of a designer, you need to be able to combine and balance these tones with the goal—and the result—that clear communication is guiding your design decisions.

## White Space

*White space—or blank space free of text or artwork—is one of the most undervalued and misunderstood fundamentals of design.*

White space provides contrast and serves as a resting point for readers' eyes. White space can take many forms:

- **The open area surrounding a headline.** The attention-getting power of a headline is increased more by adding extra white space around it rather than by using larger type.

- **The page margins of an advertisement or publication.** Wide margins direct the readers' attention into the center of the page.

- **The vertical space between columns of type.** The wider the columns, the more space needed between them.

- **The space created by ragged line endings of unjustified type.** This space relieves the monotony of large expanses of evenly measured text.

- **Paragraph indents and extra line space between paragraphs.** These small but effective increments of space can open up a page layout.

- **Leading between lines of type.** Tightly packed lines of type darken a publication page.

- **The space inside photographs and illustrations.** Also incremental in nature, these spaces contribute to the total amount of white space on a page.

## TIP

White space doesn't have to be white. If your publication is printed on colored paper stock (e.g., ivory or tan), white space lets more of the background color appear. This is also true for Web pages that use rich backgrounds of colors, textures, and patterns.

## Techniques for Tone & White Space

Because any element surrounded by white space will attract attention, you can emphasize important information anywhere on a page.

*Specific arrangements of the tones and space—when used appropriately—signal logical relationships for readers.*

Because any element surrounded by white space will attract attention, you can emphasize important information anywhere on a page. You can also establish connections for readers with variations in the amounts of space used between elements. For example, more white space above a headline and less below it visually cues the readers that the headline and the text that follow are related.

Remember, white space alone—or too much of it—isn't likely to be useful unless there are noticeable contrasting elements. Gray values in photos, text patterns, and screen tints bring some contrast. Black tones from bold type, reverse blocks, and rules bring sharper contrast and potency to the other tones and the whole project. It's the balance achieved by combining all three tones that yields exciting results.

## Sinks

*One of the easiest ways to enliven your publication is to include a sink—a band of white space, also called a "drop"—at the top of each page.*

This white space draws attention to the text below by adding contrast. It can also dramatize headlines.

### WHEN YOU GO...

One of the easiest ways to enliven your publication is to include a drop–a band of white space, also called a "sink," at the top of each page. This white space draws attention to the text below by adding contrast.

It can also dramatize headlines. Another visually interesting device is placing photographs so they slightly extend into the drop, rather than align with the top text margin. One of the easiest ways to enliven your publication is to include a drop–a band of white space, also called a "sink," at the top of each page.

This white space draws attention to the text below by adding contrast. It can also dramatize headlines. Another visually interesting device is placing photographs so they slightly extend into the drop, rather than align with the top text margin. One of the easiest ways to enliven your publication is to include a drop–a band of white space, sometimes referred to as a "sink," at the top of each page.

This white space draws attention to the text below by adding contrast. It can also dramatize headlines. Another visually interesting device is placing photographs so they slightly extend into the drop, rather than align with the top text margin. One of the easiest ways to enliven your publication is to include a drop–a band of white space, sometimes referred to as a "sink," at the top of each page.

This white space draws attention to the text below by adding contrast. It can also dramatize headlines. Another visually interesting device is placing photographs so they slightly extend into the drop, rather than align with the top text margin.

One of the easiest ways to enliven your publication is to include a drop–a band of white space, also called a "sink," at the top of each page. This white space draws attention to the text below by adding contrast.

It can also dramatize headlines. Another visually interesting device is placing photographs so they slightly extend into the drop, rather than align with the top text margin. One of the easiest ways to enliven your publica-tion is to include a drop–a band of white space, also called a "sink," at the top of each page.

This white space draws attention to the text below by adding contrast. It can also dramatize headlines. Another visually interesting device is placing photographs so they slightly extend into the drop, rather than align with the top text margin.

It can also dramatize headlines. Another visually interesting device is placing photographs so they slightly extend into the drop, rather than align with the top text margin. One of the easiest ways to enliven your publica-tion is to include a drop–a band of white space at the top of each page.

You can place photographs to slightly extend into the sink, rather than align with the top text margin.

A consistent sink provides important page-to-page continuity throughout your publication. Notice how publication unity is destroyed when the text begins at a different level on each page.

## Vertical White Space

*Depending on relationships with other elements on the page, vertical white space can be perceived as crisp, elegant, fresh, contemporary, or stark—any of which communicates a positive message.*

Vertical white space—by omitting a column of text—can add personality to your project. Ideally, most of the column is kept open, but it can provide space to extend a front-page table of contents, publishing information, or pull quotes.

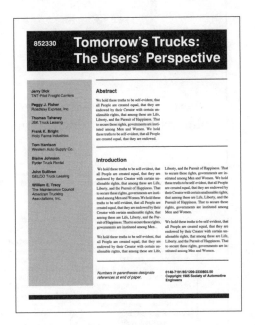

## Rules

*Imaginative use of rules can reinforce your project's layout and add impact. Deceiving in their simplest forms, rules can perform many vital functions including separating and organizing information, emphasizing and framing content, and guiding your reader's eyes into the content.*

Rules are lines that can be used to emphasize or frame various page elements such as headlines, pull quotes (short sentences that summarize key points of an article or paragraph), headers, and so on. Although they are sometimes considered embellishments, rules can be powerful.

From centuries of printing, many ornate varieties of rules are available. They can be horizontal, vertical, angled, thick, thin, solid, dotted, dashed, patterned, or graphical.

Rules are lines that can be used to emphasize various page elements such as headlines, pull quotes, and subheads.

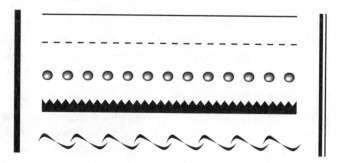

Vertical rules, called *downrules*, are often used to separate columns, particularly when type isn't justified.

Lorem ipsum dolor sit amet, consectetuer adipiscing elit, sed diam nonummy nibh euismod tincidunt ut laoreet dolore magna aliquam erat volutpat. Ut wisi enim ad minim veniam, quis nostrud exerci tation ullamcorper suscipit lobortis nisl ut aliquip ex ea commodo consequat.

Duis autem vel eum iriure dolor in hendrerit in vulputate velit esse molestie consequat, vel illum dolore eu feugiat nulla facilisis at vero eros et accumsan et iusto odio dignissim qui blandit praesent luptatum zzril delenit augue duis dolore te feugait nulla facilisi. Lorem ipsum dolor sit amet, consectetuer adipiscing elit, sed diam nonummy nibh euismod tincidunt ut laoreet dolore magna aliquam erat volutpat.

Ut wisi enim ad minim veniam, quis nostrud exerci tation ullamcorper suscipit lobortis nisl ut aliquip ex ea commodo consequat. Duis autem vel eum iriure dolor in

hendrerit in vulputate velit esse molestie consequat, vel illum dolore eu feugiat nulla facilisis at vero eros et accumsan et iusto odio dignissim qui blandit praesent luptatum zzril delenit augue duis dolore te feugait nulla facilisi.

Nam liber tempor cum soluta nobis eleifend option congue nihil imperdiet doming id quod mazim placerat facer possim assum. Lorem ipsum dolor sit amet,sed diam nonummy nibh euismod tincidunt ut laoreet dolore magna aliquam erat volutpat. Ut wisi enim ad minim veniam, quis nostrud exerci tation ullamcorper suscipit lobortis nisl ut aliquip ex ea commodo consequat.

Duis autem vel eum iriure dolor in hendrerit in vulputate velit esse molestie consequat, vel illum dolore eu feugiat nulla facilisis. Lorem ipsum dolor sit amet, consectetuer adipiscing elit, sed diam nonummy

Dolor sit amet, consectetuer adipiscing elit, sed diam nonummy nibh euismod tincidunt ut laoreet dolore magna aliquam erat volutpat. Ut wisi enim ad minim veniam, quis nostrud exerci tation ullamcorper suscipit lobortis nisl ut aliquip ex ea commodo consequat.Lorem ipsum dolor sit amet, consectetuer adipiscing elit, sed diam nonummy.

Duis autem vel eum iriure dolor in hendrerit in vulputate velit esse molestie consequat, vel illum dolore eu feugiat nulla facilisis at vero eros et accumsan et iusto odio dignissim qui blandit praesent luptatum zzril delenit augue duis dolore te feugait nulla facilisi. Lorem ipsum dolor sit amet, consectetuer adipiscing elit, sed diam nonummy nibh euismod tincidunt ut laoreet dolore magna aliquam erat volutpat.

Ut wisi enim ad minim veniam, quis nostrud exerci tation nonummy ullamcorper suscipit lobortis nisl ut

Horizontal rules can be used to separate topics within a column or to draw attention to subheads.

Horizontal rules are often used to draw attention to pull quotes.

Choose rules that harmonize with the tone of your document. Thick rules darken a document unless they are set off by white space.

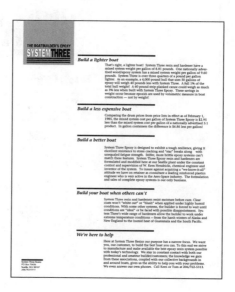

Thin rules are often appropriate for documents with a lot of copy.

Another useful technique is to use rules similar in width to the thickness of the strokes of the letterforms used in a newsletter nameplate or an ad headline. This can add an interesting graphic element to the type treatment.

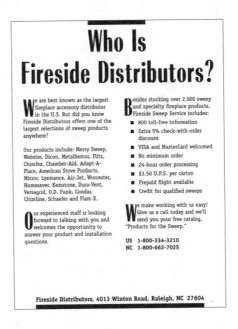

## Borders

*Use borders to frame and draw attention to the "live area"—the space in which text, display type, and artwork appear.*

Well-executed borders work with white space to determine the publication's visual and emotional tone. Borders can be tangible or assumed. Tangible borders are rules or graphics that outline a document. Assumed borders aren't visible but are created subconsciously as the reader encounters the edge of the live area of a document.

The basic tangible border is a large frame surrounding the contents of a page. With most desktop publishing programs, it's easy to create a border by using the box-drawing tool. Either single or double lines, thick or thin, can be used. Full-page boxes can provide unity to pages with several different kinds of information.

All four borders don't have to be the same, however. Different styles of rules can be used for the vertical and horizontal sides.

Well-executed borders work with white space to determine the publication's visual and emotional tone.

Borders don't have to extend the full height or width of a publication's live area.

Boxes can also be used to isolate the table of contents or masthead, a list of publication staff members and their titles. With assumed borders, the edges of text columns and artwork create the illusion of borders.

With assumed borders, the edges of text columns and artwork create the illusion of borders. Use boxes for emphasis or to separate parts of a publication. Sidebars, short articles that supplement longer feature articles are often set in boxes.

Boxes can also be used to isolate the table of contents or masthead, a list of publication staff members and their titles. With assumed borders, the edges of text columns and artwork create the illusion of borders. Use boxes for emphasis or to separate parts of a publication. Sidebars, short articles that supplement longer feature articles are often set in boxes.

Boxes can also be used to isolate the table of contents or masthead, a list of publication staff members and their titles. With assumed borders, the edges of text columns and artwork create the illusion of borders. Use boxes for emphasis or to separate parts of a publication. Sidebars, short articles that supplement longer feature articles are often set in boxes.

Boxes can also be used to isolate the table of contents or masthead, a list of publication staff members and their titles. With assumed borders, the edges of text columns and artwork create the illusion of borders. Use boxes for emphasis or to separate parts of a publication. Sidebars, short articles that supplement longer feature articles are often set in boxes.

Boxes can also be used to isolate the table of contents or masthead, a list of publication staff members and their titles. With assumed borders, the edges of text columns and artwork create the illusion of borders.

Use boxes for emphasis or to separate parts of a publication. Sidebars, short articles that supplement longer feature articles are often set in boxes. Boxes can also be used to isolate the table of contents or masthead, a list of publication staff members and their titles. With assumed borders, the edges of text columns and artwork create the illusion of borders. Use boxes for emphasis or to separate parts of a publication. Sidebars, short articles that supplement longer feature articles are often set in boxes.

Boxes can also be used to isolate the table of contents or masthead, a list of publication staff members and their titles.

With assumed borders, the edges of text columns and artwork create the illusion of borders.

## Boxes

*Boxes can be used to emphasize or separate parts of a publication.*

Sidebars (short articles that supplement longer feature articles) are often set in boxes.

You can use boxes to create reader-response coupons. Most desktop publishing programs let you create boxes with dashed borders to clearly identify the coupon.

Boxes can also be used to isolate the table of contents or the publication's masthead (a list of staff members and their titles).

Boxes often define the boundaries of a visual. By using boxes to enclose light-colored or indistinct edges of a photograph or illustration, you prevent the visual from blending into the background and thereby create a publication that appears unfinished.

## Drop Shadows

*Skillfully used, drop shadows create attention-getting, three-dimensional effects.*

Drop shadows can draw attention to boxes or visuals. They can help emphasize a photo, illustration, or checkbox by isolating it from its background.

### WHEN YOU GO...

One of the easiest ways to enliven your publication is to include a drop–a band of white space, also called a "sink," at the top of each page. This white space draws attention to the text below by adding contrast.

It can also dramatize headlines. Another visually interesting device is placing photographs so they slightly extend into the drop, rather than align with the top text margin. One of the easiest ways to enliven your publication is to include a drop–a band of white space, also called a "sink," at the top of each page.

This white space draws attention to the text below by adding contrast. It can also dramatize headlines. Another visually interesting device is placing photographs so they slightly extend into the drop, rather than align with the top text margin. One of the easiest ways to enliven your publication is to include a drop–a band of white space, sometimes referred to as a "sink," at the top of each page.

This white space draws attention to the text below by adding contrast. It can also dramatize headlines. Another visually interesting device is placing photo-

graphs so they slightly extend into the drop, rather than align with the top text margin. One of the easiest ways to enliven your publication is to include a drop–a band of white space, sometimes referred to as a "sink," at the top of each page.

This white space draws attention to the text below by adding contrast. It can also dramatize headlines. Another visually interesting device is placing photographs so they slightly extend into the drop, rather than align with the top text margin.

One of the easiest ways to enliven your publication is to include a drop–a band of white space, also called a "sink," at the top of each page. This white space draws attention to the text below by adding contrast.

It can also dramatize headlines. Another visually interesting device is placing photographs so they slightly extend into the drop, rather than align with the top text margin. One of the easiest ways to enliven your publication is to include a drop–a band of white space, also called a "sink," at the top of each page.

This white space draws attention to the text below by adding contrast. It can also dramatize headlines. Another visu-

Like all desktop publishing tools, use drop shadows with discretion. Because they are easily created, they tend to be misused and applied too frequently. Be sure that the three-dimensional effect that accompanies a drop shadow is important to communicating the content. If it's not important, don't use it—it will distract your readers.

## Screens

*Screening adds contrast and defines various elements of a document, such as sidebars or boxes that contain important information.*

Screens can make or break a page layout. Experiment with the percentage of black (or color) to find the screen that best suits your needs. (Also see Chapter 8, "Working With Color, " for more about screens.)

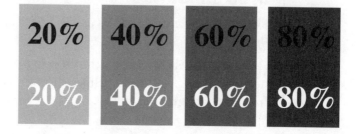

Screens can be effective in adding "color" to a page, breaking up the monotony of black and white. Adding a screened rule to an ad, for instance, breaks up the type block and makes the document more visually appealing.

Screening a sidebar or a chart sets that information apart from the rest of the text and draws attention to it.

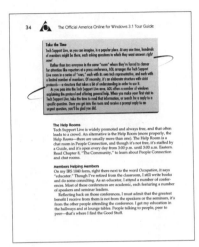
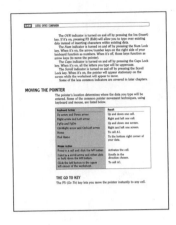

# Bleeds

*Some of the most dynamic design results are achieved with bleeds.*

A printed image that extends beyond the text margin to the edge of a page is called a bleed.

An oversize initial cap, or chapter number, can bleed to the top or side edges of a title page of a manual or book.

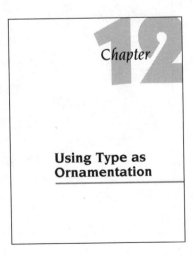

A photograph can gain "motion" when it extends to the edge of a page.

Horizontal rules that bleed to one or both sides of a page add continuity to pages.

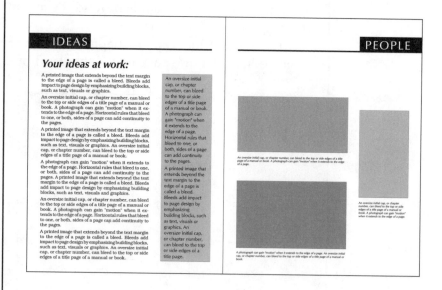

Newsletter nameplates gain impact when their backgrounds bleed to the top or sides of the page.

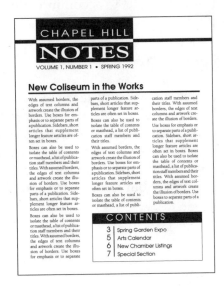

Cost can be a consideration when using bleeds—check your budget and hardware resources. Commercial offset printers have to use oversized sheets of paper and trim it to actual publication size after printing, thus the increased cost. (See Chapter 9, "Working With Service Bureaus.")

Sometimes you can successfully use bleeds with 8-½ x 11-inch paper with your laser printer. The printing area of most laser printers is approximately a quarter-inch smaller than the physical size of the paper. (High-resolution output devices—1270 or 2540 dpi—do not have this limitation.) You can print your pages at a slightly reduced size (90% of the original size) and then increase them (111%) on a photocopier or offset press. You'll need to test this for complex projects since type distortion and disturbances in letter spacing and word spacing can occur.

Bleeds work particularly well with two-color brochures in which the entire front and back covers are printed in a second color, with headlines reversed out. (See Chapter 8, "Working With Color.")

Bleeding can be overdone, of course. Some readers become annoyed with magazines that routinely forfeit page numbering, for example, to accommodate advertisements covering the physical page.

## Moving On

Now that you've learned the basics about layout, type, and graphic elements, let's explore the different kinds of illustrations you can add to your documents. The next chapter addresses the importance of such visuals as illustrations, clip art, charts, and graphs that you can use not only to emphasize and enhance your message but to organize and present your information too.

# 5

# The Art of Illustration

## Overview

- Remember that tones of an image or illustration affect the balance of your layout.

- Use white space to frame and balance images and illustrations.

- Choose a style of illustration to complement your content and typography.

- Focus on the essential details of an illustration, select an appropriate size, and remove irrelevant aspects.

- Pay close attention to direction and motion conveyed by images.

- Effective presentation and position of illustrations are based partly on the content of your message.

*Images can be decorative or informative. When used to inform, visual images in a document communicate your message at a glance.*

New designers often fall into the trap of using illustrations whenever they want to fill up a page, break up copy, or generally add visual spice to a document. You can avoid this trap and other problems by putting some forethought into illustrations.

Graphics, art, and pictures are used to help deliver your message. An effective design communicates the message—but don't expect graphics and pictures to do all the work.

Regardless of the role illustration and artwork play in your layout, you'll want to give them careful consideration. Understanding how, where, and when illustrations are best used assures your document's uniqueness and power.

## Working With Illustrations

*Using professional illustrations can significantly enhance the effectiveness of your message and the overall attractiveness of your page.*

The reproduction and creation power of today's publishing programs goes beyond most designers' imaginations. The programs help you manipulate and modify your illustration to suit your page layout and overall design.

### TIP

You may be relieved to know that not every professional designer is also a talented artist. Luckily, with today's technology and choices, you don't need to master drawing skills to illustrate your ideas. Your ability to think visually is much more important. Still, you'll want to develop at least a shorthand method of visually representing ideas. Then you can look for an existing image (be mindful of copyrights!) or commission an artist to create one that effectively communicates your ideas.

The expression of an idea through illustrations enjoys a wide variety of form and style. Such a vast resource can be overwhelming but it doesn't have to be. You can start by becoming familiar with a few forms and styles and then add others to your design arsenal gradually as you move from project to project.

Consider each alternative in relation to your design and how well each one reproduces for final output. You can choose from many types of illustrations, including:

- Scanned images
- Bitmapped images
- Text shapes
- Traced pictures
- Painted creations
- Thumbnail sketches
- Photographs
- Line art
- Clip art
- Charts, graphs, maps, and tables
- Picture fonts

All of these possibilities make this area an exciting one. You can combine a variety of these effects or manipulate any single one.

You can enliven your materials even with a low image inventory. Impact can be achieved by:

- Inverting a positive to a negative.
- Successive repetition that targets the main focus.
- Flipping and reversing.
- Distorting.
- Autotracing a full image to its outline form.
- Creating shapes with text.
- Creating illustrations with text.

Ultimately, the effect needs to elucidate your message or decorate it in a fitting style.

## Using Illustrations Effectively

*Your message can get lost in a sea of illustrations when graphics and artwork are used as filler or substitutes for content.*

Images and illustrations are an integral part of design. Image and text frequently combine to tell a story, make a point, reveal a different perspective, make a comparison, and condense or expand an idea.

If you add an inappropriate illustration—or use a graphic in a way that doesn't serve the reader—you are asking for trouble.

Here are a few common sense guidelines you can follow that will help you effectively integrate your illustrations into an attractive layout:

- **Don't crowd your artwork.** Leave generous borders around illustrations so the eye flows to them naturally.

- **Vary illustration size and shape.** Running lots of illustrations at roughly the same size and shape gets boring. Be creative with the size, shape, and placement of each image.

- **Be consistent.** Using a vastly different range of illustration styles in a document can make it appear disjointed and uncomfortable.

- **Less is more.** It's usually the case that running fewer illustrations at a larger size yields a higher visual impact than lots of smaller ones—it also gives you more bang for your illustration buck.

Don't forget the designer's motto: Rules were made to be broken (when you know what you're doing). You can achieve specific and unique effects by following steps that might normally yield unsightly pages. But in general, crowded repetitive illustrations make for an unattractive document.

## Illustrations vs. Photographs

*Designers with years of experience can (and often do) disagree over whether a particular layout calls for a photo or an illustration.*

Illustrations are the logical choice to evoke a particular mood or depict a complex object.

Photos are generally used to report or document an event or realistically portray an individual or group of people. Illustrations are the logical choice to evoke a particular mood or depict a complex object such as the internal structure of a high-suspension bridge. While recent advances in computer imaging are blurring the line between photos and illustrations, they are treated as separate subjects in this book.

For more on selecting and using photos in your documents, see Chapter 7, "Communicating With Photographs." Many of the design concepts covered in that chapter hold true for working with illustrations as well as photos.

## Illustrious Possibilities

*Illustrations offer far more opportunities for interpretation than photos do.*

You can selectively organize and emphasize information as you want it to be seen, read, and interpreted. Therefore, artwork can convey accuracy, skewed information, atmosphere, or aesthetics.

For example, a draw-type program can be used to render an image of a person's hand, either literally or in abstract form.

Cutaways (line diagrams) of objects are often used in technical manuals and documents and—in this age of computer graphics—they're easy to include. These illustrations can show the internal structure of an object with more clarity than photographs of the various components of the object.

## Build an Image Database

*Collecting and cataloging your image and illustration inventory will save you hours of hunting and sorting.*

If you're not yet connected to the Internet, obtaining images is only one good reason to try it out. There are large repositories of useable art and images—some are free and part of the public domain, some have usage restrictions (you may need to credit the originator), and others can be purchased. These images are useful for both desktop publishing and for Web pages. Check Appendix B, "Clip Art, Photographs & Font Resources" in the back of this book for Internet resource sites.

### TIP

Today's technology makes it easy to acquire and radically alter images—with little respect for copyrights. Copyright myths abound, so you need to pay attention. For example, just because an image appears on the Internet and you can save it on your hard drive, it does not automatically mean you can use that image without violating copyright laws. Make sure you're clear about copyright licenses, laws, privileges, and ownership before you grab and use an image. Read and follow the author's restrictions.

You'll find the Image Bank on the Companion CD-ROM a great place to start looking for images. Use the cataloging program to store and catalog others that you find.

# Ready-Made Art

*Use ready-made art to save time and to try out a number of illustrations in a page layout program before making a final choice.*

Ready-made art is any illustration, image, photo, or artwork that you did not originally create but you have permission or license to use.

Using a page layout program, you can try out any number of different illustrations on a page before making a final choice. And with the wide proliferation and low cost of ready-made art such as electronic clip art, background textures, patterns, and other forms of illustration, designers have never had more options to choose from:

- Clip art comes on floppy disk, CD-ROM, and over the Internet. Clip art offers the designer nearly unlimited access to digitized art ranging from the simple to the masterful.

- Background textures and patterns, rules, icons, and boxes are packaged and distributed much like clip art.

- Dingbat sets are fonts that contain numerous images accessible via keystrokes that would ordinarily yield letters. Instead of printing letters, these special fonts yield dingbats, bullets, icons, or other pictures.

## Clip Art

*Use clip art to add pizzazz and professionalism to ads, brochures, menus, and newsletters—but understand the risks you take.*

Clip art consists of files of existing artwork that can be dropped into your desktop published documents. Clip art can save you lots of time and money by letting you brighten your publication without having to create your own illustrations.

Still, clip art has its drawbacks. Charges can add up when you consider that one or two images in dozens are actually useful. Not all clip art vendors create art of equal quality—some clip art is poorly drawn or is outdated in style. You also take the risk of seeing your art in someone else's work. None of these disadvantages are meant to deter you from using clip art. You'll want to use it often—just pay attention to its quality and freshness when you do.

There are many different styles of clip art. Some of it is strictly functional, such as maps and anatomical drawings.

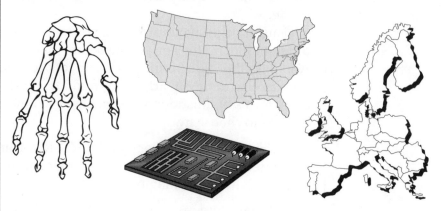

Other clip art is more artistic, mimicking the look of hand-drawn images, watercolors, or woodcuts.

Clip art is often used for borders. There are hundreds of unique and specific clip art border treatments.

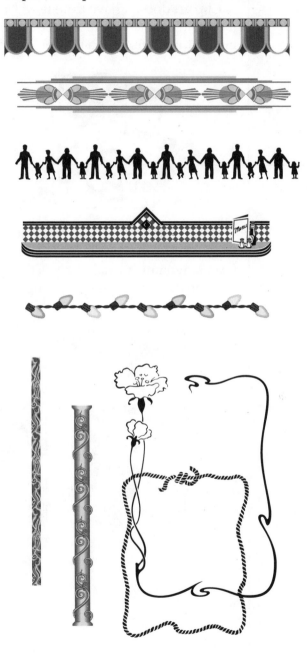

There are tens of thousands of other clip art files available to suit any conceivable subject or interest.

Clip art doesn't have to be used "as is." You can often customize it by using some special techniques. For example, you can crop an image, that is, use just a portion of it, but greatly increase its size.

Another technique involves combining several clip art images. For example, individual clip art items can be brought together to form a dynamic visual, such as the still life superimposed on the geometric figure in the following example.

## Background Textures & Patterns

*You can achieve some nice effects and impressive results with patterns and textures.*

Background textures and patterns, which are either created by professional graphic artists or scanned from actual objects like marble or fabric, can be used to lend a touch of elegance or respectability to any layout from print to Web pages.

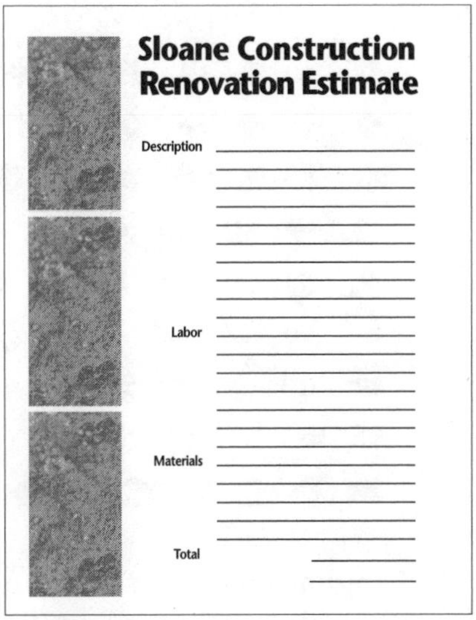

**Sloane Construction Renovation Estimate**

Description _____

Labor _____

Materials _____

Total _____

Unlike clip art, background textures and patterns are used more to lend color or weight to a document, not to illustrate a particular part of the text. They are effective for ads, brochures, invitations, and flyers. Another popular application for this kind of art is its use as a backdrop over which text is placed. This is especially useful when creating electronic pages for use on the Internet or in another electronic medium.

As with clip art, you don't have to use textures or patterns as they originally appear. A little editing and manipulation go a long way toward making commercially created artwork look like a unique graphic.

Background textures and patterns are used to lend color or weight to a document.

## Dingbat Sets & Picture Fonts

*Image fonts are an often overlooked source of illustrations.*

Although most designers don't turn to fonts when they're looking for a particular illustration, a host of companies produce
dozens of non-text fonts that can be used to illustrate everything
from books to flyers. Most designers are familiar with dingbat
collections, such as the popular Zapf Dingbats, named after
Hermann Zapf, who also created the typeface Palatino.

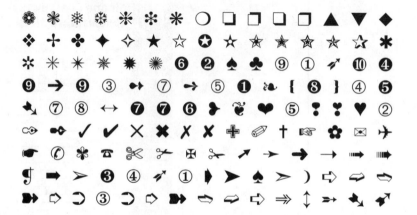

Dingbat sets are useful sources for clean and effective bullets,
slugs, icons, and other small pictures. And since they are actually
fonts, dingbats are conveniently imbedded in lines of text, so
there's no placing or importing to worry about when using page
layout programs. But bullets and slugs are just the beginning.
You may be able to solve many of your illustration needs using
picture fonts.

## Shopping for Ready-Made Art

*It's important to know what you need and can use before buying commercial graphics.*

There's no shortage of sources for clip art and graphics, and each vendor offers a huge array of products. But to make sure you're buying the right graphic for the job, here are a few guidelines you can follow:

- Graphics are saved in a number of file formats. Images saved in TIFF or EPS formats are usually compatible with any software program.

- Graphics come on floppy disk, CD-ROM, and via online services. Make sure the source medium your graphics vendor uses is compatible with your system.

- Be sure to find out how many images are included on each disk, CD, or package purchase. Ask your graphics vendor if the graphics are provided in color, black and white, or both.

- Some graphics are in a form that you can edit with a paint or draw program, while others aren't. If you plan to alter individual objects in an image, make sure your software is capable of working with it in its format.

## Screen Captures

*Computer documentation often contains a specialized form of art, called screen captures.*

Screen capture capabilities accompany most popular programs today. They take a "picture" of the computer screen (you determine how much of the screen to capture by selecting options) with a command or hot key. Once captured, you can save the image as a file.

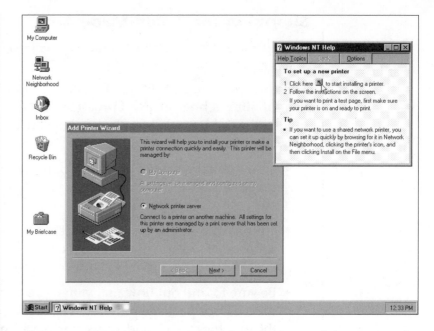

Screen captures are very useful in software training manuals.

# Manipulating Illustrations

*Most images and illustrations can be manipulated in a number of dramatic ways.*

Most page layout, paint, and draw programs let you enlarge, reduce, and stretch an image.

There are a number of special techniques (besides the simple cut-and-paste and cropping techniques discussed in the "Clip Art" section of this chapter) that you can use to manipulate or otherwise change an illustration to suit the needs of a specific layout. Many software packages allow you to edit images in a variety of dynamic ways.

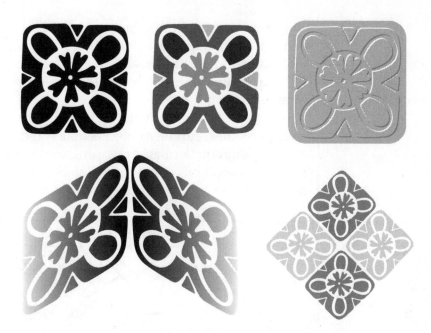

Generally, computer-generated illustrations are created using either a paint program or a draw program.

Images in "paint" formats are bitmaps—a huge collection of tiny squares that make up the larger picture. Enlarging a bitmapped image causes the individual squares to become more clearly visible, yielding jagged or chunky results.

You can't typically manipulate individual objects or single items in a bitmapped graphic, although some programs provide tools that emulate this capability. You can, however, use special techniques and filters to change the appearance of the entire bitmapped graphic.

Images in "draw" formats, on the other hand, are composed of a series of lines, curves, or objects that you can usually edit using a draw program. Because draw programs use equations to define the curves and lines in individual objects, the resulting images have the same quality of smoothness at practically any size.

Using a draw program, you can isolate and edit specific objects in a larger image, while leaving the rest of the graphic unchanged.

The kind of effects you can create using ready-made art depend largely on the software at your disposal and the format of the image itself, but nearly every program that handles graphics will allow you to stretch, size, and crop an image, regardless of its format.

## Presenting & Positioning Illustrations

*A dynamic illustration or image can lose its impact if it isn't presented and positioned to fulfill its purpose and role.*

Present an illustration in a way that allows it to fulfill its function without disrupting the flow of information for the reader.

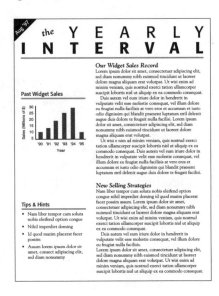

Balance the black or dark tones of a photograph with other heavy and contrasting elements on the page. In the following layout, the nameplate and bold headline balance the photo at the bottom.

Illustrations can occupy any part of the page including top, bottom, middle, left or right sides, and diagonal corners. Some guidelines you can follow include:

- Use the content of the image to direct the readers toward the corresponding text.

- When photographs are the central focus of your project, highlight them by using simple type.

- Be consistent in size and shape when using multiple images on the same page. Different shapes—as when one image occupies three columns and another occupies two—can give the layout a miscalculated and disjointed look.

- Leave even margins of white space when the text wraps around an image.

- Sometimes the content of the image can spur your creative juices and give you ideas for positioning and presentation.

- Illustrations can help you organize content, especially if your project contains different kinds of information.

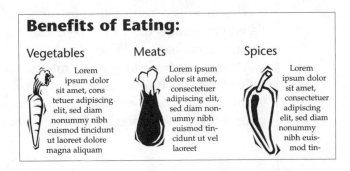

- When working with contrasting forms of illustrations—for example, some drawings and one photograph—give one form more breathing room than the other, and make sure their styles are complementary.

## Moving On

Illustrations add an important dimension to a document. Use them to add "color" to your overall page and to support and communicate your message.

The various manipulation features included in desktop publishing programs can be a mixed blessing. Overdoing it is an occupational hazard. When used with restraint, these features can transform ho-hum visuals into exciting ones.

Now let's focus on information graphics—maps, charts, graphs, and tables—and how to use them effectively to make your designs look good in print and your content crystal clear.

# 6

# Information Graphics

## Overview

- Information graphics require a high degree of design clarity to perform well.

- Significance, not style, determines when to use an information graphic.

- The form an information graphic takes is based on the kind of information being depicted; one method will make the information visually clearer than another.

- Use information graphics to make understanding greater and easier.

- Effective statistical graphics depend both on form and delivery.

Statistical graphics—charts, diagrams, tables, maps, pictograms, and even forms, checklists, and applications—project information embodied in numbers, words, and ideas. They can transform a series of unconnected numbers to a pattern that makes sense of statistics, maps out an idea, or invites our participation.

When we use information graphics, we generally use numbers and number relationships in picture form to communicate. Their purpose is to make visible certain facts that would otherwise remain hidden in a mass of lists, figures, and reports. Numbers and number relationships can become visually clearer in picture form.

Information graphics can inform audiences and draw attention to trends, comparisons, and organizational structures. They can be used to categorize and relate information about ideas, points of view, and events.

You can create these kinds of illustrations easily using clip art and your desktop publishing program's drawing tools. Or, you can create them with separate drawing programs.

The widespread use of information graphics in publications such as *USA Today* and *Time* shows that charts, diagrams, and tables can be presented in visually exciting ways. With today's affordable multicolor printing, you're likely to be using information graphics more and more in your publications and presentations.

You'd be surprised how you can assemble impressive graphics from nothing more than combinations of circles, straight lines, fill patterns (such as parallel lines or dots), and clip art. Yet to be powerful, these kinds of graphics need to clarify meaning rather than be an exercise in technological prowess.

## Charts & Diagrams

*Charts and diagrams translate numbers and values into visual images so that readers don't lose their way through a matrix of unconnected figures and information.*

Charts quickly communicate comparisons, relationships, and trends. The first step in choosing the appropriate type of chart is to define its purpose and identify which chart will be the most effective to present that concept to the reader or viewer.

Pie charts best display parts-to-whole relationships.

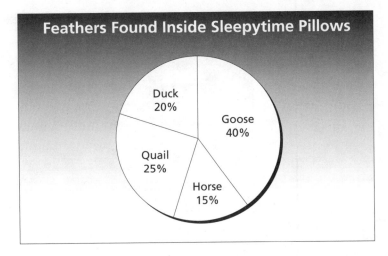

Pie charts best display parts-to-whole relation-ships.

Pie charts work best when the slices are large and few. Dividing a pie chart into too many slices results in confusion.

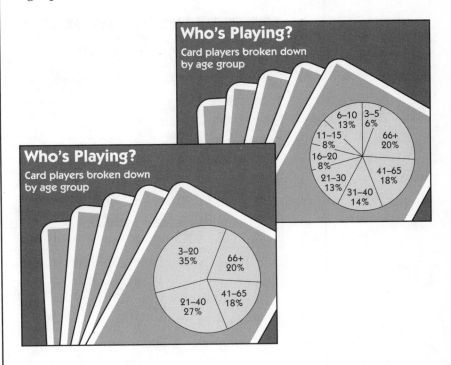

Bar charts make comparisons.

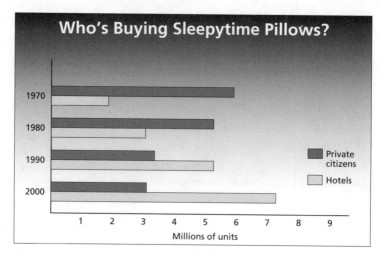

Stacked bar charts display the parts that contribute to the totals.

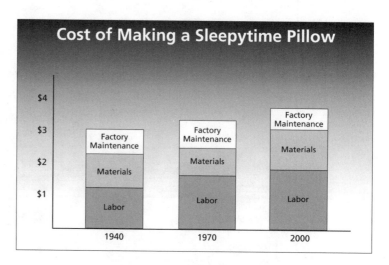

The bars can be drawn vertically, horizontally, or sometimes as objects instead of bars. Using objects can be misleading, because both area and volume information are present. In these cases, the difference in apparent volume is incorrect and misleading although the effect is dramatic. For example, you'll see tiny objects next to big ones where usually only height is being compared.

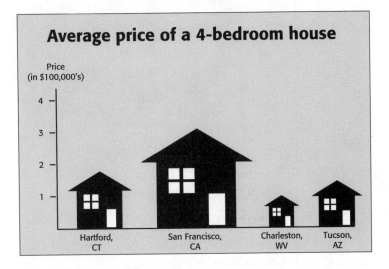

Line charts show trends.

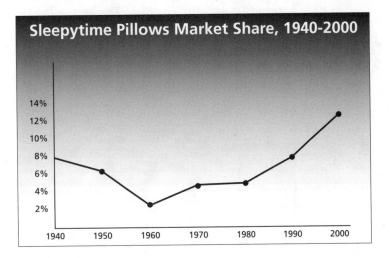

You can also combine chart types. This compound chart shows both total yearly sales and departmental contributions to the total yearly sales.

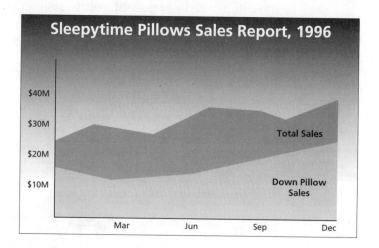

## Diagrams

*Choose diagrams rather than charts when you want to emphasize relationships and sequences rather than numbers.*

Organizational diagrams are one of the most frequently encountered types of diagrams. These display dominant/subordinate, "who reports to whom," relationships.

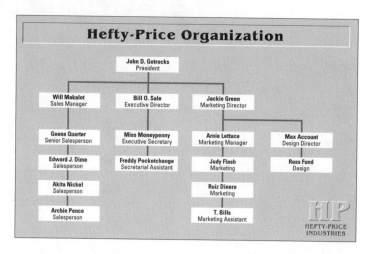

Flow, or process, diagrams are used to display sequences—
what must be done first, what must be done second, and so on.

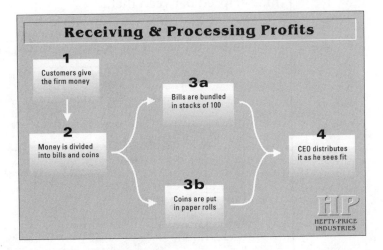

Choose a PERT—Program Evaluation Review Technique—
diagram when you want to display both sequence and the length
of time it will take to accomplish each step. PERT diagrams
communicate both sequence and time, because all elements are
drawn to the same scale.

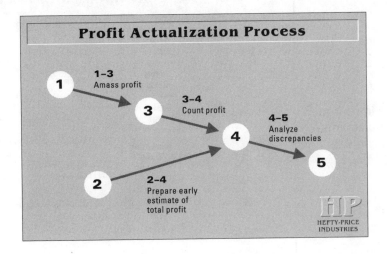

Timelines help you visually communicate historical perspectives. You can show when certain events occurred and how much time elapsed between them.

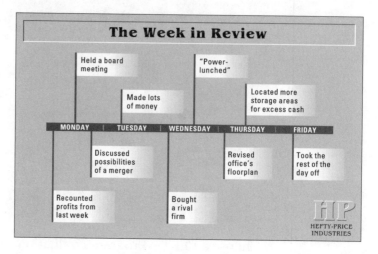

Diagrams can also be used to display spatial relationships. Floor plans, cutaway product drawings, and maps are examples.

Add impact to your diagrams by using size and color.

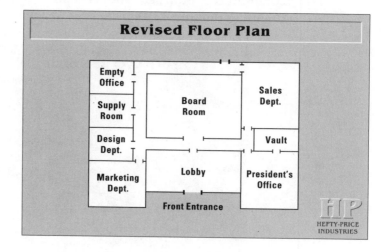

Add impact to your diagrams by using size and color. Size can be used to indicate time and color can be used to draw attention to critical parts. You can also enhance your drawings by "exploding" them—isolating the most important part and making it larger.

You can increase the impact and communicating power of your charts and diagrams by doing the following:

- Include a title that summarizes the purpose or importance of the information being displayed.

This title lacks impact:

## 1992 Sales by Region

But this title commands more attention:

## Projected 1992 Sales Increases

- Use labels to indicate the exact amounts displayed in each chart segment or bar graph column.

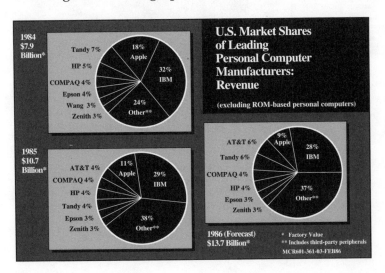

- Include background grids that provide a frame of reference by indicating the major numeric divisions.

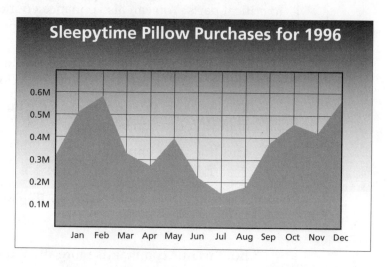

- Include tick marks that define subdivisions.

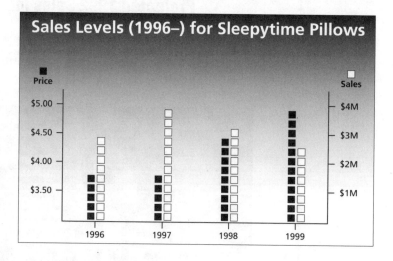

- Use a legend in a chart or diagram to identify symbols and units of measure.

- Use shades, patterns, and colors that complement each other. Avoid adjacent colors that fight or that blend together.

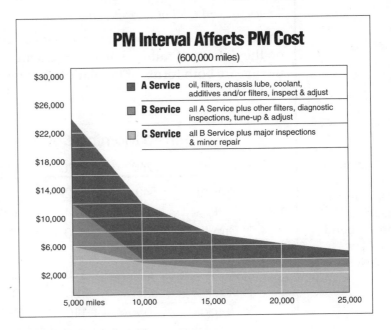

## Enhancing Charts & Diagrams

*You can improve a visual's communicating power by modifying the type specifications.*

Here are some of the ways you can selectively enhance the typography in your chart or diagram:

- Choose a different typeface and increase the type size of pie or bar charts or of diagram value labels.

- Reset X- and Y-axis annotation in a larger type size to improve legibility.

- Make the legend more noticeable by using a larger type size and adding white space around it.

# Tables

*Tables present a lot of information in a concise and orderly way.*

Tables are useful when you want to focus your reader's attention on the data itself rather than on representations. Price lists and menus are both forms of tabulation that represent numbers and words.

When placing information in tables, be sure to leave enough "breathing room" around the text or numbers.

### Preferred Morning Beverage (1,000s)

| COFFEE | 1960 | 1970 | 1980 | 1990 |
|--------|------|------|------|------|
| Instant | 540 | 562 | 580 | 590 |
| Perk | 453 | 444 | 420 | 410 |
| Drip | 622 | 690 | 725 | 950 |
| **TEA** | | | | |
| Black | 325 | 320 | 315 | 250 |
| Herbal | 105 | 110 | 160 | 200 |

Charts and diagrams show trends and comparisons. Tables let you easily read down or across to compare specific information in adjacent rows and columns.

A table can often replace several sentences. Tables are frequently used in proposals and reports to buttress arguments and conclusions. Tables are also used in slides and overheads to elucidate concepts and ideas.

When placing information in tables, be sure to leave enough "breathing room" around the text or numbers.

Make row and column headings significantly larger or bolder than the information they introduce. Screens can also be used to set off header information.

| Preferred Morning Beverage (1,000s) | | | | |
|---|---|---|---|---|
| **COFFEE** | **1960** | **1970** | **1980** | **1990** |
| Instant | 540 | 562 | 580 | 590 |
| Perk | 453 | 444 | 420 | 410 |
| Drip | 622 | 690 | 725 | 950 |
| **TEA** | | | | |
| Black | 325 | 320 | 315 | 250 |
| Herbal | 105 | 110 | 160 | 200 |

Avoid including more detail than necessary. Instead of including all digits in large numbers, round the numbers off to the nearest hundred, thousand, or million. (Be sure you prominently indicate the scale you're using.)

Although column headings are often centered, flush-right alignment can be used for row identifiers. This locks the information together.

| Preferred Morning Beverage (1,000s) | | | | |
|---|---|---|---|---|
| **COFFEE** | **1960** | **1970** | **1980** | **1990** |
| Instant | 540 | 562 | 580 | 590 |
| Perk | 453 | 444 | 420 | 410 |
| Drip | 622 | 690 | 725 | 950 |

When tables contain numbers, decimal alignment ensures that the numbers will line up, regardless of the size of the number or the number of decimal points after it.

| | |
|---|---|
| 1,567.98 | 1,567.98 |
| 257 | 257.00 |
| 3,410.3 | 3,410.30 |
| 957.69 | 957.69 |
| 2,113.54 | 2,113.54 |

Avoid using thick rules that darken a table and overwhelm the information presented. Notice that the horizontal and vertical rules can be of different thickness, as can the border rules.

| Preferred Morning Beverage (1,000s) | | | | |
|---|---|---|---|---|
| **COFFEE** | 1960 | 1970 | 1980 | 1990 |
| Instant | 540 | 562 | 580 | 590 |
| Perk | 453 | 444 | 420 | 410 |
| Drip | 622 | 690 | 725 | 950 |
| **TEA** | | | | |
| Black | 325 | 320 | 315 | 250 |
| Herbal | 105 | 110 | 160 | 200 |

# Maps

*Maps can take many forms. Like ideas and numbers, maps are understood when we see them in relationship to something else.*

Maps show reference. The simplest map locates a point by referencing it to known landmarks.

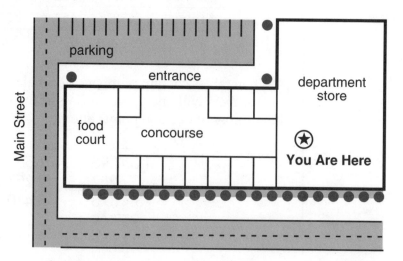

Maps, especially aerial maps, can also show size in relationship to other objects or places.

Map design requires an understanding of the information needed for clarity and a sense of what information can be omitted without diminishing its purpose. This is the vital difference between describing something and understanding it enough to represent it accurately.

## Moving On

Information graphics in its myriad of forms allows plenty of room to confuse aesthetics with performance. Part of your responsibility as a designer is to continually ask how your documents and their elements function. Good-looking documents perform well.

Now let's focus on photography and how to use it effectively to make your designs look good in print.

# 7

# Communicating With Photographs

## Overview

- Make sure each photo conveys a subtle message; check for appropriateness.

- Review all the elements in a photo—theme, characterization, setting, and mood.

- Choose your shots carefully.

- Edit photos to properly fit your layout.

- Give your photos "looking room"—allow for ample white space to frame a photo.

*Sometimes words alone seem inadequate to communicate your message.*

As many desktop publishers are learning, photographs can add power and impact to a layout.

Just as desktop publishing has made using illustrations and drawings as easy as clicking a few buttons, advances in scanning, printing, and other imaging technologies have made photos accessible to many desktop publishers.

## Why Use Photographs?

*Photographs bring realism and authenticity to a document.*

Photos offer a few things that other kinds of illustrations and artwork can't match. The most obvious is that photos seem real—they offer concrete visual proof to back up your text. This is why newspapers and magazines use photos for hard news stories, but use illustrations for more abstract articles.

# Walking a Political Tightrope

Bill Clinton struggles to balance competing interests

For the past week, the factions have hounded Bill Clinton. They all want a piece of the pie. Five hundred years ago, Christopher Columbus was on his knees in throne rooms throughout Europe, scrambling to finance his first voyage to the New World. Meanwhile, his Venetian countryman Aldus Manutius—scholar, printer, and entrepreneur—was establishing what would become the greatest publishing house in Europe, the Aldine Press. Like Columbus, Aldus Manutius was driven by force of of intellect and personality to realize a lifelong dream.

Aldus' greatest passion was Greek literature, which was rapidly going up in smoke in the wake of the marauding Turkish army. It seemed obvious to Aldus that the best way to preserve this literature was to publish it—literally, to make it public. The question was, how?

Although it had been forty years since the advent of Gutenberg's perss, most books were still being copied by scribes, letter by letter, a penstroke at a time. Because of the intensity of this labor, books were few and costly. They were also unwieldy. Far too large to be held in the hands or in the lap, books sat on lecterns in private libraries and were seen only by princes and the clergy.

One day, as he watched one of his workers laboring under the load of books he was carrying, Aldus had a flash of insight: Coopuld books from the Aldine Press be made small enough to be carried without pulling a muscle? And could How could he produce the elegant, lightweight volumes he imagined and still sell them at an attractive price?

The first problem was how to print more legible words per page and thus reduce the number of pages. Aldus needed a smaller typeface that was both readable and pleasing to the eye.

**Health Care Policy Summary**

The new typeface enabled Aldus to print portable and highly readable books. Besides the first edition of Dante's Divine Comedy, Aldus published the essential texts of Greek literature: the histories of Herodotus and Thucydides, the tragedies of Sophocles, the epics of Homer, and the treatises of Aristotle, thus rescuing them from relative oblivion.

The timing was perfect. With the growth of the merchant class in Venice, Florence, Naples, and Rome, a new market ripe for books had recently emerged. This newly prosperous middle class was flush with money and ankshious for intelligent ways to spend it. The new books from the Aldine Press were an immediate success.

As more books became available, the middle classes in Italy—and ultimately in all of Europe—grew more literate and the Aldine Press became more prestigious.

Numerous studies show that readers are more likely to believe a story, statistic, advertising claim, or other assertion if it features a photo.

Studies show that readers are more likely to believe a story, statistic, advertising claim, or other assertion if it features a photo.

Photos can also evoke a greater sense of urgency and drama from readers than illustrations can. If you try to recall the most important events of the last 50 years, odds are you associate the events you remember with photos you've seen.

Black-and-white photos are generally considered to be more authentic or "real" than color photos. Despite advances in technology, it's still easier to work with black-and-white. So this chapter will focus on the elements of using black-and-white photos effectively. (For more on working with color photos, see Chapter 8, "Working With Color.")

## Choosing Good Photographs

*Half the battle of producing professional, attractive layouts with photos is making sure you choose the best shots available.*

You don't have to be a shutterbug to know that not all photos are created equal. A good photograph stands apart from the rest because it both feels right and looks good. It captures our attention, conveys emotion, and tells a story. Photographers must expose and print the photograph properly, meeting basic standards of clarity and quality. A combination of the artistic and technical produces a winning photo.

A good photograph captures our attention, conveys emotion, and tells a story.

NORM KERR

## Evoke a Feeling

*Choose your shots carefully, not only for their visual quality and content, but also for the emotional impact they will have on the viewing audience.*

Good photographers are handy with a camera, but also have an eye for where to point the lens and when to click the shutter to capture emotion. For example, a tight close-up of a person talking tends to focus on that individual's qualities and heighten the dramatic effect of what the person is saying. Compare this to the distant and cool effect of a full-length shot of the same subject.

Most often it's much easier to recognize a great photo than it is to take one (or describe one for that matter). Yet every good photograph shares a few common elements:

- **A decisive moment.** Any shot of a person or event that suggests to the reader that it was the optimum instant to snap the picture.

- **Emotional context.** Even photos of cars or toothpaste tubes are loaded with emotion and implied meaning. If the image is devoid of feeling, it won't evoke a strong response.

- **Powerful visual imagery.** The underlying geometry, tone, and composition of a photo can make the difference between a mediocre shot and a great one.

- **Strong cropping and framing.** While you can always crop (or cut) an image, you can't get more from an image than the photograph originally offered. On the other hand, cropping can make or break a photo.

## Technical Fine-Tuning

*Desktop publishers need to be able to recognize a technically correct photo.*

Numerous technical factors influence how a photograph looks. A correct shot fulfills a number of common, related requirements:

- **Focus.** Above all, a photo must be in proper focus. Except when striving for a particular effect, fuzzy, vague, or blurry pictures look unprofessional.

Above all, a photo must be in proper focus.

- **Clarity.** It's possible for a negative and print to be in proper focus, but for the resulting image to appear grainy or diffuse.

- **Contrast.** Black-and-white photos must have balanced contrast. Too much contrast makes whites look too light and blacks look too dark; not enough contrast makes the entire image seem gray and washed out.

- **Brightness.** In simple terms, a correct shot is neither too dark nor too light, regardless of its subject matter.

A correct shot is neither too dark nor too light.

## TIP

You can easily determine where your potential reader's will tend to focus on a shot. Mentally divide the image into thirds vertically and horizontally. Viewers will focus where the lines intersect.

Intentionally blurring, overexposing, or otherwise altering technical aspects of a photo can yield dramatic and effective results. But, these are special circumstances that call for breaking the conventions of good photography in an effort to produce a particular effect.

# Designing With Photographs

*Good design is as important to photos as it is to type and illustrations.*

Working with photographs involves paying attention to a few important design concepts and conventions. As with illustrations, using photographs appropriately is all-important in realizing their effectiveness and impact.

## Use Dominant Photos

*Dominant photos tell readers where to look first.*

When running several photos on a single page or spread, choose one as the dominant image and position it prominently.

### The Road to Recovery

*Today's farmers are embracing new methods—and their open-mindedness is paying off*

Lorem ipsum dolor amet, consectetuer adipiscing elit, sed diam nonummy nibh euismod tincidunt ut laoreet dolore magna aliquam erat volutpat. Ut wisi enim ad minim veniam, quis nostrud exerci tation ullamcorper suscipit lobortis nisl ut velit aliquip ex ea commodo consequat.

Duis autem vel eum iriure dolor in hendrerit in vulputate velit esse molestie

nonummy nibh euismod tincidunt ut laoreet dolore magna aliquam erat ut volutpat.

Ut wisi enim ad minim veniam, quis nostrud exerci tation ullamcorper suscipit lobortis nisl ut aliquip ex ea commodo consequat. Duis autem vel eum iriure dolor in hendrerit vulputate velit esse molestie consequat, vel illum dolore eu feugiat nulla facilisis at vero eros et

placerat facer possim assum. Lorem ipsum dolor sit amet, consectetuer adipiscing elit, sed diam nonummy nibh euismod tincidunt ut laoreet dolore magna aliquam volutpat. Ut wisi enim ad mini veniam, quis nostrud exerci tation ullamcorper lobortis nisl ut aliquip ex ea commodo.

Duis autem vel eum iriure dolor in hendrerit in vulputate velit esse molestie consequat, vel illum dolore eu feugiat nulla facilisis.

Lorem ipsum dolor sit amet, consectetuer adipiscing elit, sed diam nonummy nibh euismod tincidunt ut laoreet dolore magna aliquam erat volpat. Ut wisi enim ad minim veniam, quis nostrud exerci tation ullamcorper suscipit lobortis nisl ut aliquip ex ea commodo consequat.

Duis autem vel eum iriure dolor in hendrerit in vulputate velit esse molestie consequat, vel illum dolore

eu feugiat nulla facilisis at vero eros et accumsan et iusto odio dignissim qui blandit praesent luptatum zzril delenit augue dolore te feugait nulla. Consectetuer adipiscing elit, nonummy nibh euismod tincidunt ut laoreet dolore aliquam erat volutpat.

Ut wisi enim ad minim veniam, quis nostrud exerci tation ullamcorper suscipit lobortis nisl ut aliquip ex ea commodo consequat. Duis autem vel eum iriure dolor.

consequat, vel illum dolore eu feugiat nulla facilisis at vero eros et accumsan et iusto odio dignissim blandit praesent luptatum zzril delenit augue duis dolore te feugait nulla facilisi. Lorem ipsum dolor, consectetuer adipiscing elit, sed diam

accumsan et iusto odio dignissim blandit praesent luptatum zzril delenit augue duis dolore te feugait nulla facilisi.

Nam liber tempor cum soluta nobis eleifend option congue nihil imperdiet doming id quod mazim

Multi-photo layouts without a dominant image can look uninspired and confusing.

Multi-photo layouts without a dominant image can look confusing.

# The Health Care Puzzle

## Americans come together to create a new set of standards for healing the sick

One day, as he watched one of his workers laboring under the load of books he was carrying, Aldus had a flash of insight: Coopuld books from the Aldine Press be made small enough to be carried without pulling a muscle? And could he produce the elegant, lightweight volumes he imagined and still sell them at an attractive price to the buyer?

The first problem was how to print more legible words per page and thus reduce the number of pages. Aldus needed a smaller typeface that was both readable and pleasing to the eye. The work of the Aldine Press had attracted the notice of the finest typographic artists in Europe, so Aldus was able to enlist the renowned Francesco Griffo da Bologna to design a new one. But that was just the beginning of a new era. Under Aldus' direction, Griffo developed a typeface that was comparatively dense and compact and that imitated the calligraphy of courtly correspon-

dence. The result of this Aldus-Griffo collaboration was the ancestor of italic type.

The new typeface enabled Aldus to print portable and highly readable books. Besides the first edition of Dante's Divine Comedy, Aldus published the essential texts of Greek literature: the histories of Herodotus and Thucydides, the tragedies of Sophocles, the epics of Homer, and the treatises of Aristotle, thus rescuing them from relative oblivion and obscurity.

The timing was perfect. With the growth of the merchant class in Venice, Florence, Naples, and Rome, a new market ripe for books had recently emerged. This newly prosperous middle class was flush with money and ankshious for intelligent ways to spend it. The best aspect of this is the new books.

As more books became available, the middle classes in Italy—and ultimately in all of Europe—grew more literate

and the Aldine Press became more prestigious. And Aldus, the publisher who put books in the hands of the people, eventually lent his name to the company that put publishing in the hands of the people.

The first problem was how to print more legible words per page and thus reduce the number of pages in each of the new books he printed. Aldus needed a smaller typeface that was both readable and pleasing to the eye.

The work of the Aldine Press had attracted the notice of the finest typographic artists in Europe, so Aldus was able to enlist the renowned Francesco Griffo da Bologna to design a new one. But that was just teh start of an era. Under Aldus' direction, Griffo developed a typeface that was comparatively dense and compact and that imitated the calligraphy of courtly correspondence. The result of this Aldus-Griffo collaboration was the ancestor of what we now call italics.

# Lines of Force

*Each photo has its own internal geometry that influences a page's overall design.*

Photos have their own underlying lines of force, regardless of how they're arranged on a page. The internal lines and geometry of a photo play an important role in how a page or spread will appear.

The internal lines and geometry of a photo play an important role in how a page or spread will appear.

For instance, if a person in a photo is pointing or gesturing in a particular direction, the reader's eyes will want to follow that gesture. Being aware of the lines of force in a photo can help you add impact and influence to your design.

We've got what it takes to make you look good in print.

When it comes to professionals who know how to make your printing work look perfect, nobody beats the Print Haus.

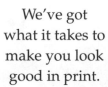

the Print Haus
183 Raymond Lane
Barwick, CA 83127
818/555-1894

## Follow the Horizon

*Be aware of a photo's inherent direction and balance.*

Just as people can keep their balance on a pitching ship by watching the horizon, you can get a good idea if a photo in a layout is straight by making sure the horizon (or other flat objects like desktops, tables, floors, or ceilings) is parallel with other horizontal lines on the page, including the caption, headlines, and other lines of type.

Likewise, objects like telephone poles, flagpoles, and tall buildings need to appear at a correct angle to the horizon.

### Achieving Motion Through Sequences

*You can imply time and motion by using a sequence of still photos.*

By running several similar photos—taken quickly from the same angle—in a sequence, you can impart a sense of movement to the reader.

## Altering Photographs

*Expecting a photo to fit perfectly in a layout without alterations is not generally realistic.*

Since editing is typically a prerequisite to working with photos, how you edit a photo for publication is an important factor in your page design. Fortunately, publishers have a number of tools and techniques at their fingertips to edit and change a photo to suit a document.

### It's All in the Crop

*Cropping is the simplest, most powerful tool for improving photos.*

Cropping is one of the most important ways you can improve the quality and impact of photos. Cropping a photo trims away the extraneous elements of the image and lets you present the reader with only the most important part of the photograph. A good crop heightens the message, impact, and attractiveness of any photo.

A good crop heightens the message, impact, and attractiveness of any photo.

Mug shots (close-up photos of people's faces) tend to be cropped far too loosely. Since mug shots are usually run at small sizes, crop them tightly to make sure the subject's face is the dominant focus.

Crop mug shots tightly to make sure the subject's face is the dominant focus.

While you look for ways to clarify and simplify an image through cropping, don't become so zealous in your efforts that you crop out important details.

Keep an eye out as well for crops, especially when working with photographs of people. Cutting away entire limbs and heads yields embarrassing results.

Keep an eye out as well for crops, especially when working with photographs of people.

## Enlarging & Reducing Photographs

*Enlarging a photo improperly can cause it to look grainy or fuzzy.*

When cropping a photo for maximum impact, designers often enlarge it at the same time. Enlarging a photo can sometimes make the details of a photo look fuzzy or grainy.

When enlarging photographs, work from the largest print available, and begin with the proper resolution. See Chapter 8, "Working With Color," for more about resolutions.

## Flipping & Flopping Photographs

*Reversing photos can improve the impact of a layout.*

Designers sometimes reverse an image so that its lines of force lead into the page—drawing the reader's interest inward, rather than outward. This is an effective technique for ensuring that each image on the page guides the reader into the layout.

But flipping (reversing top-to-bottom) and flopping (reversing side-to-side) an image can cause trouble if you don't pay close attention to details.

Because reversing a photo creates a mirror-image of the original, not only will text read backwards, but other subtle gaffes can also appear, like soldiers delivering left-handed salutes or watches and rings appearing on the wrong hand. (For more on this matter, see "Photographs, Technology & Ethics" later in this chapter.)

## Adjusting Contrast & Brightness

*You can electronically enhance a photo's contrast and brightness.*

Many page layout programs let you change the contrast and relative brightness of a photo you've imported. This can be an effective method of optimizing an image for your specific print-ing parameters; it's also a handy technique for correcting minor problems in the original photo.

It's important to experiment with contrast and brightness because each output device (printer, monitors, inks, and paper) will interpret the relative lightness or darkness differently. Be sure to test-print your image using various levels of contrast and brightness to find its optimum appearance.

## Touching Up Problem Spots

*Touch-up work can be done conventionally or on the computer.*

Both the conventional airbrush and its electronic counterparts let you eliminate blemishes and minor imperfections from photos.

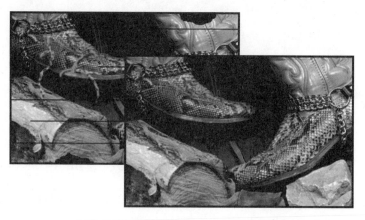

Keep in mind that touching up a photo is not recreating it from scratch using image-editing software. If a photo needs extensive overhauling, you're probably better off with a different photo.

## Special Effects With Photographs

*When used sparingly, photo effects can have a dramatic impact on a layout.*

As with type, you can achieve numerous special effects by manipulating photographs electronically. Digital image editing can now be done with relative ease by most desktop publishers using software bundled with a common flatbed scanner.

Silhouetting an image can achieve eye-popping results for a minimum of time and money.

It's not difficult to make subtle or dramatic changes to an existing photo, or even combine parts of two separate images to create a new photo illustration.

As with type, you can achieve numerous special effects by manipulating photographs electronically.

And ready-made filters and special add-on modules produce startling effects at the touch of a button.

But remember that any special effect you use too often will lose whatever "special" quality it might have if it becomes too familiar to the reader.

## Photographs, Technology & Ethics

*The power of modern imaging technology brings up a number of ethical questions worth considering.*

While many designers may never consider the responsibility they face when working with photographs—especially when altering or dramatically changing the context or content of a photo—manipulating photos carries a certain amount of ethical accountability.

You'll need permission from the photographer (written is best), whose work you're publishing. In general, you should have the permission of any people who appear in the photos you plan to use, although obtaining permission can be difficult.

Whether you're using stock photos, professionally-shot images, or snapshots you took on vacation, use common sense when running or editing photos—especially photos with people in them. Don't portray unsuspecting people in derogatory contexts.

## Moving On

Photographs lend authority and realism to a publication. Frequently, you can accomplish far more with a single image than with a comparable amount of text.

In the next chapter, "Working With Color," we'll take a look at the life and vitality that colors add to your documents. We'll also learn how to achieve professional results on tight schedules and small budgets.

# 8

# Working With Color

## Overview

- Adding one color and applying it selectively to highlight a few words can be very effective.

- Two colors can be used in creative ways to capture the purpose of a layout.

- Color combinations can have strong effects on legibility. Avoid very light colors for small typefaces.

- Full- or four-color printing has the potential to add enormous impact to your documents. But when overused, full color can saturate the reader's eye and reduce the impact.

- Some colors work well together, others do not. Develop a color plan based on relationships that work well rather than randomly adding colors.

- A major design decision is to determine the intent and purpose of using color in your project. Then select the appropriate color output device to support your color decisions.

*How you use color in your documents—or whether you use it at all—plays a tremendous role in the power of your message.*

As a design tool, color can be used to attract readers' attention, set a mood, influence emotions, or brighten up pages. Color can add impact and beauty to a layout. In some cases, it can command more respect and attention than black ink on white paper.

Color can add impact and beauty to a layout.

Great-looking color documents used to be impossible to produce from a desktop. Then it became possible but expensive. With today's printers, it's possible and affordable. Although capability and affordability mean a lot, they aren't the most important considerations in designs that use color.

Some color combinations are more pleasing than others. Certain colors work with each other, while others do not.

## Learning About Color

*Basic color concepts and a few guidelines can help you use color effectively.*

A color wheel shows the relationship between colors and illustrates how they are related to each other. You need to know that there are several color systems—each of which is very workable and easily grasped when visualized as a color wheel.

In this wheel, red, yellow, and blue are the *primary colors* from which all other colors can be mixed. Colors that result from a mix of primary colors are known as *secondary colors*. For example, mixing the primary colors red and yellow will result in the secondary color orange.

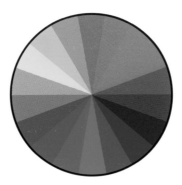

You can create any color by combining various percentages of the three primary colors: red, yellow, and blue.

You can create any color by combining various percentages of the three primary colors: red, yellow, and blue.

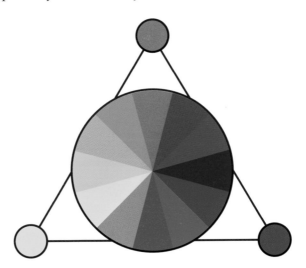

*Analogous colors* are any three or four consecutive colors on the wheel. Since they are similar they tend to work well together. For beginning designers, using analogous colors as a basic color plan is a good idea.

Choosing analogous colors will help your documents have a unified look. Of course you can still add accents in other colors.

Colors located opposite each other on the color wheel are *complementary colors*.

Color combinations composed of a single complementary color from each of the three primary sections of the color wheel are called *triads*. Choosing complementary triads helps you establish palettes of colors that also work well together.

Complementary colors seem to be made for each other, establishing a pleasing visual flow or creating an interesting contrast.

You'll find that—in the correct proportions—complementary colors are accents that can add excitement and visual tension. Complementary colors seem to be made for each other, establishing a pleasing visual flow or creating an interesting contrast.

## Warm & Cool Colors

*You can train yourself to feel color relationships. You'll then want to use these relationships to get your message across.*

Most colors carry emotional and psychological implications that can help or hurt your design. People have different reactions to different colors. In spite of this, there are some constant—or reasonably predictable—expectations that accompany certain colors. Most colors can be easily categorized as warm or cool. Warm colors tend to advance toward the viewer; the colors appear to get closer.

Bright warm colors get attention. You can use them to highlight the important elements in your design.

Most colors carry emotional and psychological implications that can help or hurt your design.

Cool colors tend to recede and appear to move away. Blue is cool. It can be aloof and detached, or soothing and reassuring.

A listing of resources for film, video, television broadcast & production, and multimedia.

Keeping the movement of warm and cool colors in mind, a designer can keep backgrounds cool and foregrounds warm.

Keeping the movement of warm and cool colors in mind, a designer can keep backgrounds cool and foregrounds warm. This is a good guiding principle for new designers to follow.

However, when it comes to color, you'll make your own rules because colors have variations. Cool colors have warm variations and warm colors have cool variations, such as cool reds and warm blues.

It's typically to your advantage to choose either a cool theme or a warm one for your project, rather than spotting the design evenly with warm and cool colors. Then in a warm document you can use a cool color as an accent. In a document based on cool colors, you can use warm colors to add contrast or accent.

One phenomenon to watch is the effect of background colors on foreground tones. Backgrounds can alter the foreground color and its impact. In the figure below, both inner circles are the same shade of blue.

 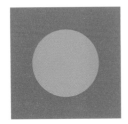

## Color Relationships

*Take advantage of color relationships in your designs.*

When designers talk about color, they usually discuss a few basic properties or color relationships: value, hue, and saturation.

*Value* is the measure of where a color lies between white and black. Each color has a value. Yellow is closer to white, while some blues are closer to black. Colors work well together when their values are either very close or very far apart.

Value is the basis of screening. *Screening* is a process by which you use a percentage (or lower value) of a full color, creating a lighter shade of the original. For example, a block of green color screened at 40 percent would have a lower value of green than one screened at 80 percent.

*Hue* is the actual shade or color itself. Violet, for instance, is a darker hue than yellow.

*Saturation* is the relative brilliance or vibrancy of a color. The more saturated a color, the less black it contains. If a color has very little saturation, it will appear dark and dull.

By manipulating the various properties of color, using the relationships between different hues, and adjusting the values and saturations of colors, you can achieve a wide range of effects from just a handful of different shades.

Most publishing and illustration programs provide you with one or more color models. HSB (hue, saturation, and brightness) and RGB (red, green, and blue) are two popular methods. You can create colors using the model you're most comfortable with.

# Colors & Computers

*Colors on your computer screen are created from red, blue, and green light sources. You'll want to pay attention to differences between colors on your monitor and the final output of your project.*

Because printing presses—even multicolor presses—can only print in one color at a time, each color you specify in your project must be printed separately: one print for each different color. Known as *color separations*, this separation process, along with differences among devices, can make color materials expensive. Two-color projects require two printing plates and two passes through the press; three-color requires three plates, and so forth. In most cases, costs make four-color offset printing impractical if the print run is only a few hundred.

You'll need to determine how your final project will be printed. Will it be printed from your laser printer or through a service or imagesetter?

A color management system built into your publishing software must take into account all factors involved for all the devices used for color acquisition, viewing, and reproduction. It can account for the monitor, printer, and a scanner.

Red, green, and blue are the component colors in one of three basic color models that are used for creating process colors in many desktop programs.

A *gamut* is the range of colors a device can reproduce. Both the human eye and photographs are devices through which large ranges of color can be reproduced; they have large color gamuts. A monitor, with its RGB gamut, can also display many colors. If you use colors outside of the printer's gamut, your publishing program may ensure that those colors are mapped into the printer's gamut as accurately as possible.

When making color decisions, you'll need to ask yourself if the colors will reproduce well on your system. If you plan to use a service, it's best to coordinate with the service during the planning stages of your project.

The color system developed by printers uses three subtractive primaries of cyan (near blue), magenta (near red), yellow, and standard black. CMYK displays on color monitors. Normally, when you print two or more colors to a color printer the colors are described in CMYK inks.

## Uses of Color

*It's as important to know when to use color as to know how to use it.*

As with any design element, color must be used carefully to achieve maximum impact. Slapping a few random colors onto a page rarely works well. Your use of color needs to follow a specific plan. Color for its own sake is often a costly design mistake.

You can emphasize type or graphics with even a subtle use of color.

In a world drowned in catastrophic floods, with an atmosphere of fierce hurricanes and seas of tidal waves only one sanctuary dominates this ruined world: The land of the Dragons.

Pushed to the edge of extinction, man has risen above the planet creating a brave new world powered by the sun and wind. By a marvel of 40th century technology and with the help of the Knight - brave and heroic - a wonderful world exist: earth, where man lives in peace. However the Flying Dragon must constantly venture to the earth's surface to search for Amber Crystals that powers their world and keeps them suspended above the earth. But for how much longer.

Knight
By William Thorn

Maps, technical drawings, charts, diagrams, and information graphics work especially well with color. Simple, clean line art also gains impact from color.

This advertisement becomes more powerful and more memorable when rendered in color.

## Tone

Color can be used to set the tone of your project for your readers long before they actually begin reading the content. Subtle uses of cooler colors can provide a casual, elegant, or stark appearance.

Deep, warm colors signal excitement or immediacy.

## Impact

Adding one color to a black-and-white document not only creates a more visually stimulating page, it also directs the reader's eye to a point of focus. Related information can be offset with spot color, or colored rules can be used to separate different elements or content. Avoid the trap of using too many colored elements on a single page or your reader will not know where to start or what to look at first.

Avoid the trap of using too many colored elements on a single page or your reader will not know what to look at first.

## Visual Guideposts

Colors are not only decorative; they can be practical and functional. Designers use color in projects as *visual guideposts*. Special repeated columns or sections are frequently color coded so readers can quickly locate what piques their interest. For example, bars of different colors along the outside edge of each page can separate the product advertising section from the featured stories section.

A drop-cap character is generally recognized as the starting point of text, however coloring that drop cap adds flair and visual stimulation.

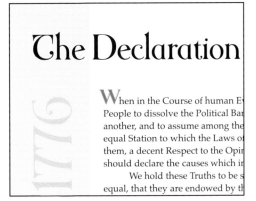

A small, colored graphic can be used as the end mark of long editorials or to break the appearance of an otherwise gray page. As a design tool, color can quickly establish consistency within a page, document, or larger publication.

ngress, Assembled, appealing to the Supreme Judge
r the Rectitude of our Intentions, do, in the Name,
rity of the good People of these Colonies, solemnly
eclare, That these United Colonies are, and of Right
ree and Independent States; that they are absolved
ance to the British Crown, and that all political
tween them and the State of Great-Britain, is and
tally dissolved; and that as Free and Independent
ve full Power to levy War, conclude Peace, contract
blish Commerce, and to do all other Acts and
Independent States may of right do. And for the
s declaration, with a firm Reliance on the Protection
idence, we mutually pledge to each other our lives,
and our sacred Honor. ❧

Color combinations can also have strong effects on type legibility. In addition to the standard black ink on white paper, black and yellow, along with orange and white, are highly visible and legible color combinations. Think of the colors used in most roadside caution signs.

Other combinations make type virtually unreadable. Yellow type on a pink background, for instance, may grab the reader's attention, but its "electric" appearance—created by the contrast and interplay between the two colors—makes for difficult reading.

## Choosing Colors

*Before making your final choice, experiment with different colors.*

It's important to know early in a project's schedule how, where, and why you intend to use color. Keep in mind the tone of your content. For example, is the tone of your project meant to inform, convey urgency, persuade, or educate? The colors you choose will influence the message you're sending to your readers. Make sure the colors complement rather than distract or conflict with the content.

It's important to know early in a project's schedule how, where, and why you intend to use color.

If you're unsure about your choices for color you can follow current trends. Color, like fashion, often follows popular trends. Don't be timid about borrowing color ideas and combinations from other sources that may work for your project.

Above all, use color with restraint. It's a tool for you to attract and guide your readers into the content and keep them there. Don't let color become a distraction.

## Working With Spot Color

*Two-color printing may be the affordable answer to your color needs and the best color decision for the project.*

Black-and-white pages are often enhanced with the addition of an extra color. In the spot-color process, a second color is added to the single color normally used (black is the traditional single color in most print jobs).

Even where there is no room for graphics, using a second color as a tint behind text can enliven a text-heavy page.

O͟n February 8, 1996, the world wide web turned black. People who were "surfing the net," browsing the World Wide Web, noticed that a large number of homepages, sites, had turned there background black. Everywhere they turned was another page that was black. Yahoo, Netscape, Webcrawler, and over 20,000 other sites were black for the same reason, to protest the passage of the new Telecommunications Bill. It was signed into law by President Clinton that day, February 8, 1996. It had been passed by overwhelming majorities in both the House of Representatives (414-16) and the Senate (91-5). The bill has an amendment, called the Communications Decency Act or CDA, which outlaws "indecent" and "patently offensive" material on the web, to protect children. This amendment censors the entire web, and restricts what American adults can freely put on the web. It is in direct conflict with the First Amendment of the Constitution of the United States of America which granted the right of free speech to all American citizens. The CDA is filled with vague and undefined language that will affect more sites than it was initally planned to ban. The internet will be distorted and negatively affected by this bill until it can be repealed by the courts for being unconstitutional.

# Communications
# Decency Act

The Communications Decency Amendment to the Telecommunications Bill of 1996 has provisions in it that relate to the use of computers and the internet. The bill applies to "Whoever . . . uses any interactive computer service to display in a manner to a person under 18 years of age . . . any comment, request, suggestion, proposal, image, or other communication which is obscene or indecent" (CDT). This means that anything that is "indecent" that is made available to the general public, one can do this through the world wide web, ftp, email, and many other ways, will be against the law to have there. The CDA can make vast areas of the internet illegal and have them banned. The Government of the United States has decided that they need to regulate the internet for the safety of our children.

The regulation of the internet provided by this bill violates the First Amendment. This very important Amendment gives us, the American people, the right to free speech (Constitution). The internet is no exception to the Amendment, and the government has no right to restrict what is on and what is not on the internet. They are overstepping their bounds set by the constitution with this regulation. In a bookstore the authors and writers are protected by the First Amendment, but if they put the same material on the internet, some of them would be breaking the law, according to the CDA. The First Amendment has no limits on the internet, but this bill would like to force limits upon it.

The government's ultimate goal is to protect the children from "indecent" materials, and the way they came up with this was to create limits to the internet and ban all the "bad sites." This method is laborsome, costly, ineffective, and unconstitutional. The easiest and most efficient way to protect the children is to have their parents filter the internet for them. Parents do not need to watch their kids twenty-four hours a day, all they need to do is get some new filtering software. This new software will allow them to filter their connection to the internet, and thereby prevent their children from accessing pornography on

Printing a black design on colored paper is popular for low-budget projects that need to attract attention. Be careful about printing photographs on colored paper. Don't portray unsuspecting people in a derogatory context or color. For instance, flesh tones on green or blue paper, or grass on red paper doesn't typically work.

## The Spot Color Secret

*Some of the most effective projects, large and small, are created with only spot color.*

Newspapers, tabloids, mail-order companies, and direct-mail firms have long known the secret of spot color. Pages that might seem drab, or at best ordinary, come alive with a little strategically placed spot color. Browse through one of your favorite magazines and you'll notice the strategic use of spot color in many ads as well as feature articles.

Flyers, letterhead, brochures, and newsletters can undergo a dramatic, eye-catching transformation from simply adding a second color.

# RECYCLE *Weekly*

## Recognizing environmental contributions

If recognition of a job well done is the top motivator of employee performance in general, then it follows that recognition of employees' environmental contributions should also be a top motivator to encourage increased environmental actions. Personal recognition indicates that someone took the time to notice the achievement, seek out the employee responsible and personally tell the individual that their achievement was impressive.

Book after book on human resource management tells

managers to deliver "one-minute praisings", "pats on the back" or "bravo cards" to motivate employees to higher levels of achievement. The principle also applies when encouraging employees to take greater personal responsibility for reducing negative environmental impacts at work.

Thoughtful, personal recognition of an employee's contribution is invaluable  both to the employee and to the positive effects it can have on the workplace. The best informal act of recognition is one that

creates a story  that the person can tell her/his colleagues and family.

It's also important to use the person's name around the office  let others know that you're impressed by someone's efforts. The best kind of office gossip is when word gets back to you  that your boss has been saying good things about you. Or, if you hear from another employee about someone's environmental efforts, be sure to repeat it back to the individual: let them know that you have heard what they are doing and that you are impressed with their initiative.

## It's always time to recycle

No time to recycle? It doesn't have to be a burden, says Joe Heimlich, waste management specialist with the Ohio Extension Service.

Once a system is set up, recycling should only take about five minutes a week per family member, Heimlich says. The trick is setting up a pattern: "It's

hard to get people to that point," Heimlich says. "I tell people to fit recycling into their own kitchen set-up, so it doesn't become a pain."

For example, Heimlich suggests putting a recycling container where the trash bin is now. "Make it easier to recycle than to throw items away--that's what works," he says.

Heimlich also suggests letting glass containers soak in dishwater left over from dirty dishes. Any grease in the warm soapy water helps labels peel off. Just rinse the glass items out later and put them in a recycling container, perhaps under the sink, he says.

### Biological diversity

Biological diversity... is the key to the maintenance of the world as we know it... This is the assembly of life that took a billion years to evolve. It ... created the world that creates us. It holds the world steady."

Scientists estimate that 50-100,000 species are made extinct each year. This means that every day on the planet 100-300 species disappear forever...

"...The [Chernobyl] catastrophe caused thousands of deaths....It continues to reach into the future to claim new victims and indeed the spectre of another Chernobyl continues to hang over the region..."

## Stop Ocean Dumping

As part of a wider campaign against dumping, Greenpeace has maintained from the start that it is wrong in principle to dump oil installations at sea.

To dump structures, such as the Brent Spar, in areas of high marine biodiversity with poorly understood ecology infringes the precautionary  principle and

presents unknown environmental risks.  To do so would set dangerous precedents for future dumping of wastes at sea. It ignores the impact of

Restraint with spot color keeps your pages tasteful and inviting. It's important to know when not to run an item in spot color. Overuse of spot color creates so much contrast that readers won't logically know where to begin and won't take the time to look.

Overuse of spot color creates so much contrast that readers won't logically know where to begin and won't take the time to look.

# RECYCLE *Weekly*

## Recognizing environmental contributions

If recognition of a job well done is the top motivator of employee performance in general, then it follows that recognition of employees' environmental contributions should also be a top motivator to encourage increased environmental actions. Personal recognition indicates that someone took the time to notice the achievement, seek out the employee responsible and personally tell the individual that their achievement was impressive.

Book after book on human resource management tells

managers to deliver "one-minute praisings", "pats on the back" or "bravo cards" to motivate employees to higher levels of achievement. The principle also applies when encouraging employees to take greater personal responsibility for reducing negative environmental impacts at work.

Thoughtful, personal recognition of an employee's contribution is invaluable  both to the employee and to the positive effects it can have on the workplace. The best informal act of recognition is one that

creates a  story  that the person can tell her/his colleagues and family.

It's also important to use the person's name around the office  let others know that you're impressed by someone's efforts.  The best kind of office gossip is when word gets back to you  that your boss has been saying good things about you.  Or, if you hear from another employee about someone's environmental efforts, be sure to repeat it back to the individual: let them know that you have heard what they are doing and that you are impressed with their initiative.

### Biological diversity

Biological diversity... is the key to the maintenance of the world as we know it... This is the assembly of life that took a billion years to evolve. It ... created the world that creates us. It holds the world steady."

Scientists estimate that 50-100,000 species are made extinct each year. This means that every day on the planet 100-300 species disappear forever...

"...The [Chernobyl] catastrophe caused thousands of deaths....It continues to reach into the future to claim new victims and indeed the spectre of another Chernobyl continues to hang over the region..."

## It's always time to recycle

No time to recycle? It doesn't have to be a burden, says Joe Heimlich, waste management specialist with the Ohio Extension Service.

Once a system is set up, recycling should only take about five minutes a week per family member, Heimlich says.  The trick is setting up a pattern: "It's

hard to get people to that point," Heimlich says.  "I tell people to fit recycling into their own kitchen set-up, so it doesn't become a pain."

For example, Heimlich suggests putting a recycling container where the trash bin is now.  "Make it easier to recycle than to throw items away--that's what works," he says.

Heimlich also suggests letting glass containers soak in dishwater left over from dirty dishes.  Any grease in the warm soapy water helps labels peel off. Just rinse the glass items out later and put them in a recycling container, perhaps under the sink, he says.

## Stop Ocean Dumping

As part of a wider campaign against dumping, Greenpeace has maintained from the start that it is wrong in principle to dump oil installations at sea.

To dump structures, such as the Brent Spar, in areas of high marine biodiversity with poorly understood ecology infringes the precautionary  principle and

presents unknown environmental risks.  To do so would set dangerous precedents for future dumping of wastes at sea. It ignores the impact of

Use spot color to highlight only vital or unique elements, especially items that can help direct the reader's eye.

## Screening Spot Color

*You can create the illusion of using several colors in a document by screening spot color.*

Tint screening is a process by which you use a lower percentage of a solid color, creating the appearance of a lighter shade. By screening one—or both—of your colors, you can achieve the effect of printing in multiple colors. For example, a dark blue box screened to a 20-percent value produces a paler, sky-blue color.

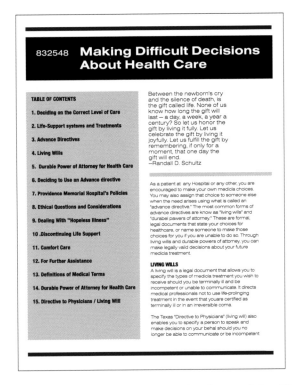

Screening a color produces lighter shades and the illusion that a new color has been added to the page. In the example below, darker shades of blue are used to create the illusion of four different colors.

## Creating Duotones

*Adding a single color to black-and-white photographs—creating a duotone—can bring depth and richness to photos and emphasize detail that otherwise may have been lost.*

In the standard duotone, you'll use the black ink to print most of the shadow tones, while specifying the second ink (yellow in the above example) to print most of the mid-range and highlight tones.

Be careful when choosing a second color on a document that contains photographs. Unexpected surprises can await you. For example, if you decided to use dark blue rules and bullets for highlights in text, your duotone will consist of your primary color (black) and blue. All your photographs will then gain a blue cast from the mid-tone and highlight treatments.

## Printing Two-Color Jobs Without Black Ink

*If you're careful, substituting a different color for black in a two-color job can be an effective way to draw attention to flyers, ads, and brochures.*

If your project doesn't contain lots of text, such as bumper stickers, banners, and small signs, you might consider printing it in two different colored inks, rather than black ink and a single second color. This can be an effective technique for simple flyers that sport eye-catching artwork and only a tiny amount of type.

## Working in Full Color

*Advances in new technology allow virtually any desktop publisher and designer to quickly graduate to a new league: full-color documents.*

With color printers now mainstream, full-color is often mistakenly interpreted as simply adding more colors to a spot, or two-color, process. Full-color, also called four-color process, has its own rules. To successfully design with full color, you need to know the tasks that today's technology hides.

Conventionally, full-color projects required a coordinated effort of a fairly large staff, including copywriters, designers, illustrators, photographers, film specialists, plates experts, and press operators, each with an important task.

Now, easy access to scanners, clip art, and stock photos often replaces the need for photographers and illustrators; image-setters take care of film work, color separation, and plate burning; and many desktop publishers act as both copywriter and designer.

Your design decisions are directly tied to the level of finished color output you need for your project. For example, inkjet and color laser technology are well established in the personal and home office market segment. On the other hand, larger business and industry needs dictate that their projects use more high-end output services and technology, such as service bureaus and publishing houses.

The trade-off in technology can be measured in terms of quantity, speed, and cost restraints. Inkjet and laser technologies have the advantages of immediacy and lower costs for short runs yet are constrained in output quality. Service bureaus and printing houses offer high-quality output with more options in paper stocks, binding, and trim sizes all at increased run quantities and costs. (See Chapter 9, "Working With Service Bureaus," for more.)

Your decision on when to use your desktop printer and when to use a service bureau is based on the purpose of your project, as well as its content and message. If your project is a high-profile, image-building job such as creating marketing brochures, annual reports, and national magazine advertising, then your best choice may be a service bureau. Even small businesses that regularly use inkjet or laser technology for most of their publishing projects opt for service bureaus when specific jobs are high profile and high impact.

## Inkjet Printers

*For short-run and cost-conscious projects, inkjet and color laser technologies are desktop standards.*

The obvious advantage of using color today is the availability of color printing. The drawbacks are less well known. Using inkjet technology for full-color pages works best for most text- and art-based projects, but will prove less than satisfactory for jobs with full-color photographs that demand high quality.

There are two kinds of inkjet printers: color-capable and full-color systems. Color-capable printers have one color cartridge that mixes cyan, magenta, and yellow (CMY) to create a wide range of colors including black. Mixing CMY to produce black will actually result in a lighter shade (composite) of black rather than a true black. You cannot produce a color piece and have true black on the same page.

Full-color inkjets have two cartridges: one (true) black and one CMY. Both types of inkjets are fine if you print mostly text and only need to accent your design with small amounts of color.

Whether you have (or are contemplating using) full-color or color-capable inkjet technology, keep in mind the drawbacks. These printers spray liquid ink onto paper with varying degrees of accuracy. In the process, significant control over dot shapes and spacing is forfeited and takes a toll on photographs or other graphics where you need to retain crisp, sharp images.

You'll also want to pay attention to paper types, quality, and environmental variations such as humidity and dryness. They play an important role in your color design decisions for inkjet printing.

Some color and color-capable printers require special paper to achieve their highest quality print. Special papers smooth the paper surface and increase contrast. Such papers may be treated with additives or coatings. To find out which papers are best for your projects, request samples. Many paper suppliers are happy to send you a few sample sheets of their products for you to test.

Still with these drawbacks, inkjet printers serve designers and desktop publishers well. For small runs and special projects like invitations and simple flyers, inkjets can add brilliant color. Inkjets are also great as an inexpensive color proofing system.

## Color Laser Printers

*For higher volume, speed, and quality color printing, color laser technology is becoming the choice of many designers and desktop publishers.*

An alternative to color inkjet technology is a color laser printer. To produce colors, the color laser printer contains four toner cartridges: cyan, magenta, yellow, and black (CMYK) instead of the inkjet technology which uses one or two print cartridges.

You'll get crisper, sharper images with laser than with inkjet. If you use color full-time with specific applications and if color performance is important, a laser color printer is probably a better choice. However, you still won't get the true photographic quality that you'll see from an imagesetter and printing house.

Let's say you design a color graphic for mass-mailing labels. In this case you design a simple cartoon that contains the name of the recipient in the "balloon." The graphic is used to personally appeal to readers and get their attention. It is therefore an important application in which a color laser printer can perform best. Annual reports or sales brochures, on the other hand, are likely to be sent to a service where a high-resolution imagesetter is used.

Tim's Scooters
1247 Fast Lane
El Paso, Texas 79925

Many of the drawbacks of inkjet technology apply to color laser printers as well. They do not accommodate different paper sizes, and tint screens and halftones are too coarse to use for any "prestige" pieces.

## Resolution Confusion

*It's easy to get and stay confused about printer resolution.*

Resolution is typically defined as the number of dots the printer can fit vertically and horizontally in one square inch of paper. The more dots per inch (dpi), the higher the resolution and the sharper the image. In theory, there's no confusion—the issue is black and white! In practice, printer resolution is complicated and affected by many other factors, which often results in confusion.

Ultimately, seeing is believing. If the results you expect aren't on the printed page, the dpi rating and resolution claims don't really mean much.

Another source of "resolution confusion" is color scanner technology. The major confusion lies in the resolution options you have at your disposal to capture a color image versus output resolutions. Do you scan:

- At resolutions to match your video monitor (72 dpi) for the best view?

- At a resolution to maximize a laser printer (300 dpi or better)?

- At a different (often very high) resolution for an imagesetter?

Color scanners today can often scan anywhere from 50 dpi to well over 4,000 dpi. But do you really need this ultra-high resolution for color jobs going to a laser printer, inkjet, or imagesetter? Usually not.

These printing devices can't print shades of any color. The imagesetter is strictly black and white; laser printers and inkjets both simulate colors by mixing CMYK. These machines are designed to translate solid color information into a series of dots of varying sizes that produce the desired shade.

By scanning in higher resolutions than you need, you could be inadvertently sending well over 10 times the amount of information that an output device can actually use.

In this translation process, much of the color information in your scan is necessarily discarded. The same thing happens on your computer screen whenever the scanner sends a 300 dpi image to your monitor. You've sent 300 dpi of information to a 72 dpi device that subtracts what it doesn't need to display (output) the image.

These three devices must translate some information and ignore what they can't use. By scanning in higher resolutions than you need, you could be inadvertently sending well over 10 times the amount of information that an output device can actually use. To find out which scan resolution best fits an inkjet or color laser printer, some trial and error may be in order. (Hint: If you're really desperate to know, read the manual, although it's not really guaranteed to be in there either!) For an imagesetter it's best to contact your service bureau. The point is, you usually don't need high-resolution scans to work with full color.

## Moving On

When working with color, how you plan to execute your color decisions is as important as the color decisions you make. The keyword is planning. Develop a clear and concise color plan at the beginning of your project; don't plan as you go or you'll never get back.

A well-crafted plan includes a logical beginning and ending with clear methods in place to get there. Once your plan is in place, stay on course; resist the urge to change direction in midstream.

In order to take full advantage of the technology at your fingertips—especially in the world of printed color—your best partners are a service bureau and printing press. In the next chapter, we'll look at commercial printing avenues and pre-press details.

# Putting Your Knowledge Into Action

9

# Working With Service Bureaus

## Overview

- Laser printers can't produce true typeset quality. When you need quality high resolution, it's time to use a service bureau.

- Check several service bureaus in your area and find the one that fits your needs.

- A reputable service bureau is ready, willing, and able to provide you with all the information you need to make your jobs run smoothly and quickly through their system.

- Check with your service bureau ahead of time and make a checklist for yourself of all the component files you will need to give them.

- For projects that use large databases; require calculations, sorting, and cross-indexing; or have large amounts of tabular data, you can save time and cost with a specialty service bureau.

- Pay attention to pre-press details. Choose a single color matching system for all your color work.

*A good service bureau can help you sidestep problems that trap many designers and desktop publishers.*

Although computers are supposed to make document creation easier, sometimes technology seems only to complicate matters. This is especially the case when you're using an untested technique, trying out new software, or working with new hardware.

If you're working with color or digital photography, or if you plan to work with a service bureau for high-resolution output, the advice in this section will save you money and hours of frustration.

## The Role of the Imagesetter

*Today, you—the designer—have more control and choices over typesetting issues and placement of graphics and photos than ever before.*

Prior to desktop publishing, designers specified type style and size, and leading and column widths to traditional type houses that manually phototypeset *galleys*. These galleys—long strips of typeset paragraphs—were then returned to the designer for the *paste-up* process. After considerable slicing and dicing, adding acetate overlays for color separation, and graphic or photo placement, the finished *camera-ready* art was sent to the print shop.

At the print shop another multistep process began. Film work created the necessary negatives to produce the final printing plates for the presses. This usually included such tasks as adding tint screens, half-toning photographs, creating traps, spreads, and stripping the final negatives (the film version of paste-up). For a complex finished piece, this preparation process could not only consume a considerable amount of time but was prone to human error.

By now, you have discovered—probably by trial and error—that you make these choices and also have the added responsibilities of a typesetter and imagesetter as well as an entire pre-press staff. At the push of a button (or a few mouse clicks), you can instantly select typefaces and create color separations.

Even after your often hasty education to overcome some hurdles, there is still an insurmountable roadblock. Laser printers can't produce true typeset quality.

To fill in this missing link—and recover from the millions of dollars lost by type houses to desktop systems—typesetting equipment manufacturers created laser imagesetters. Designed to read a customer's desktop files, these imagesetters, with resolutions from 1,200 dpi, create true typeset quality output.

Laser printers can't produce true typeset quality.

## Laser Printers vs. Imagesetters

*Laser printer technology is more related to the office copier than a phototypesetter or imagesetter.*

Laser printers electrostatically charge a drum that picks up powdered toner, places it on paper, and "irons" it on to make it permanent. It's an indirect process.

If you've ever removed a jammed sheet of paper from a copier or laser printer that hasn't yet made it to the hot fusing rollers and it smears, you know what it's like. Costs for a laser printer can range from a few hundred dollars to several thousand depending on the options that come with the machine.

On the other hand, using a laser imagesetter is a direct process. The internal laser beam scans back and forth on roll-fed, photo-sensitive paper, exposing the image (or page). This paper, like a photograph, then undergoes a developing, fixing, rinsing, and drying process usually handled by an external processor.

Most imagesetters can expose directly to film negatives and, in some cases, can bypass the paper or film and directly create printing plates. The costs for an imagesetter, depending on the options, can range from $30,000 to $80,000 and up. There's usually no need for you or your company to make this kind of investment—your friendly service bureau already has.

# The Role of a Service Bureau

*By definition, a service bureau takes your desktop files and creates high resolution output—positive or negative—on paper or film.*

Most desktop publishers, from the home office to medium-sized business segments, can't afford to park a $50,000 imagesetter in their office. For typeset quality output, it makes sense to use a service bureau and pay only for the part of an imagesetter you use, namely the output.

In theory this is perfect: pop in a desktop file and pop out paper or film, take it to your favorite print shop and viola! You're done. Sound too good to be true? It usually is.

Just as there are companies that offer only typesetting and companies that offer printing in conjunction with typesetting, there are service bureaus, and then there are print shops that operate service bureaus.

How much "service" can you expect when you choose a service bureau or when you choose a print shop/service bureau for price or convenience? How much your service bureau knows about your software and hardware is as important as how much you know. You shouldn't think of handing a last minute job to a service bureau you've never used before and expect perfect results. A reputable service bureau is ready, willing, and able to provide you, ahead of time, with all the information you need to make your jobs run smoothly and quickly through their system. After all, it's in their best interest.

There are plenty of affordable and outstanding service bureaus. Many of them have preprinted booklets or specification sheets that outline the various program files they support in addition to helpful tips that make using their service a breeze.

The combination service bureau/print shop has a distinct advantage. Their imagesetters can usually take your files and go directly to printing plates bypassing paper and film altogether. However, if this is the case, proof your job very carefully or request plain paper proofs. Printing plates are more expensive to replace than paper or film; making one little typographic error costs plenty.

The bottom line is to check a number of service bureaus in your area and find the one that provides the kinds of services you need and has the knowledge and skill to do the job right.

## Getting Files From Here to There

*In ancient desktop history (10 years ago), almost all jobs were delivered on diskette to the service bureau via "Sneaker-Net." And every six months or so, you needed a new pair.*

These days, transporting files from your desktop to a service bureau can be as simple as a mouse click. There are private bulletin board services (BBSes) as well as the Internet that allow you to send your entire job without leaving the comfort of your chair.

With a telephone line, modem, and appropriate communications software, you can be in the process of sending one job to a service bureau while you're busy designing the next.

Getting your project to a service bureau is only half the task, making sure you get *all* of it there is another. Desktop systems don't automatically pile everything into one nice, neat file. For example, if you have a job that uses 2 typefaces, 12 pieces of clip art, and 6 scanned photos, you may have to provide your service bureau with 21 (or more) files. That's the main file, both type font files (if the bureau doesn't have them), the 12 clip art files, and 6 scanned photo files. Luckily, almost all desktop systems will allow you to move all the files necessary for printing to one area, directory, or folder on your hard disk. You select the option; it handles the inventory for you.

It's wise to check with your service bureau ahead of time and make a checklist for yourself of all the component files you may need to give them whether by BBS, Internet, or Sneaker-Net. Your service bureau will also be able to advise you of the various file formats you need to provide for graphics and scanned photos, as well as which data compression software—for speed of transmission or to conserve diskette space—they can support.

# Choosing a Service Bureau

*A small investment of time before you decide which service bureau is right for you will ultimately save costly and time-consuming problems later.*

Every designer—and every piece they design—has unique needs when the job reaches the final output stage. Whether it's simple brochures, advertising pieces, or highly technical manuals crammed with hundreds of finely detailed illustrations and photos, choosing a well-rounded service bureau requires some forethought.

In the fast-paced world of desktop publishing, it's true that no surprise is a good surprise. You can minimize this potential surprise factor with a few simple questions directed to a number of prospective bureaus in order to narrow your selection:

- **What file formats does the service bureau require or prefer?** Are they compatible with your software? Some service bureaus require that all files be submitted as encapsulated PostScript files (EPS). If your software not only allows you to save your jobs as EPS files but offers several varieties of EPS formats, find out which is best suited for that service bureau. Also ask about saving your file with or without image headers (color or black and white), and text as curves.

    Different file formats can create vastly different file sizes and in some cases this can have a direct bearing on the amount of time (and money) it takes to output your job. Scanned color photos saved as a tagged image file format (TIFF) can quickly grow to an unmanageable size. Service bureaus with four- or five-year-old equipment—ancient by today's standards—might charge a premium if your job ties up their machinery for hours, if they can output your job at all!

- **Do you need to provide any typefaces with your job?** Get a list of the typefaces available from the service bureau but don't expect similarities in typeface names to be the same typeface you use. Just because the names are similar— like Optima and Ottowa—doesn't mean there aren't differences in character shapes and spacing. There usually are slight differences that could result in many of your line endings or special characters being changed in the final output.

- **Can the service bureau make last-minute corrections?**
  If you've just sent your job and then notice a small typographic error, you should know if your service bureau can make corrections for you and at what cost. This will depend on the file format you've provided and whether it's "editable" or not. If the service bureau runs the same operating system and desktop software (as well as the same version) that you use and requested files in that format, they can most likely edit your files.

- **What is the average turnaround time?**
  If you've never used this service bureau before, allow some extra time. Do find out if they charge a premium for rush service and find out what's the best method of getting your jobs to them. If it's on diskette (Sneaker-Net), will they pick it up for free or do you need to deliver it? If they use their own BBS, it may take a day or two to set up an account and password for you on their system and provide you with communications software or instructions to configure your software. If it's via the Internet's e-mail system, do you send the files as attachments or directly embed them in the body of your e-mail? And finally, do they offer (free) delivery when the job is finished?

- **How do they price their services?**
  Do they charge per page, by time (or both), or do they custom quote each job? If you have the service bureau create the job for you, will you be able to get a copy of the files?

Finding out how much service you really get from a service bureau will come from other customers. Call a few of their customers to get their impressions—both success and horror stories will give you a better perspective. Like your car, the best way to ensure that your jobs won't go flat on you at the last minute is simply to keep a spare handy. Become familiar with two service bureaus in case one runs into equipment problems, can't deliver on time, or has other unforeseeable problems.

**TIP**

For data-intensive projects, you can find specialty service bureaus like Graphion on the Internet. Contracting these types of service bureaus can free your time so you can concentrate on the design-intensive side of a project. Graphion's Web address is http://www.slip.net/~graphion/.

## Other Pre-Press Details

*Like just about everything else in desktop publishing, the duties of the pre-press technician are often now a part of your design and publishing obligations.*

Here are a few more pre-press details you'll want to watch for: trapping, spot color preparation, and color matching.

### The Color Trap

*Trapping* is the process of determining how much overlap or spacing to leave between color elements to ensure clean, clear printing, even if you only encounter slight problems with alignment.

Trapping is the process of determining how much overlap or spacing to leave between color elements to ensure clean, clear printing.

While trapping was traditionally handled by the printer on any given job, most desktop publishing and illustration packages provide for some means of electronic trapping control. As with most other aspects of color pre-press and printing, the details of this process vary widely.

Poor trapping can be worse than no trapping at all. Trapping options are available in most desktop publishing programs when you start the color separation process. It's best to consult your software manual, service bureau, or print shop for the details and help you'll need.

## Preparing Spot Color for Printing

Printing spot-color work is only slightly more involved than printing single-color work. If you've planned and set up your document carefully, printing a spot-color job is no more complicated than a regular one-color document.

Printing a separation proof creates two pages of output for each single page in your electronic document: one page with all items in black, and another for all items in spot color.

Printing a composite proof gives you a single page where both colors are printed, showing you how the final product will look. Of course, you'll need to output to a color printer for realistic color composites.

You can also use separation and composite proofs to check the trapping, the alignment, or registration of the items in your document.

## Color & Computer Technology

Computers make designing and producing color documents easier, but they aren't foolproof. Just as advances in technology have made working with type more predictable, the disparity in color on the computer and color off the press is shrinking every day.

Part of the problem in matching color on the computer to the color of the final product lies in the media:

- Monitors produce colors by creating light as they illuminate your screen. Printed documents rely on toners, dyes, inks, and reflected light.

- Monitors use red, green, and blue (or additive color) to create all other colors, while the printing process uses cyan, magenta, and yellow (or subtractive color) as its palette.

Various techniques and systems have been developed to help compensate for the differences between colors on the computer and the printing press. For more information about color differences between devices, see Chapter 8, "Working With Color."

Color matching is the process by which the colors you choose for your computer-generated documents are matched to existing color standards. The final printed product is also checked against a set of standard colors to ensure accuracy at the final stage.

There are a number of different color matching standards, including the Pantone Matching System (PMS), in which you use a color sample book and an electronic color library to match colors with standard inks that most printers can use.

It's important to choose a single color matching system for all your color work. Your software package, color choices, and production and printing methods play a major role in determining which matching system, if any, you should use. Consult your software manuals, service bureau, and print shop for advice on color matching standards.

Color calibration techniques involve using special software and hardware devices to compensate for the differences between computer-generated and printed colors. Most desktop publishing programs include color calibration utilities.

Color calibration technology has not yet fully developed, and just as with color matching systems, competing vendors and platforms will struggle to develop a universally accepted standard.

Regardless of the sophistication of your color software and hardware—when printing a computer-generated color document—there's no substitute for a well-trained eye. Some colors are particularly difficult to reproduce faithfully—watch out for unrealistic flesh tones, for example.

> It's important to choose a single color matching system for all your color work.

## Moving On

Now you're familiar with the basic concepts of design and some of the finer technical aspects and industry secrets. You have the tools you need to create great-looking print projects.

Another important skill most designers develop typically comes from less-than-successful designs. Recognizing problems and solving design errors is a valuable skill. In the next section, we'll look at common design mistakes and how you can recover from them and develop your problem-solving skills.

# 10

# Distribution Media: Newsletters, Tabloids & Newspapers

## Overview

- Build your publication around a distinctive nameplate that identifies the subject matter and editorial focus.

- Display volume and issue numbers and dates prominently.

- Identify the source of your publication by logo, address, and contact information.

- Use teasers on the front cover to direct the reader's attention inside.

- Clearly separate articles from each other.

Newsletters, tabloids, and newspapers are often a montage of dissimilar bits of information including stories, reports, news, reviews, editorials, and pictures. Although it may appear simple, successfully integrating such varied content can be surprisingly complicated unless you have a plan.

Successfully integrating varied content can be surprisingly complicated without a plan.

Overall styles can range from formal, news-laden, and serious to informal, chatty, and entertaining. Whatever style you choose, though, make sure that your type choices and illustrations are appropriate for that style.

A strong grid design ensures a visual order for mixed content. A minimum of three columns, but not more than six, gives you a workable grid system with plenty of flexibility. You can use gutters, rules, and boxes to separate different items from each other.

You can also change the style and presentation of each kind of information to suit various sections. Be sure you keep the overall design consistent and visually coherent. Sound tricky? Read on.

# Newsletters

*Newsletters are major beneficiaries of the desktop publishing revolution.*

Highly-specialized newsletters that once were impractical because of high typesetting and paste-up costs can now be produced using the most basic desktop publishing and word processing software. Desktop-published newsletters also provide associations and retail and service establishments with a cost-effective advertising medium.

Although they may appear simple, newsletters are surprisingly complex. The typical newsletter contains numerous elements that must be successfully integrated—often under last-minute deadline pressure.

## Repeating Elements

*Successful newsletters are built around a number of elements that appear in every issue.*

While the content changes, some features remain constant including the nameplate, logo, publication information, credits, and mailing area.

## Nameplate

*Your nameplate provides immediate visual identification and communicates your newsletter's purpose.*

Devote some time and thought to the design of the nameplate and logo. They're the most noticeable features and are essential for promoting identification and continuity. Successful nameplates are simple in design and are easily recognized.

Successful nameplates are simple in design and are easily recognized.

Nameplates are generally found at the top of the first page and sometimes extend across the full width of the page. However, equally effective nameplates can be placed centered, flush-left, or flush-right.

You can also place nameplates approximately one-third of the way down from the top of the page. This location leaves room for a feature headline and article to appear above it.

Vertical orientation can draw more attention to an important headline.

## Publication Information

*You want your readers to identify the source of the newsletter quickly and easily.*

Be sure to tell readers who you are by leaving space for your organization's logo or name, as well as your address and phone number.

You can place a logo at the bottom of the front cover, relegate it to the back cover, or totally eliminate it, as long as your organization is identified in some way.

In many cases, a logo or name appears on the front cover or page. It's large enough to be noticed but small enough to avoid competing with the nameplate.

The volume and issue numbers and date should be prominently featured. This allows both you and your readers to refer easily to back issues.

## Credits

*If your newsletter is designed to provide employees or members with opportunities to express themselves, identify authors by name, department, division, and position.*

If possible, personalize feature articles by including a photograph or drawing of the author. Photos can become organizers for features.

## Mailing Information

*If your newsletter is a self-mailer, be sure to provide sufficient space for a mailing label and other mailing information.*

A newsletter's mailing area normally appears at the bottom of the back page.

Be sure to include your organization's return address next to the mailing label. Sometimes when fulfillment (mailing list maintenance and addressing) is handled by an outside firm, you'll put that firm's return address in the mailing area.

In the mailing area, clearly indicate whether your newsletter is first- or third-class mail. In either case, to avoid licking stamps, include your firm's postal permit number.

Adding "Address Correction Requested" above the mailing label area helps you keep your customer or prospect mailing list up to date. If you include "Address Correction Requested" in the mailing area of your newsletter, you'll be informed of the new address when a recipient moves.

## Using Variables Consistently

*While some elements are fixed and appear in each issue, you'll use other elements to create distinct visual patterns between mixed types of information.*

Headlines, teasers, and lead-ins can add enough contrast to make your newsletters come alive. You'll need to formulate your own house rules for these different components and keep their style consistent within each issue.

For instance, just because your last issue of a newsletter used a single dominant headline doesn't necessarily mean that each succeeding issue must also. You can vary these elements and often content will require that you do.

Headlines, teasers, and lead-ins can make your newsletters come alive.

## Headlines

*You can vary the use of headlines to accommodate the number and length of articles included in each issue.*

If you plan to feature a single in-depth article plus a few shorter pieces in each issue of your newsletter, you'll use a single, dominant headline.

On the other hand, if you feature several short articles, the front page can be designed to accommodate more than one significant headline.

Typically, headlines are placed above the articles they introduce. However, you might consider placing the headline next to the article as well.

## Teasers

*Use teasers to invite readers inside your newsletter.*

A short table of contents on the front cover can draw attention to articles and features inside or on the back cover.

The table of contents should be a focal point. Experiment with different locations and typographic treatments to help it stand out on the page.

You can also let the entire front cover serve as your table of contents. Include photographs that relate to the articles inside, with photo captions that tease the reader to find out more.

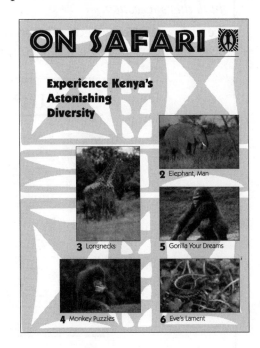

Many publications, like newsletters and direct mail pieces, appear in the reader's mailbox with the address label up. You may want to place the table of contents next to the mailing label area where it can't be overlooked.

## Lead-ins

*Use subheads and short summaries to provide transition between headlines and body copy. (For example, the previous sentence is a lead-in to this subsection.)*

Lead-ins can be placed between the headline and text. Frequently, lead-ins span more than one column.

A lead-in is often placed within the text, set off by horizontal rules or some other device.

## Size

*Although smaller formats are possible, a standard newsletter is created by folding an 11- x 17-inch sheet of paper, called a signature, into four 8½- x 11-inch pages.*

Newsletters with 8, 12, or 16 or more pages are assembled by using additional 11- x 17-inch sheets.

## TIP

"A sizes" refer to paper sizes measured in metric units. You can choose from A3, A4, and A5 sizes using the page setup or layout tools in most word processing and publishing programs. Three- and four-column grids are suitable for A4 newsletters. Five and six columns can also work for A3 newsletters.

## Distribution

*How you distribute your publication is a design consideration.*

Newsletters can be mailed full-size or folded; or they can be self-mailers or enclosed in envelopes.

Decisions about distribution need to be made early in your planning process. Self-mailers avoid the cost of envelopes but you also lose valuable editorial or selling space because you must leave room for the address area. Additionally, its pristine condition off the press might not withstand the rigors of today's automated physical mail delivery system. Often—especially in lightweight papers—tears and creases can mar an otherwise good-looking piece. To test the durability of your publication, mail one to yourself.

While a multiple-fold newsletter is easier to mail, the nameplate and headlines aren't visible until the folds are opened. You also lose the advantage of presenting the recipient with the "billboard effect" of a full-size 8½- x 11-inch newsletter.

## Tabloids

*Designing tabloid-sized newsletters, newspapers, and other publications is a logical progression from 8½- x 11-inch newsletters.*

The need to maintain issue-to-issue consistency while accommodating a constantly changing mix of text and visuals is apparent in tabloids and newspapers. For example, they need high-impact headlines that don't compete with the nameplate or with each other. It's also important to organize photographs of varying size as effectively as possible.

Similar to newspapers, tabloids feature a larger page size, allowing more design flexibility.

Similar to newspapers, tabloids feature a larger page size, allowing more design flexibility. The typical tabloid page is 11 x 17 inches, although those dimensions vary from newspaper to newspaper and printer to printer. Some tabloids, for example, are 11 x 14 inches.

Tabloids often are printed on a web press, which feeds the paper to the press from a large roll. As a result, the actual image area of the tabloid is slightly smaller than the page size of 11 x 17 inches.

Laser printers can be used to prepare tabloids, although the coarse paper used for most tabloids absorbs ink and consequently reduces the high-resolution sharpness normally achieved in phototypeset images.

Most laser printers, however, are not designed to handle paper sizes larger than 8½ x 11 inches. (Tabloid-sized laser printers are available.) To get around that limitation, desktop publishing programs offer a tiling feature that automatically overlaps, or tiles, a series of 8½- x 11-inch pages that can then be pasted together to create one large tabloid page.

## Front Cover

*Larger page sizes can accommodate large, bold headlines and large photographs.*

The most effective tabloid covers contain a dominant visual element. For important or urgent news stories, the headline should probably be the primary focus.

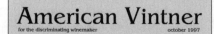

# American Vintner
for the discriminating winemaker                                    october 1997

## 258 Bottles of Priceless Bordeaux Discovered in Abadoned Cellar

Lorem ipsum dolor sit amet, consectetuer adipiscing elit, sed diam nonummy nibh euismod tincidunt ut laoreet dolor magna aliquam erat volutpat. Ut wisi enim ad minim veniam, quis nostrud exercitation ullamcorper suscipit lobortis nisl ut aliquip ex ea commodo consequat.

Duis autem vel eum iriure dolor in hendrerit in vulputate velit esse molestie consequat, vel illum dolore eu feugiat nulla facilisis at vero eros accumsan et iusto odio dignissim blandit praesent luptatum zzril delenit augue duis dolore te fegait nulla facilisi. Lorem ipsum dolor sit amet, consectetuer adipiscing elit, sed diam nonummy nibh euismod tincidunt laoreet dolore magna aliquam erat volutpat.

Nam liber tempor cum soluta nobis eleifend option congue nihil imperdiet doming id quod mazim placerat facer possim assum. Lorem ipsum

dolor sit amet, consectetuer adipiscing elit, sed diam nonummy nibh euismod tincidunt ut laoreet dolore magna aliquam erat volutpat. Lorem ipsum dolor sit nihil imperdiet doming id quod mazim placerat facer possim assum. Lorem ipsum dolor sit amet, consectetuer adipiscing elit, tincidunt ut laoreet dolore magna aliquam erat volutpat.

Lorem ipsum dolor sit amet, consectetuer elit, sed diam nonummy nibh euismod tincidunt ut laoreet dolor magna aliquam adipiscing elit, sed diam nonummy euismod. Lorem ipsum dolor sit amet, consectetuer elit, sed diam nonummy nibh euismod tincidunt ut laoreet dolor magna aliquam erat volutpat. Ut wisi enim ad minim veniam.

Duis autem vel eum iriure dolor in hendrerit in vulputate velit esse molestie consequat, vel illum dolore eu feugiat nulla facilisis at vero eros accumsan et iusto odio dignissim blandit praesent luptatum zzril delenit augue duis dolore fugait nulla facilisi. Lorem ipsum dolor sit amet, consectetuer, sed adipiscing elit, sed diam nonummy nibh euismod tincidunt ut laoreet dolore magna aliquam erat volutpat. Lorem ipsum dolor sit nihil imperdiet doming id quod mazim placerat facer possim assum. Lorem ipsum dolor sit amet, consectetuer adipiscing elit, tincidunt ut laoreet dolore magna aliquam erat volutpat. Duis autem vel eum iriure dolor in hendrerit in vulputate velit esse molestie consequat, vel illum dolore eu fugiat nulla facilisis at vero eros accumsan et iusto odio dignissim blandit praesent luptatum zzril delenit augue.

If your headline is more evocative than informative, you might wish to let a photograph or an illustration dominate the page.

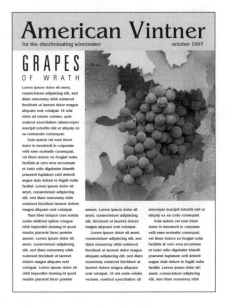

For an extravagant look, you can mimic a magazine cover by using a full-page photo.

## Inside Pages

*Choose a consistent format for the inside pages of your tabloid.*

Design your tabloid as a series of two-page spreads. Include your organization's logo or publication title at least once on every spread, typically in a running footer. Another ideal place for such items is in a *drop*, which is a deep top border.

Include your organization's logo at least once on every spread.

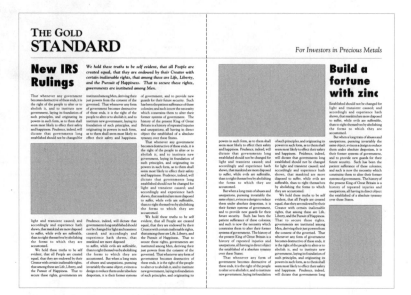

Choosing a three-column format lets you use a variety of photograph sizes.

A five-column grid creates even more design flexibility.

## Planning for Ads

You can mix information and advertising in your publication to enhance your firm's credibility and image. You can also pre-sell prospective customers on your firm's competence and professionalism and expand the market for your products by answering basic questions first-time buyers might have.

You can creatively mix editorial and selling space. You can highlight editorial information in several ways:

- Between parallel rules on the top half of each page.

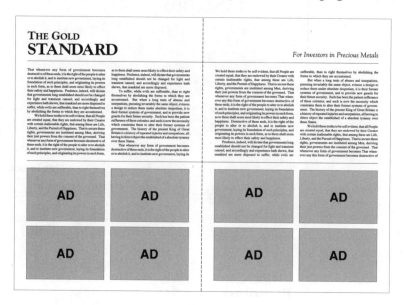

- In vertical columns adjacent to the selling area.

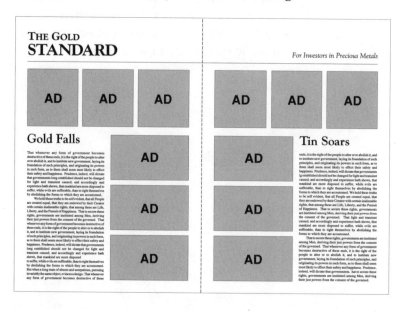

- Between the selling areas.

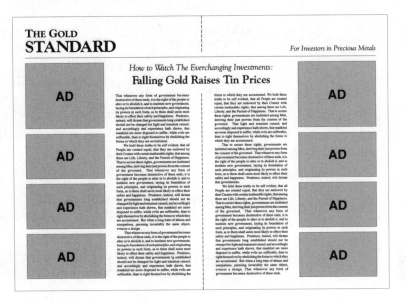

- At the bottom of each page.

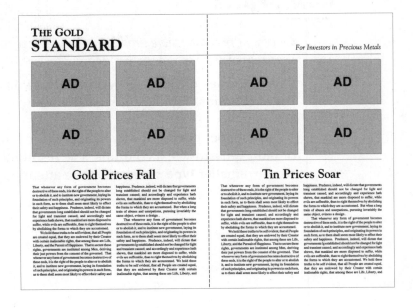

- With a screen to integrate editorial material into one unit.

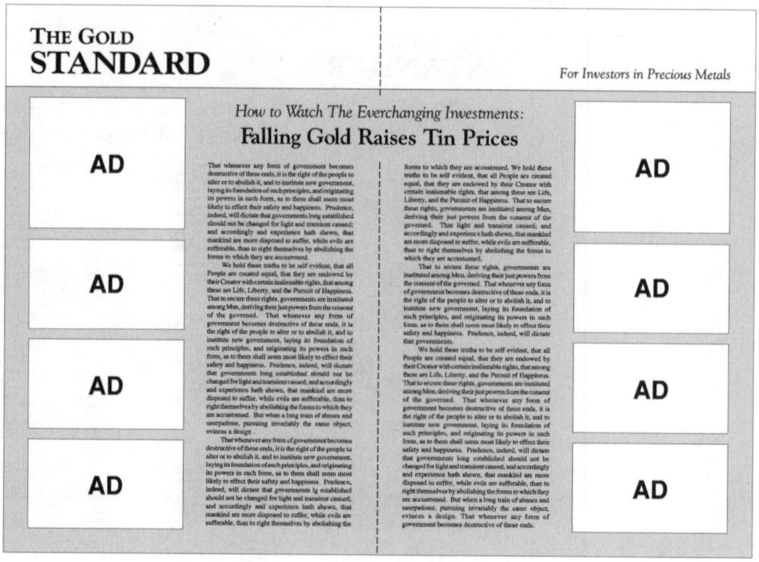

THE GOLD
**STANDARD**

*For Investors in Precious Metals*

*How to Watch The Everchanging Investments:*
**Falling Gold Raises Tin Prices**

AD

AD

AD

AD

AD

AD

AD

AD

# Newspapers

*Once you're comfortable producing tabloid-size newsletters, you'll find it easy to step up to newspaper design.*

One of the key differences between the two formats is the number of columns. Tabloids are usually set up on fewer, wider text columns.

Newspaper pages, however, are divided into many—often six or more—narrow text columns. The resulting shorter line lengths require smaller type sizes and more attention to hyphenation and letter and word spacing.

## Headlines

*An important challenge that faces newspaper designers is working out a hierarchical order among the various articles that will appear on the same page.*

The type size of the headline should reflect the importance of the story. Make sure there's some variation; confusion will reign if all articles are introduced by the same size headline.

Let the top of the page carry most of the weight. Your layout will look unbalanced if you place your larger headlines near the bottom.

## Photographs

*Newspapers must accommodate a wide variety of photographs of differing size and degree of importance.*

In a typical newspaper, the front page alone often contains more photos than are found in an entire newsletter issue.

Arrange multiple photographs so that each is placed appropriately in relation to the others and to the page design as a whole.

Arrange multiple photographs so that each is placed appropriately in relation to the others and to the page design as a whole.

Whereas many newsletter photographs are often simple head shots, newspaper photos include a variety of subjects, shapes, and sizes.

## Teasers

*Because of a newspaper's greater size and complexity, it's even more important to provide front-page teasers to attract readers to the inside.*

Attention must be drawn to special features and high-interest articles inside. Readers also want clear direction to specific items such as classified listings, calendars of events, and other sections.

## Article Jumplines

*Another peculiarity of newspapers is the large number of articles continued on inside pages.*

Long articles are often broken into several segments placed on subsequent pages. Each segment requires jumplines to help the reader locate the continuation. Jumplines present a challenge to the designer: they must be easily noticed but also easily distinguished from headlines and subheads.

---

**Article doesn't quite fit**

Ut wisi enim ad minim veniam, quis nostrud exerci tation ullamcorper suscipit lobortis nisl ut aliquip ex ea commodo consequat. Duis autem vel eum iriure dolor in hendrerit in vulputate velit esse molestie consequat, at vero eros et accumsan et iusto odio dignissim qui praesent luptatum zzril delenit augue duis dolore te feugait nulla facilisi.

Nam liber tempor cum soluta nobis eleifend option congue nihil imperdiet doming id quod mazim placerat facer possim assum. Lo-

rem ipsum dolor sit amet, consectetuer adipiscing elit, sed diam nonummy nibh euismod tincidunt nisl ut aliquip ex ea commodo consequat.vel illum dolore eu feugiat nulla facilisis at vero eros et accumsan et iusto odio dignissim qui blandit praesent luptatum zzril delenit augue duis dolore te feugait nulla facilisi nam liber tempor soluta.

Nam liber tempor cum soluta nobis eleifend optional congue nihil imperdiet domin. Duis autem vel iriurent

*(Continued on p. 7)*

## Advertisements

*Advertising is a necessary ingredient, and in fact, pays the bills for most newspapers.*

Advertisements must neither compete with nor be over-shadowed by adjacent editorial material.

It's often impossible to be sure of the number and sizes of advertisements you'll run until the last minute. Many newspapers adhere to the specifications of the Standard Advertising Units to simplify page makeup (check this with your local newspaper). These include a variety of standard ad sizes that can be used as building blocks in assembling pages.

For more about design and placement of advertisements, see Chapter 13, "Advertising Materials: Response & Collection."

## Moving On

Successful design of distribution media includes consistent and appropriate treatment of repeating elements that appear in each issue. For information that varies from one issue to the next, designers create distinct visual patterns between them. Distribution methods will also affect your design decisions for these media.

In the next chapter, we'll explore how to design successful sales materials.

# 11

# Sales Materials

## Overview

- Consider the intended target readership.

- Convey a sense of immediacy and excitement.

- Prioritize your information so that your readers do not have to wade through information that is not relevant to a purchase.

- For larger materials like catalogs, consider how well your design can handle changes, such as pricing.

- Make it easy for readers to respond by providing complete ordering information in an easy-to-use format.

- Include pre-paid reply envelopes if needed.

*Designers are alert to graphic and style devices that help identify different groups of people and position products (or services) within the buyer's reach.*

Special considerations must be made for the different needs met by sales materials, including information distribution and the response and collection of information.

One key to presenting different types of products and services is to accurately identify your intended market. The more precisely you do, the more your design for that market is likely to elicit the response you're looking for.

Successful sales materials require careful planning. They can be prepared in a wide variety of shapes and sizes. Choosing an approach depends on many factors including the following:

One key to
presenting
different types
of products and
services is to
accurately
identify your
intended
market.

- The number, complexity, and cost of products and services being advertised. Will the sales piece focus on a single item, or must it accommodate a variety of products and services?

- The targeted point in the purchase cycle. Will materials be designed for a wide range of potential buyers or aimed specifically at prospects who are ready to make a purchase now?

- The choice of whether to appeal to the buyer's emotions. Is the item utilitarian, or will it be perceived as an enhancement to the buyer's lifestyle and self-image?

- The production time and relative longevity of the sales piece. How much time is involved in producing it, and how long will it last?

- The appropriate overall style. Does the project match the style expected by the target audience?

- The anticipated use of the sales piece. Is it intended for casual browsers or is it intended to close a sale?

You'll need to consider how sales materials are generally used. Many people enjoy browsing through catalogs and brochures randomly, while others use them as a reference to find specific items that interest them.

Menus and order forms as sales materials differ in their regular use as convenient lists. You can treat them as point-of-sale ads with equal attention paid to design that attracts the reader and design that encourages further reading.

Next, know your stuff. Product research is frequently neglected, or worse, invented! For all your work in design and layout, ultimately you'll be judged for accurate content and how well your design and layout match and support the content . Remember design is meant to be transparent so that it reveals your message. When a copywriter other than yourself is involved in your project, you'll need to work hand-in-hand with them during the design stage.

If there is a single component for successful design for sales materials, it is placing the product (or service) firmly and undoubtedly in the buyer's sphere of interest. To do this you need to know product features in order to develop a graphic style that hits the mark.

Your knowledge of product and market are essential to the design of all kinds of sales materials. They help you formulate an approach, organize content, and deliver the appropriate message.

## Brochures

*Brochures can follow different themes but all share three common design requirements:*

- A front-cover headline that summarizes the primary benefits of the product or service being offered.

- Facts and figures that connect ideas and relationships for readers and encourage a positive customer decision.

- Prominently displayed, clear reader-response instructions. You want to make it easy to do business and remain as flexible as possible to the preferred buying methods of your potential customers.

Avoid boxing or bordering each page uniformly. This can interfere with the reader's natural progression from panel to panel.

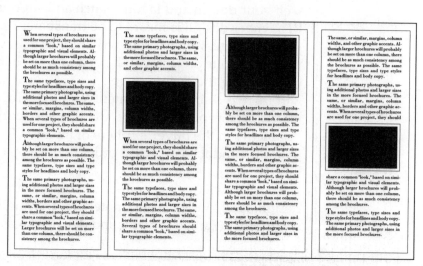

Also keep in mind that brochures distributed to a large audience early in the purchase cycle may not need to be as detailed—or expensively printed—as those distributed to qualified prospective buyers who are ready to pull out their checkbooks.

Brochures describing a standard line of products or services can be used over an extended period of time. They are typically supported by detailed product sheets (see the "Product Sheets" section later in this chapter), which present a more detailed look at a single product. This saves money because individual product sheets can be revised and reprinted as products are updated, without making the full line of brochures obsolete.

## Design Consistency

*Consistency in design can help you achieve a unified package of various materials.*

Here are some ways to build consistency across a series of brochure projects:

- Consider the same typefaces, type sizes, and type styles for headlines and body copy.

- Use a primary photograph (perhaps cropped differently), with additional new photos and larger sizes in the more detailed brochures of your series.

- Keep margins, borders, and graphic accents consistent.

- Place photos in the same position from one page to the next.

When several types of brochures are used for one project, you'll want them to share a common look based on similar typographic and visual elements. You want to relate them to each other while at the same time define their unique characteristics.

- This is especially important when you offer more than one product.

- Variation along a theme can help you give a unique personality to each piece that reflects its purpose.

- Vary the layout. For example, in a three-column layout, consider filling all columns in one piece and for the next piece leave one column blank.

- Use a symbol in slightly different ways from one piece to the next. You may want to change the color of a particular symbol from one piece to the next, or use the same symbol but larger (or smaller) and in a different fixed location.

## Types of Brochures

*Understanding your product (or service) and your target audience will help you choose a suitable brochure type and style.*

Three common types of brochures are service, line, and product-specific brochures.

*Service brochures* describe a firm or association's goals and products or services. A health maintenance organization's brochures might describe its preventive medicine and long-term care plans, while a performing arts group's brochures might provide concert and instruction schedules.

*Line brochures* feature one category or even one item of a product line. An audio/video manufacturer might have separate brochures for compact disc players, videocassette recorders, and car stereo systems.

*Product-specific brochures* focus on a specific purpose. A college alumni association, for example, might prepare a brochure in conjunction with a fund drive to raise money for a new building.

As for size, brochures run the gamut—from a single 8½ x 11-inch sheet of paper, folded into thirds and printed in one color on both sides, to 16 four-color pages. You'll want to include a simple index for multipage pieces that carry several categories or items. You can use a symbol or a color to identify each category and serve as an index system.

In addition to the various sizes and editorial approaches, brochures can also be categorized by their level of depth and breadth of information. These consist of teasers, tell-alls, and impressers.

## Teasers

*Teasers are brochures targeted to prospective buyers early in the decision-making process.*

Teasers don't pretend to tell the whole story; their purpose is to direct the reader to the next level of action, such as calling a toll-free telephone number.

Teasers are frequently printed on single sheets of paper, then folded into panels (to fit into a Number 10 business envelope). They're inexpensively produced so that they can be distributed to as many prospective buyers as possible. Teasers are also displayed conspicuously in free-standing or countertop racks so that anyone can feel free to take one.

The future is now. Introducing the Axon Impulse.

photo

FINALLY, a fax machine that makes use of a logic circuit. Imagine a fax machine that can collate your document, remove any spelling errors, and deduce the recipient's phone number—even if you don't know it yourself. Now stop imagining. It's already available.

Call **1-800-IMPULSE** for your free brochure.

In the future, fax machines will operate on artificial intelligence...

AXON

## Tell-all Brochures

*Tell-all brochures target qualified buyers.*

Tell-all brochures are designed for the next level of readers— serious potential buyers who are closer to the moment of truth. They contain more information and often conclude with detailed specifications of the products or services being offered.

Tell-all brochures are often printed on standard 8½- x 11-inch paper or on larger sheets requiring a 9- x 12-inch envelope. In fact, a great deal of flexibility is possible. The size, shape, and quality of paper used for these brochures can help set your presentation of a product or service apart from competing ads. You can even use square or other nonstandard page sizes if they enhance your design.

**It collates.**
Lorem ipsum dolor sit aet, consectetuer adipiscing elit, sed diam nonummumy nibh euismod tincidunt ut laoreet dolore aliquam erat volutpat. Ut wisi enim ad minim veniam, quis notrud exerci tation ullamcorper suscipit lobortis nisl ut aliquip ex ealut commodo.

**It spell-checks.**
Duis autem vel eum dolor iriure dolor in hendrerit in vulputate velit esse molestie consequat, vel illum dolore eu feugiat nulla facilisis at vero eros et accumsan iusto odio dignissim qui blandit.

**It cleverly deduces phone numbers.**
Praesent luptatum delenit augue duis dolore te feugait nulla facilisi. Lorem ipsum dolor sit amet, consectetuer adipiscing elit, sed nonummy nibh euismod tincidunt ut laoreet dolore magna erat volutpat.

**More great office stuff available from AXON**
- Lorem ipsum
- Dolor sit aet
- Consectetuer
- Adipiscing elit sed diam
- Nibh euismod tincidunt
- Laoreet dolore
- Aliquam erat volutpat

**It makes toast.**
Lorem ipsum dolor sit aet, consectetuer adipiscing elit, sed diam nonummumy nibh euismod tincidunt ut laoreet dolore aliquam erat volutpat. Ut wisi enim ad.

You'll find that tell-all brochures tend to be either copy- or illustration-oriented. Combining large and small photographs with expanded captions is another option you may want to consider.

## Impressers

*Impressers approach the quality of booklets or small magazines in design sophistication.*

Impressers follow up and reinforce the message at the last crucial phase before purchase. They combine sophisticated graphic design with high-quality printing and paper. An impresser brochure is frequently designed to be part of the product—the high quality of the sales materials implies high quality in the product or service.

Impressers are appropriate when the products or services are either emotionally important to the buyer or in cases where benefits can't be measured until after the purchase is made. Examples include luxury items such as expensive automobiles, complex technical products and services, and intangibles like public relations or financial services.

## Catalogs

*The nature of a product can carry a whole range of associations with it. The character of your company, the type of goods and services, and the target market will influence the overall catalog style.*

Catalogs are similar to brochures, except they usually contain more pages and are more product-oriented. The challenge is to integrate numerous visual elements, captions, and prices into an effective and appealing design.

Catalogs are usually produced once or twice a year. Because of their longevity, they're often printed on more expensive paper and include more color.

In many cases, particularly in the retail business, catalogs evolve from newsletters. Often, page size is sacrificed for volume, which increases the perceived "reference value" of a catalog and contributes to the long life of the catalog.

Many catalogs use a lot of color, which also increases their perceived value and selling power. The often necessary expense of full-color for dynamic catalogs requires acute design skills to maximize cost returns.

Catalogs are similar to brochures, except they usually contain more pages and are more product-oriented.

## Covers

*Catalog covers often are printed on a different paper stock than the inside pages.*

Often, a heavier, glossy (or smooth) paper stock is used to provide higher quality photo reproduction and better color saturation.

You'll often see a single photo of the company's most popular product used on the cover to communicate an identity and promote sales. The cover can also feature a collage, or grouping, of photos or illustrations, calling attention to the diversity of products described inside.

Like newsletters, catalog covers often contain a nameplate that clearly reflects the content and provides a strong identity.

Like newsletters, catalog covers often contain a nameplate, or title, that clearly reflects the content and provides a strong identity.

## Inside Pages

*Often a catalog's inside front-cover spread describes the company and its policy. Frequently there's a "Letter From the President" explaining the company's philosophy.*

Inside catalog spreads are generally more complex than newsletter pages. Space is allotted into sections for product photos, captions, and prices.

You can use varying sizes of artwork.

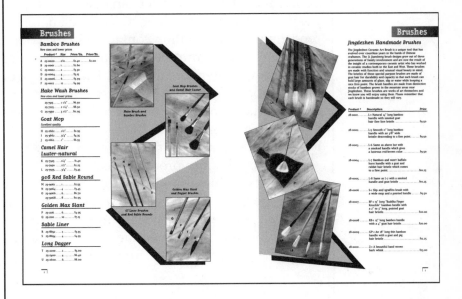

## Ordering Information

*Ordering information and forms are typically printed as part of the catalog. However, response is encouraged by providing a separate, postage-paid, self-addressed order form inserted into the middle of the catalog.*

Inviting readers to respond by offering easy-to-use order forms and placing toll-free telephone numbers in the catalog can greatly increase sales.

You want to let your readers know clearly how to become your customers and allow them to do that easily and conveniently.

For online projects, design your ordering information to let your customers know how to buy, what security measures you follow, and when to expect delivery, but also provide traditional methods for ordering like a toll-free telephone number.

## Product Sheets

*Product sheets are more complex than flyers.*

Product sheets provide detailed information and specifications about a product or service and are usually printed on high-quality paper stock. The front cover can display a large photograph of the product, a paragraph or two of explanatory material (often repeating the information contained in the company's full-line brochure), plus an outline of the product features and benefits.

Back covers are more detailed. They include one or more photographs of products being used, followed by specific product information and any related accessories and supplies.

Product sheets are often three-hole punched, so they can be inserted in binders or added to proposals.

Often you'll notice product sheets created for an entire series of products within a single product line. For example, a manufacturer of pens can have separate series of product sheets: one for ball point pens, another for felt-tipped instruments, and still another for calligraphic pens and inks. A simple graphic can unify single product sheets into a series.

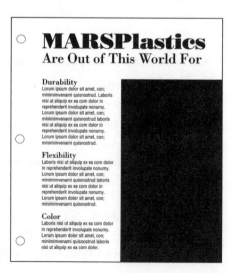

Consistent placement of a graphic can provide the continuity necessary to tie various product sheets together. This graphic symbol is often printed in a different color on each product sheet, to help distinguish it from other products.

You can build consistency by using the same sizes, styles, and placement for borders, columns, visuals, and logos.

# Order Forms

*Order forms are more than a handy list.*

Order forms often double as price lists. Designers consider order forms on two equally important levels. The readers' ease in relating items with part numbers and prices is the main focus of a logical and coherent design. Second, the design style that suits the business and the intended customer is assessed. A graphic style for women's sportswear may need to be fresh yet not too wild. Fashion clothes for teenagers can have a more carefree, fun-loving appeal and presentation—perhaps even bordering on the wacky.

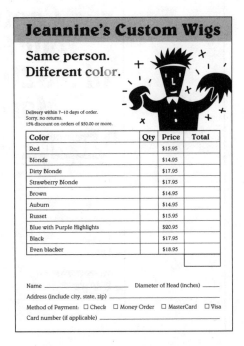

Sales materials of all types are aimed at generating interest from the beginning—often at a glance, keeping interest all along the way and effectively requiring the reader to move into action either immediately or in the near future.

## Flyers

*Flyers are typically used to advertise a special, limited-time promotion of a single product or service.*

Flyers contain time-sensitive information printed on one side of a sheet of paper. They're ideal when you have a small budget and you have to get the information out right away. They can also be hung on walls, placed on countertops, or used as shopping bag inserts.

Flyers are appropriate vehicles for promoting a drug store's specially priced vitamins, a nightclub's upcoming performance of a popular jazz musician, an office supply dealer's sale on file folders, or a music store's sale on a certain label's compact discs.

Flyers contain time-sensitive information printed on one side of a sheet of paper.

For flyers to capture an audience's attention, they must include the following:

- Large headlines.

- A catchy phrase leading them to read more.

- Attention-getting visuals or graphic accents.

Since the primary goal of sending out flyers is to get the message out to as many people as possible, they're usually printed inexpensively in only one or two colors on a cheaper grade of paper.

Printing your flyers on low-cost colored paper produces attention-getting two-color effects for a one-color price.

Although most flyers are printed on standard 8½- x 11-inch paper, larger sizes are possible. In terms of visual impact and amount of information communicated, tabloid-sized 11- x 17-inch flyers can almost be considered as mini-billboards.

Today, flyers are also delivered via fax machines. This means of delivery sends a message of urgency that often grabs attention.

## Direct Mail Pieces

*For direct mail pieces, you need the kind of graphic signals that achieve the best response in a few short seconds. Impact is the key word in this area of design.*

The life span of direct mail is very short and those pieces that don't survive are called junk mail. Many direct mail pieces arrive in an envelope. You have to get your readers to open the envelope first, then actually scan the information. You must grab attention with the envelope before your whole piece hits the trash can unopened.

Direct mail demands the immediacy of an advertisement. Images must instantly grab attention, interest, and focus on persuasive content. There are no shortcuts for designing winning direct mail. Your designs will need to be sophisticated and quick to compete with other mailers—some 60 billion pieces annually are distributed in American mailboxes. See Chapter 13, "Advertising Materials: Response & Collection," for more about designing advertising pieces.

Here are some tips to help fine-tune your direct-mail design. Make sure that:

- The hierarchy of information matches the target market's interests.

- The sense of movement across the page(s) is strong.

- Color and color accents draw the readers in.

- Continuity of style is established early on the cover (and envelope).

- Graphic images work on the reader's intuitive and conscious levels.

Unless you're very confident, you'll want to avoid rotated and fit-to-path text elements. All too often they diminish and overwhelm otherwise compelling buy signals.

Sort through the collection of direct mail that arrives in your mailbox daily. Examine those pieces that you find interesting. Note what the mailer was intended to achieve and what graphic style the designer used to achieve it.

## Menus

*A restaurant's menu is its most important advertising medium.*

Menus require special care in organizing the material and creating a design that presents an appropriate image.

A menu is an excellent candidate for the application of desktop publishing technology. You can create menu templates that can be easily updated as prices change or new items are added.

Indeed, many fine restaurants print new menus each day using color printers. This allows each menu to feature the freshest produce and special of the day.

Borders, typefaces, and visuals used in the menu's design play a major role in projecting the restaurant's character.

Stylized serif typefaces and ornate borders can communicate an Old World atmosphere. A contemporary atmosphere is suggested by sparse, angular, or geometric sans serif type.

Menus present an ideal opportunity to use clip art to establish a mood. Clip-art publishers offer a variety of country, urban, and atmosphere themes.

In creating a layout, remember that patrons want to quickly locate food categories. Subheads set in a contrasting typeface, type size, or type style are easy to distinguish.

Categories can be boxed or separated by horizontal rules and white space.

One of the clichés of menu design is separate columns with leader dots connecting descriptions to prices. Unfortunately, the result is often a distracting horizontal pattern. Also, isolated prices place undue emphasis on the price rather than on the cuisine. As an alternative, try centering descriptions in two or three columns across the page.

Each item can be introduced by a centered, one- or two-word identifier—perhaps in boldface italics—followed by a two- or three-line (mouth-watering) description. The price can then be discreetly and clearly included at the end of the description. This approach focuses the reader's attention on one item at a time.

## Moving On

Let's move on to other types of business communication—letterhead, logo, and business cards—which are as much a part of marketing as they are functional items. In the next chapter, you'll see how to design business communication that sells.

# 12

# Business Communication

◀ **Overview**

- Make sure your design accurately reflects your company's philosophy and way of doing business.

- Include all necessary information, such as area codes, fax numbers, Internet addresses, post office box numbers, and street addresses.

- Make your logo legible, proportionate to other elements, and connected to the whole.

*Letterhead, logo, and business cards—and other types of business communication—are as much a part of marketing as they are functional items.*

Business communication materials graphically establish a company's style and purpose. They are both functional and informative in nature.

As vehicles for correspondence and communication, you want to design them for maximum leverage. This includes using the design patterns for an entire range of stationery from letterhead to envelopes to fax cover sheets.

# Letterhead

*A good letterhead communicates subliminal as well as practical infor-
mation at a glance.*

Letterhead design is not as obvious as it may seem. It's important
to express something about the nature or character of your firm
or association in your letterhead design, in addition to providing
its name, address, and phone number as response information.
For instance, a district attorney requires a different letterhead
style than a tanning salon.

These are the basic components of a letterhead:

- Firm or organization name

- Logo

- Motto or statement of business philosophy

- Street address and mailing address (if different)

- Telephone number(s)

- Telex and/or fax number

- Electronic and online addresses and contact information

Corporate and nonprofit letterheads often list officers or board
members as well. All too often, however, that leaves little space
for the actual message area and presents a real design challenge.

## Logo Size & Placement

*The size of your logo must be proportional to the amount of supporting
information.*

Logos must be large enough to be noticed, yet not so large they
visually overwhelm the letterhead. In the following example, the
logo detracts from the message area.

Logos must be large enough to be noticed, yet not so large they visually overwhelm the letterhead.

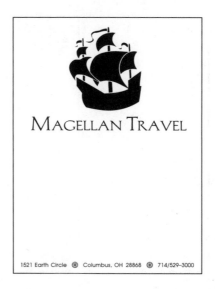

Placement can be flexible. Although logos are frequently centered above the letterhead, there is no reason why they can't be placed differently, as long as you observe basic rules of good design.

For example, logos can be set flush-left or flush-right at the top of the page.

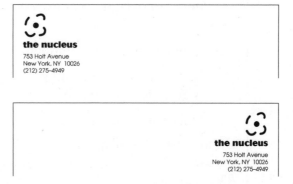

The letterhead can be designed on an asymmetrical grid. This will leave a vertical band of white space along the left-hand side of the letterhead. This type of layout presents vital information in a long, narrow, elegant column.

MAGELLAN
TRAVEL

1521 Earth Circle
Columbus, OH 28868
714/629-3000

## Contact Information

*Be sure to include all the information that the letter's recipient needs in order to respond.*

Insufficient address and phone information can cause problems for your correspondents.

Letterhead design becomes a bit more complicated when you must include:

- Telephone and fax numbers

- Both street address and post office box number—sometimes with different zip codes

- Online information

One common mistake is to print a telephone number without the area code. That will put long-distance callers at a distinct disadvantage.

Placement of telephone and address information usually depends on logo placement. When the logo is centered at the top of the letterhead, telephone and address information is often centered in a smaller type size along the bottom.

When telephone and fax numbers are included, as well as a separate street address and post office box number, the information is often divided into thirds and placed across the bottom of the letterhead. For example, the street address can be aligned flush-left on two lines, telephone and fax numbers centered on two lines in the middle, and post office box number placed flush-right.

| 1845 United Terrace<br>Salem, Oregon 12345 | PHONE 987/765-5432<br>FAX 987/765-2345 | P.O. Box 1659<br>Salem, Oregon 12345 |
|---|---|---|

When fewer items are included, they can be placed on one line and separated by white space and oversized bullets.

P.O. Box 146 ◆ Kittering, PA 15401 ◆ 900/735-8976

Another option is to indent logo and address information from the left-hand edge of the letterhead. The logo is placed at the top of the page, while address and telephone information is placed at the bottom.

753 Holt Avenue ▲ New York, NY 10026 ▲ (212) 275-4949

## Mottos

*You can include your motto in your letterhead, especially when it's part of your business identity.*

Mottos often run along the bottom of a letterhead, forming an umbrella over address and phone information. In these cases, the motto is typically set slightly larger, and the italic version of the motto's font is used for the address and the telephone number.

## Message Area

*Don't forget the message area.*

The final challenge is to effectively set off the letterhead elements so they don't interfere with the contents of the document. One way to do this is to box the message area.

A screened column or panel or a second color can also be used to isolate supplementary information. This technique works well for listing board members or officers of an organization. Careful, screens that are too strong will adversely affect legibility.

## Envelope Design

*Letterhead designs and logos—in a scaled down size—are repeated on the business envelope.*

Letterhead designs and logos—in a scaled down size—are repeated on the business envelope.

Some businesses use window envelopes, which eliminate the need for addressing separate envelopes or labels. In such cases, the letterhead design must allow for properly positioning the inside address. The recipient's name and address are placed on the page so they can be seen through the window when the letter or form is folded and inserted into the envelope.

Often a "family" of envelopes is created: a small, inexpensive envelope for sending invoices and paying bills; a Number 10 envelope printed on the same paper stock as the letterhead for standard correspondence; and a 9 x 12-inch envelope for formal proposals or oversized documents.

Sometimes logo and address information are rotated 90 degrees and placed vertically along the side of the envelope.

# Business Cards

*Business cards are too often—and mistakenly—considered strictly functional pieces.*

On a business card, a lot of information must be presented in a relatively small amount of space—typically 3½ x 2 inches. Not only are the address, phone and fax numbers, online information and a logo included, but an individual's name and title are also prominently displayed.

Traditionally the *quadrant* technique is used as a solution to small space constraints. The firm's logo is placed flush-left in the upper left quadrant of the card. The logo is balanced by the phone number set flush-right in the upper right quadrant. The street address is set flush-left along the bottom of the card in the lower left quadrant while the post office box information is set flush-right in the lower right quadrant. These four elements form a framework around the individual's name and title, which are located in the center of the card.

Unfortunately, this layout ignores the marketing and information distribution sides of good and effective design. White space in the interior of this card quickly takes on a jumbled appearance, alienating elements and disrupting the unconscious reading flow. This start-stop, start-stop appearance is a tell-tale sign that the card was constructed with little regard to marketing.

A better solution is the lavish use of white space that allows each element to breathe. The shape of the card is emphasized by arranging the type to balance the logo. Good structuring of the information makes this layout functional and reflects positively on the image of the company and of the individual carrying the card.

Vertical formats also work well. They command authority and lend a modern feel to an important piece of business documentation. Once the basic card has been designed and stored as a template, it takes just a few seconds to change and update the information.

Don't forget the back side of a business card! You can use the back side of a card for company information and reserve the front of the card for personal contact information (title, phone number, fax number, and e-mail address).

Adding another color can also enhance a business card. You can add color accents to logos, graphics, or type. Adding one color and applying it selectively to highlight a few words or just your logo can be very effective. Color combinations can have strong effects on legibility. Avoid very light colors for small typefaces.

# Fax Cover Sheets

*Fax transmissions are an important part of today's business world.*

Cover sheets help ensure safe, efficient fax communications that are delivered quickly to the right people.

It's important for the fax cover sheet to indicate the total number of pages sent. This helps the recipient know that the entire transmission has been received and nothing is missing. Other important items include the following:

- Recipient's name
- Sender's name
- Logo and letterhead
- Date of transmission
- Subject matter or summary of contents

Some fax cover sheets include space or lines for a brief handwritten message. Or, a message can be set in a smaller type size to distinguish it from the items listed above.

Be careful when choosing typefaces for fax messages. Since the quality of reproduction varies, it's important to choose a typeface that remains legible under any circumstance.

Typefaces with thin strokes or detailed serifs tend to reproduce poorly and are not the most reliable choice for fax transmissions.

Cover sheets ensure efficient fax communications that are delivered quickly to the right people.

Many computers have standard fax transmission capabilities, frequently built-in with a modem and voice mail support. Privatized postal services also offer "send and receive services."

The office fax machine has carved a permanent niche for itself in today's fast-paced marketplace. Faxed documents are perceived as having more importance than printed documents such as letters. They are immediate, convenient, and arrive already "opened" inside the target office. While faxing is limited to black and white and does not offer the same advantages that color brochures do, its immediacy offsets the disadvantages of not using color presentation. A properly targeted fax offer can produce greater response rates and times than direct mail and at less cost.

Unfortunately, many people don't yet understand the limitations of fax transmissions. Most fax machines can transmit in high and low resolutions. High resolution makes it possible to send line-art drawings in a fax document, but the resolution is not high enough to reproduce photographs or backgrounds.

Since fax machines operate in black and white only, even high-resolution faxes of color pictures tend to lose detail and can appear somewhat muddy, or as an ugly smudge at the receiving end, especially when the original is dark.

Even when the sending machine is equipped for photographic quality, the receiving end may not be. Simple black and white line art—even if the original is camera-ready—won't be legible at the receiving station because of the bitmapped technology that's standard for faxes.

One solution to this problem is to fax the original oversized (twice the size, as a minimum). The recipient will need to reduce it back to the original size and perform some touch up. This only works when the fax is received via a computer fax (not for stand-alone fax machines). It also requires that the recipient know about the process ahead of time.

Most people don't understand that a fax machine scans—breaks down—the original document and sends it on its way. Nor do they understand that faxes are "reassembled" at the receiving end of a transmission. (Why would they care anyway as long as it works?)

However, it takes considerably longer to send (and receive) any document that contains a large number of vertical rules (lines) compared with a similar form that contains the same number of horizontal lines.

**TIP**

If your company regularly faxes forms that contain a large number of vertical rules, consider redesigning them. Not only will your fax be scanned faster with less vertical lines, but it will save a few pennies in phone charges with each transmission—which can amount to considerable savings for a large corporation over just a few months.

# Resumes

*A resume is direct response advertising in its purest form.*

With the skillful use of typographic elements, you can design resumes to set a tone and project a positive image. They're an ideal format for utilizing desktop publishing's ability to organize data and establish hierarchies of importance.

## Changing Resume Trends

*Today, the trend is toward less formal, more skill-oriented resumes.*

Contemporary resumes focus more on what an individual has to offer a specific company. In past years, resumes tended to be organized chronologically—focusing on the progression through a person's education, career, and activities.

Contemporary resumes focus more on what an individual has to offer a company.

Today, many paper-printed resumes include a reference to fully detailed Web pages that expand on professional skills. You can tailor each resume for each job and have an online version complete with images, diagrams, voice, and photographs.

Regardless of your format, white space, subheads, and graphic accents should be used to separate categories of information. A prospective employer wants to quickly locate relevant qualifications without playing detective.

**GEORGE TCHOBANOGLOUS**  662 Diego Place
Davis, California 95616
916/756-5747

| | |
|---|---|
| **Education** | **Ph.D., Civil Engineering**, Stanford University, 1969 <br> **M.S., Sanitary Engineering**, University of California, Berkeley, 1960 <br> **B.S., Civil Engineering**, University of the Pacific, 1958 |
| **Present Position** | **Professor of Environmental Engineering**, Department of Civil Engineering, University of California, Davis. <br> Research areas include solid waste management, innovative water and wastewater treatment systems, wastewater filtration, small wastewater treatment systems, on-site systems, and aquatic treatment systems. |
| **Honors/Awards** | Blue Key <br> Who's Who in America <br> Outstanding Teacher Award, 1980, School of Engineering, University of California, Davis <br> Gordon Maskew Fair Medal, 1985, Water Pollution Control Federation <br> Distinguished Alumnus of the Year for Public Service, 1985, University of the Pacific, Stockton, CA |
| **Society Memberships** | Association of Environmental Engineering Professors <br> Diplomat, American Association of Environmental Engineers <br> American Society of Civil Engineers <br> Water Pollution Control Federation <br> American Water Works Association <br> International Association on Water Pollution Research and Control <br> California Water Pollution Control Federation <br> American Association for the Advancement of Science <br> Sigma Xi <br> World Mariculture Society <br> American Fisheries Association |
| **Registration** | Registered Civil Engineer in California |
| **Employment** | 1976-Present: **Professor** <br> University of California, Davis, CA <br> 1971-1976: **Associate Professor** <br> University of California, Davis, CA <br> 1970-1971: **Assistant Professor** <br> University of California, Davis, CA <br> 1967-1969: **Acting Assistant Professor** <br> Stanford University, Stanford, CA |

Although many desktop-published documents use a combination of sans serif type for subheads and serif type for body copy, many resumes use the italic version of the serif type in a larger type size for subheads. This softens the contrast between subheads and body copy.

## Sell Yourself

*Resumes are designed like advertisements: selling information precedes supporting or qualifying information.*

Thus, addresses and phone numbers are subordinate to statements that convey what benefits the hiring firm is likely to gain if they hire you. Use keywords to summarize skills that are relevant to the potential employer. If you need help finding appropriate and varied keywords, call your local library. Reference librarians use keywords everyday to locate all kinds of information.

Since your resume is actually an advertisement for yourself, pay careful attention to the smallest details of letter and line spacing, as well as to typos and more serious errors. Communication skills are very important, so use a spell checker or grammar tool to avoid errors in grammar, spelling, and punctuation.

# Company Reports

*Reports are published to inform and will almost certainly include statistical and numerical data.*

When designing company reports, aim for visual styling, graphics, and typography that reinforce and reflect the company's character and image. Thematically, reports echo a company's confidence and progress.

A report for a corporate finance market will need to project an authoritative and secure image.

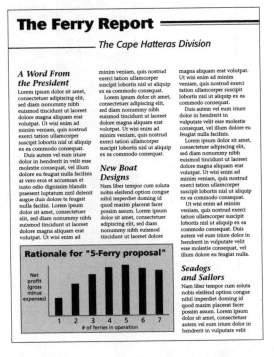

Give careful consideration to all figures, tables, and graphs, making sure readers can easily understand them. Often designers are forced to follow conventional formats in creating designs for company reports. Once you get into the habit of thinking practically about each project's formatting, you'll be able to focus on options that are both reasonable and flexible. How can you connect and present existing information in new ways?

Paying attention to content and purpose are your first clues to what you can do as a designer. These clues help you decide which layout patterns are going to be workable and appropriate for distributing this information.

Don't let yourself get caught in unnecessary layout ruts. If a document is text-intensive without photos or graphics, then you're left with text and space as your primary design tools. Consider a fresh format that promotes readability and interest, perhaps an off-center text grid that leaves a white space margin as part of the design or a two-column format.

## Moving On

Design for business communication uses reason and logic. In other types of publications you'll want to make an emotional appeal. In the next chapter, we'll explore design for advertising where moods, attitudes, and feelings are dominant in messages.

# 13

# Advertising Materials: Response & Collection

## Overview

- Clearly spell out all buying and contact information, including address, hours, and credit terms.

- Use typefaces, styles, and images that enhance the products' appeal to the target audience.

- Make the design of your ad consistent with the long-term image you want to project.

- Investigate costs, benefits, and alternative ways to add color to your work.

- Analyze collection information to detect important clues to designing performance-driven documents.

- Harmonize two-page spreads.

*Design flexibility and pragmatism are important ingredients in effective advertisements.*

Good design is particularly crucial in advertising, for the ironic reason that most viewers are content to ignore advertisements. Few media have such a built-in reluctance on the part of the reader. It requires that ads be visually striking, even flashy, to attract attention.

Unfortunately, flashiness does not always lend itself to good organization. Poorly-organized ads—many of them quite attractive—abound. They succeed in attracting attention but fail to promote any awareness of the product. Here are just a few of the things that can go wrong:

- **Too many focal points**. The best ads have one dominant visual element. Readers forced to divide their attention will probably lose their attention instead.

- **No integration of text and visuals**. An isolated visual may make readers look, but it won't cause them to read seemingly unrelated headlines and body copy. Make sure that your headlines tie in with your visual elements, and that the eye travels a logical path when moving from picture to headline to copy. If the path seems haphazard, the ad needs restructuring.

- **Missing information**. Once you've hooked your readers, don't frustrate them by withholding crucial information. If the size of the ad precludes giving all the necessary information, include instructions for finding out more.

You'll probably find that if you concentrate on organization in your ads, the problem of visual interest will take care of itself. Well-arranged graphics and text are inherent focal points.

## Newspaper Ads

*Effective newspaper ads have an underlying structure that guides the viewer's eye.*

An effective newspaper ad can be very difficult to design, due mainly to the limitations of the medium. Most newspaper ads don't fill the entire page and must compete with adjacent material for the viewer's attention. The adjacent material can be copy, headlines, or other advertisements; there's no way for the ad designer to know in advance. In the midst of all this visual competition, it's not enough to merely be eye-catching. An underlying structure is also needed to guide the viewer's eye through the content. The easiest way to attain this structure is by using a grid.

## Making Maximum Use of Grids

*The best way to design effective response and collection materials is to make maximum use of the grid as a planning tool.*

Grids make it easy to plan for the approximate number of products and text blocks necessary for marketing and promotional needs.

The first step is to create a flexible grid. In the sample grid below, a standard vertical rectangle has been divided into six columns, with each column divided into 13 equal units.

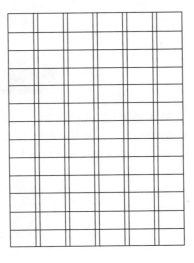

From this simple grid, a number of ways to mix text and graphics becomes possible. For example, you can divide the space from top to bottom into four areas: a two-unit-high headline area extending across the top of the page; below that, an area for visuals also extending the width of the page; then three two-column-wide text blocks four units high; and at the bottom of the page, a two-unit-high response area. The response area would contain your firm's logo, address, and perhaps a coupon.

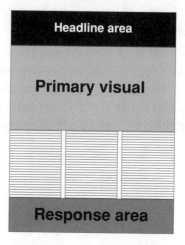

Without changing any of the proportions, notice how you can completely alter the appearance of the ad by relocating the headline below the visual.

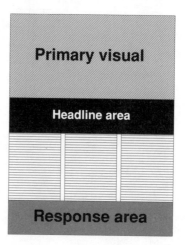

Another way to divide the space is to arrange the text in an L-shaped block surrounding a vertical photograph.

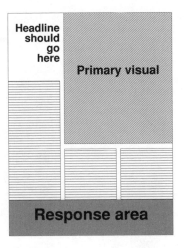

Things get interesting when you include both dominant and subordinate visual elements. For example, the combination of a large *atmosphere*—or *premise*—photograph, a column of premise copy, plus three boxes, each containing the photo, caption, and price of a specific product makes a very interesting design.

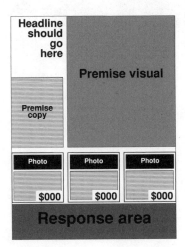

To include more products, reduce the primary photo and add another row of product photos.

Once you've finally settled upon a satisfactory grid, the actual layout process becomes very straightforward.

Grids don't limit your creative freedom; they liberate you to utilize space in more creative and cost-effective ways.

As the preceding examples show, grids don't limit your creative freedom; they actually liberate you to utilize space in more creative and cost-effective ways!

## Templates for Newspaper Ads

*Templates can save you time and effort in designing and producing newspaper ads.*

Create and save ad templates for various sizes—full-page, half-page, one-third-page, and one-quarter-page—to save yourself time. Design them all to reflect a strong family resemblance, with consistent treatments of headlines, borders, artwork, and buying information. Using grids can help you achieve these kinds of results.

By letting you predetermine the number of items you can use, grids make your planning sessions easier.

## Borders

*Because most advertisements and collection devices occupy less than a full page, pay special attention to borders.*

Strong borders separate your piece from the clutter of other page elements that surround it. The type of border you choose will often be determined by the shape of the ad.

A wide, vertically oriented ad should have strong top and bottom rules.

Strong borders separate your piece from the clutter of other page elements that surround it.

**Fetter's Office Cleaning Service**

We clean more offices than anyone else in the metropolitan area—and there's a reason we're so popular. In the dirty world of business, you don't want to trust your work area to just anyone. Give us a call.

(417) C·L·E·A·N·U·P

Thinner side rules can make small advertisements look taller than they actually are.

You can define borders with backgrounds. This type of border is more dynamic. When using backgrounds as borders be sure the overall style is appropriate to the audience, message, and personality of the firm.

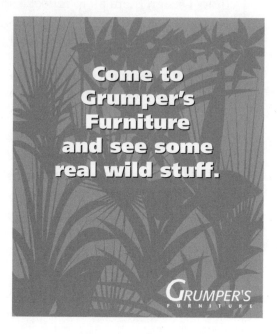

## White Space

*Use white space to further isolate and highlight your advertisement from its surroundings.*

The impact of your project can be increased by providing suffi-cient breathing room within the borders of the ad to set off artwork and text. One way to do that is to place the borders of your ad within the space allotted. As a result, there will be white space around your borders, clearly separating your copy from its surroundings.

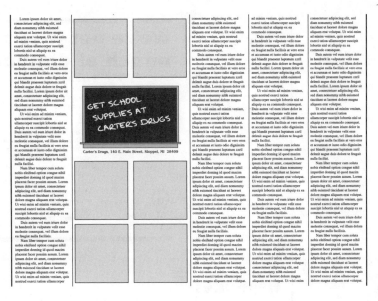

Using this technique, you can make small ads look larger by letting part of the ad break through the border into the surrounding interior white space.

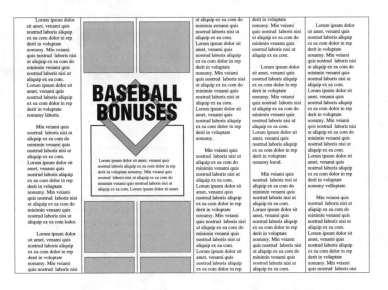

White space within ads can be created by using a multicolumn grid, indenting body copy, and allowing headlines to begin in the vertical band of white space to the left of the ad.

**We're not just a bunch of dimbulbs.**

Lorem ipsum dolor sit amet, adipiscing elit, sed diam nonummy nibh euismod tincidunt ut laoreet dolore magna aliquam erat volutpat. Ut wisi enim ad minim veniam, quis nostrud exerci tation ullamcorper suscipit lobortis nisl ut aliquip ex ea commodo consequat.

Duis autem vel eum iriure dolor in hendrerit in vulputate velit molestie consequat, vel illum dolore eu feugiat nulla facilisis at vero eros et accumsan et iusto odio dignissim qui blandit praesent luptatum zzril delenit augue duis dolore te feugait nulla facilisi.

Lorem ipsum dolor sit amet, elit, sed diam nonummy nibh euimod tincidunt ut laoreet dolore magna aliquam erat volupat. Ut wisi enim ad minim veniam.

BRIGHT IDEAS

## Headlines

*Ads, regardless of their sizes, use headline treatments to draw attention.*

A common technique is to reverse the headline out of the upper one-fourth to one-third of the area occupied by the ad.

# Everything Must Go!

After 40 years of serving the Van Nuys area, the Cobb-Hendricks Used Furniture Outlet is going out of business. Prices are dropping dramatically in an effort to empty our inventory. Our prices have never been this low! Beds, living room sets, dining room sets, sofas, chairs, and pianos are 50–70% off. So stop by and get a great deal on furniture—but hurry. After Wednesday, we'll just be a memory.

Cobb-Hendricks Used Furniture Outlet
3707 Siddown Avenue
Van Nuys, California  12345

Another effective technique is to place a graduated dark-to-light screen behind the headline and primary photograph or illustration. This allows the headline to be reversed and the text to be set in black type against a light background.

Headlines are often centered in newspaper ads, although that doesn't have to be the case. An alternate technique is to balance a strong flush-right headline with a smaller flush-left subhead. This draws the reader into the ad by speeding the transition from premise headline to supporting subhead.

## Screens

*Screens add a two-color effect to your ads.*

Screens within boxes, for example, can unify horizontal and vertical elements of the ad. Or you can place the screens behind the whole ad, which adds contrast to the boxes because of their "whiteness."

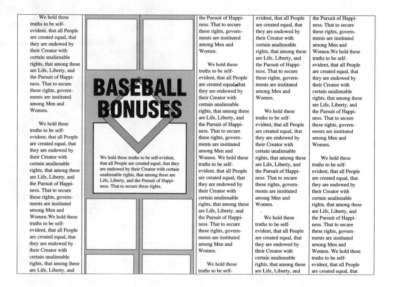

## Logos, Buying Information & Prices

*Every response and collection device necessarily requires purchasing and contact information. Make sure it's easy for potential clients to do business with you by making that information easy to find.*

Clearly visible addresses, phone numbers, and other buying and contact information make it easy for the reader to respond to the ad.

You'll want to identify the source by prominently displaying the logo of the firm running the ad. This can be achieved with size or contrast. Often the size of a manufacturer's logo is in correct proportion to the size of the visual it relates to and its surrounding information.

In this piece, the logo is relatively small, yet it's easily identified because it's surrounded by white space.

Likewise, type size used for captions and prices are proportional to the size of the photograph or artwork used to illustrate the product. Set prices in large type for large photographs, in small type for small photographs.

Practice restraint when choosing typefaces and type sizes. Avoid using a different type size for each product. Even the most product-filled ad needs no more than a few type sizes. One size for primary products and a second size for secondary products may be all the variety you need.

Remember that not every product advertised needs to be illustrated. Often, the best-looking ads simply list the products with a few representative photographs or drawings.

## Classified Ads

*Desktop publishing can produce attractive classified ads.*

Often, advertisers don't realize they can submit their own camera-ready copy rather than leaving the ad preparation to the newspaper.

The addition of a strong, high-contrast headline and prominent border can make a big difference in the response you get to your help wanted ad.

laying its foundation of such principles, and originating its powers in such form, as to them shall seem most likely to effect their safety and happiness. Minimum.

### DESKTOP PUBLISHING

Art/production person to help out three tired cowboys and one cowgirl who are working day and night to finish a graphic design book.  Must have DTP experience, willing to work long hours, meet hot deadlines and like pizza.  Must relocate to Denver, Colorado ASAP.  Send resumé to *Laser Writing Inc.*, 20 W. Bond, Denver, CO  25982.

TRUTHSAYER.  We hold these truths to be self evident, that all People are created equal, that they are endowed by their Creator with certain inalienable rights, that among these are Life, Liberty, and the Pursuit of Happiness.

NEW ASSISTANT KING.  The history of the present King of Great Britain is a history of repeated injuries and usurpations, all having in direct object the established of a absolute tyranny over these States.

Because classified pages tend to be made up of gray space, the use of white space can be a real attention-getter. Indenting body copy creates strong vertical bands of white space around your ad.

We hold these truths to be self-evident, that all People are created equal, that they are endowed by their Creator with certain unalienable rights, that among these are Life, Liberty, and the Pursuit of Happiness. That to secure these rights, governments are instituted among Men and Women.

We hold these truths to be self-evident, that all People are created equal, that they are endowed by their Creator with certain unalienable rights, that among these are Life,

Liberty, and the Pursuit of Happiness. That to secure these rights, governments are instituted among Men and Women.We hold these

## SALES MANAGER
FOR EXPANDING COMPUTER SOFTWARE COMPANY
Supervisory or extensive retail experience required.
CALL TODAY!
1-800-333-4444

truths to be self-evident, that all People are created equal, that they are endowed by their Creator with certain unalienable rights, that

among these are Life, Liberty, and the Pursuit of Happiness. That to secure these rights, governments are instituted among Men and Women.

We hold these truths to be self-evident, that all People are created equal, that they are endowed by their Creator with certain unalienable rights, that among these are Life, Liberty, and the Pursuit of Happiness. That to secure these rights, governments are instituted among Men and Women. We hold these truths to be self-evident.

## A border can also add white space.

vero eros et accumsan et iusto odio dignissim qui blandit

LOREM IPSUM DOLOR
Consectetuer adipiscing elit, sed diam nonummy nibh euismod tincidunt ut laoreet dolore magna aliquam erat volutpat. Ut wisi enim ad minim veniam, quis nostrud exerci tation ullamcorper suscipit lobortis nisl ut aliquip ex ea commodo consequat.

DUIS AUTEM VEL EUM

Iriure dolor hendrerit vulputate velit esse molestie consequat, vel illum dolore eu feugiat nulla facilisis at vero eros et accumsan et iusto odio dignissim qui blandit praesent luptatum zzril delenit augue duis dolore te feugait nulla facilisi. Lorem ipsum dolor sit amet, consec tetuer adipiscing elit, sed diam

nonummy nibh euismod tincidunt ut laoreet dolore magna aliquam erat volupat. Ut wisi enim ad vin minim veniam, quis nostrud exerci tation ullamcorper suscipit dolor lobortis nisl ut aliquip commodo consequat et miriam.

## A NEW HOUSE
3 bdrms., 2 bath, being offered by owners forced to relocate unexpectedly. Call 207/294-2428. No reasonable offer will be refused—we're desperate!

FACILIS ET VERO
Duis autem vel eum iriure dolor in hendrerit in vulputate velit esse moleste consequat, vel illum dolor eu feugiat nulla facilisis at veroros et accumsan et iusto dignisim qui blandit praesent luptatum zzril delenit augue duis dolore feugait nulla facilisi et iusto. Nam liber tempor cum soluta nobis eleifend option congue nihil imperdiet.

doming id quod mazim placerat facer possim assum. Lorem ipsum dolor sit amet.

CONSECTETUER ADIPISCING
Elit, sed diam nonummy nibh euismod tincidunt ut laoreet dolore magna aliquam volutpat. Ut wisi enim ad minim veniam, quis nostrud exerci tation ullam corper suscipit lobortis nisl ut aliquip ex ea comodo consequat. Duis autem vel eum iriure dolor in hendrerit in vulputate velit esse molestie consequat, vel illum dolore eu feugiat nulla facilisis. Ut wisi enim ad minim veniam, quis nostrud exerci tation ullamcorper suscipit lobortis.

ULLAMCORPER

Iriure dolor hendrerit vulputate velit esse molestie consequat, vel illum dolore eu feugiat nulla facilisis at vero eros et accumsan

## Quality Considerations

*It's entirely appropriate to prepare camera-ready newspaper ads using your laser printer.*

It's usually not necessary to go to the expense of having newspaper ads phototypeset, because the relatively coarse newsprint absorbs the ink to such a degree that the quality advantage offered by phototypesetting is lost.

Another advantage of desktop publishing is that you can build a library of scanned line-art illustrations to use in your ads, when appropriate, in place of photographs.

The new generation of 1,000-dot-per-inch plain-paper laser printers makes it even easier to prepare high quality newspaper ads in your office. As newspapers continue to improve their reproduction quality, however, the added clarity of images and type prepared with 1,000-dot-per-inch laser printers becomes more apparent.

In addition, scanners and desktop publishing programs are rapidly improving in their ability to handle photographs. The quality produced on some laser printers approaches the quality of newspaper photo reproduction. Thus, it's entirely feasible that you prepare complete newspaper ads, including photographs, with your desktop publishing system and laser printer.

# Information Collection

*One side effect of being in business is the necessary accumulation of all kinds of information.*

Response and collection documents are sometimes very distinct from each other and differ in their specific purposes. *Surveys* allow customers and employees to express their opinions and make suggestions. *Coupons* are valuable for providing names and addresses of prospective customers for later follow-up. *Employment application forms* help find the best candidate for the job. *Price quotations* and *order forms* make it possible to sell things to people across town or around the world.

Regardless of their specific function, response and collection media are composed of similar basic parts. Appropriate design of these parts is essential.

## Title

*Titles should clearly identify the form's purpose. The title should be set in a type face, size, or style that contrasts with the other type elements on the form.*

Like the headline of an advertisement or a newsletter article, the title of a form should be the dominant visual element, set significantly larger than the words that follow.

---

### Evaluation

Please circle one.

| Strongly agree | | | Strongly disagree | | General Session/Keynote Speaker |
|---|---|---|---|---|---|
| 5 | 4 | 3 | 2 | 1 | 1. The information presented increased my knowledge of secondary education in Howard County. |
| 5 | 4 | 3 | 2 | 1 | 2. The presentation was relevant and well presented. |
| 5 | 4 | 3 | 2 | 1 | 3. I would recommend this speaker for future conferences. |
| | | | | | Other comments or observations: _____ |

*Session One*/Title:

| | | | | | |
|---|---|---|---|---|---|
| 5 | 4 | 3 | 2 | 1 | 1. The information presented increased my knowledge of secondary education in Howard County. |
| 5 | 4 | 3 | 2 | 1 | 2. The presentation was relevant and well presented. |
| 5 | 4 | 3 | 2 | 1 | 3. The presentation will enable me to share the content with others. |
| | | | | | Other comments or observations: _____ |

*Session Two*/Title:

| | | | | | |
|---|---|---|---|---|---|
| 5 | 4 | 3 | 2 | 1 | 1. The information presented increased my knowledge of secondary education in Howard County. |
| 5 | 4 | 3 | 2 | 1 | 2. The presentation was relevant and well presented. |
| 5 | 4 | 3 | 2 | 1 | 3. The presentation will enable me to share the content with others. |
| | | | | | Other comments or observations: _____ |

## Instructions

*A successful response device gives clear directions for filling out and sending in the form or contacting the company.*

Coupon instructions should include payment options, e.g. prepayment, COD shipment, and accepted credit cards. If personal checks are an option, specify to whom they should be made out. If items are to be shipped via United Parcel Service, customers should be reminded that a post office box address does not usually provide enough information for delivery (except in some small rural communities).

Employment applications should indicate how and where the applicant can fill in education and previous employment information and references.

Surveys should carefully and clearly explain the rating scheme used—whether high numbers indicate agreement or disagreement with the statement, for instance.

Instructions are typically set in a small type size compared to other type on the page.

## Response Area

*Response areas can be designed with lines to be filled in, or ballot boxes to be checked.*

Forms with ballot boxes are easy to fill out. They are typically used for simple yes or no entries.

### Sleepytime Pillow Survey

Please take a few moments to fill out this survey. Your opinion is very important to us and these surveys help us better serve you. As an added incentive, all Sleepytime Pillow buyers who complete this survey will receive a set of Sleepytime Pillowcases absolutely free of charge. Sorry, you may not specify color.

Name _____
Address _____
_____
Phone _____
Date _____
SSN _____

1. How many Sleepytime Pillows do you own?
   - ❑ 1
   - ❑ 2
   - ❑ 3
   - ❑ 4 or more

2. How many hours do you sleep on a given night?
   - ❑ less than 3
   - ❑ 3–6
   - ❑ 6–10
   - ❑ more than 10

3. Do you ever let anyone borrow your Sleepytime Pillow?
   - ❑ yes
   - ❑ no
   - ❑ absolutely not

6. What object would you say is most comparable, in terms of softness, to a Sleepytime Pillow?
   - ❑ a cottonball
   - ❑ a sponge
   - ❑ a catcher's mitt
   - ❑ a brick

7. Do you plan to buy another Sleepytime Pillow soon?
   - ❑ yes
   - ❑ no
   - ❑ maybe

8. If someone stole your Sleepytime Pillow, would you respond with violence?
   - ❑ yes
   - ❑ no

Don't leave a lot of space between a ballot box and its accompanying label. Mentally matching up badly-spaced boxes and labels becomes tedious, and discourages respondents from completing the form.

---

**1. What made you decide to buy a Sleepytime Pillow?**
- ❒     Low price
- ❒     Softness
- ❒     Aesthetics
- ❒     Peer pressure

---

Lines accommodate names, addresses, and other detailed information that may be required. Remember to provide sufficient line length and space between lines. If you've ever tried to write in a long name or address on a tiny coupon, you know how frustrating it is, particularly if you must include additional information.

It's in the best interest of everyone involved to provide adequate horizontal and vertical space to permit a comfortable, readable handwriting size.

## Tables

Column headers should be clear and concise. Typically, they're centered over the columns.

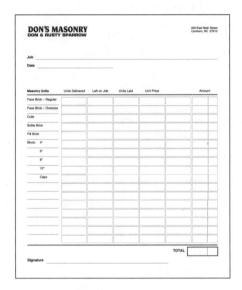

In complex tables, screening every other row helps respondents keep track of information.

### Addresses & Phone Numbers

The zip code portion of the address area should allow for the additional four-digit zip code for carrier-route sorting. Having this information can expedite mail delivery and save your organization postage costs in the years to come. It's also important to allow space to specify the country as well as the state.

Addresses for many large firms now include mail-stop information—their own internal zip codes. Unless you make it easy for users to include complete delivery information, order fulfillment or return communications can be seriously delayed.

Phone numbers should include the area code. Don't forget to include telephone extension numbers to avoid delays in case a follow-up call is necessary.

### Coupons

Coupons are typically bordered with a dashed line. Government or institution forms are often enclosed within boxed borders.

Highest response rates occur when the coupons are placed in the lower right corner of a right-hand page. (More time and effort are required for a reader to remove a coupon from a center column or the lower right corner of a left-hand page.)

## Moving On

This ends our foray through the many types of publishable media. In the next section, we'll show you how to refine the knowledge you've gained.

# Solving
# Design
# Problems

# 14

# Common Design Pitfalls

## Overview

- Make sure the design communicates the message.
- Balance tones with appropriate and ample white space.
- Make column width proportional to the type size.
- Use consistency and contrast appropriately.
- Determine an informational priority.

In all our enthusiasm for design opportunities, last minute adjustments, overload, or simple oversight can produce some unsightly and unwanted results. Below are typical examples of design hazards.

These samples show that using too many desktop publishing devices, compounded by a lack of attention to detail and time constraints, can work against the goals of straight-forward, effective communication.

### Rivers of White Space

*Watch out for "rivers" of white space that can develop vertically or diagonally through justified text.*

Rivers of white space are caused by gaps between words; they occur often when large type is justified in narrow columns.

They're especially likely to occur when two spaces instead of one are inserted after periods.

# Apartment Life

*by Sid E. Slicker*

I was so desperate to find a place to live when I first moved to New York, I signed a lease never having seen the apartment. Big mistake. The landlord, of course, gave a glowing description of the place, saying that it was "extremely well ventilated." It wasn't until I arrived at my new abode that I realized what he  meant: there were mammoth holes in the floor, ceiling and roof. I was despondent, needless to say, though at least I was sure my security deposit was safe; no further damage done to the apartment could possibly make it look any worse.

Remedies include decreasing the type size, increasing the column width, or both. You can also reset the copy with a ragged (unjustified) right margin.

# Apartment Life

*by Sid E. Slicker*

I was so desperate to find a place to live when I first moved to New York, I signed a lease never having seen the apartment. Big mistake. The landlord, of course, gave a glowing description of the place, saying that it was "extremely well ventilated." It wasn't until I arrived at my new abode that I realized what he meant: there were mammoth holes in the floor, ceiling and roof. I was despondent, needless to say, though at least I was sure my security deposit was safe; no further damage done to the apartment could possibly make it look any worse.

## Inappropriate Column Spacing

*Gutter width and type size need to be proportionate.*

As type size increases, you need more space between columns (a wider gutter) to prevent the reader's eyes from moving horizontally across columns, instead of progressing down to the next line.

As type size increases, you need more space between columns.

As type increases, more space between columns is needed to prevent the reader's eyes from moving horizontally, across columns, instead of progressing down to the next line. Be careful that you do not overdo it, however. Overly generous column spacing causes distracting vertical bands of white space.

As type increases, more space between columns is needed to prevent the

Be careful not to overdo it, however. Overly generous column spacing causes distracting vertical bands of white space. (The default column spacing for most desktop publishing programs may be too large or small for the specific typeface and type size you're using.)

## Trapped White Space

*Avoid "holes" in publications that disrupt the flow of information.*

Trapping white space between elements on a page produces a visual hole in your layout. This confuses readers and interrupts the flow of the copy and graphics.

Solutions include increasing the size of display type, enlarging the illustration, or recomposing copy.

## Claustrophobic Pages

*You'll want to provide sufficient breathing room around columns of text.*

Claustrophobic pages result when text, rules, graphics, and other elements crowd each other and the edges of the page.

Squeezing text into boxes or wrapping it too tightly around illustrations or silhouetted photographs also produces crowded pages (like a newspaper classified section).

**A VERY TIGHT FIT**

Lorum sum ipsum dolor sit amet, con; minimim venami quis nostrud laboris nisi ut aliquip ex ea com dolor . In reprehenderit in volupatate nonumy. Lorumque et ipsum dolor sit amet, con; minimim venami quis nostrud laboris nisi ut aliquip ex ea com dolor in reprehenderit in volu-patate nonumy. In reprehenderit in vo-lupatate nonumy. laboris nisi. Lorum ipsum dolor sit amet, con; minimim venami quis nostrud laboris aliquip ex ea com dolor.

**MUCH MORE COMFORTABLE**

Lorum sum ipsum dolor sit amet, con; minimim venami quis nostrud laboris nisi ut aliquip ex ea com dolor . In reprehenderit in volupatate nonumy. Lorumque et ipsum dolor sit amet, con; minimim venami quis nostrud laboris nisi ut aliquip ex ea com dolor in reprehenderit in volu patate nonumy ibsen dipsum dong.

## Whispering Headlines

*Headlines and subheads are significantly larger—and often bolder— than the text they introduce.*

Gray pages result where there's not enough contrast between headlines and text. Whispering headlines fail to attract attention to the text they introduce.

## Jumping Horizons

*Start text columns the same distance from the top of each page throughout a multipage document.*

Jumping horizons occur when text columns start at different locations on a page. The up and down effect is disconcerting to the reader and destroys publication integrity.

## Overly Detailed Charts

*Combine and simplify information presented in charts.*

To highlight the important message of a chart, combine and simplify less important information. A pie chart, for example, with more than six slices is confusing.

Group the smaller slices together to simplify the chart and direct the reader's attention to the relationship of the segments.

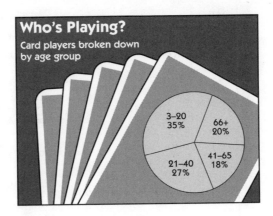

## Floating Heads & Subheads

*Position headlines and subheads close to the text they introduce, leaving plenty of room between them and the preceding text.*

The impact and purpose of a heading is weakened if readers can't immediately identify which text it refers to.

Aliquip ex ea com dolor in reprehenderit in volupatate nonumy. Ipsum dolor sit amet, con com dolor nostrud.

**Sensitivity to variations in spacing**

Minimim venami quis nostrud. Laboris nisi lorum ipsum dolor sit. Aliquip ex ea com dolor in reprehenderit in volupatate nonumy ipsum dolor.

Aliquip ex ea com dolor in reprehenderit in volupatate nonumy. Ipsum dolor sit amet, con com dolor nostrud.

**Sensitivity to variations in spacing**

Minimim venami quis nostrud. Laboris nisi lorum ipsum dolor sit. Aliquip ex ea com dolor in reprehenderit in volupatate nonumy ispum dolor.

## Buried Heads & Subheads

*Avoid headlines and subheads isolated near the bottom of columns.*

When only one or two lines of type follow a headline at the bottom of a page, that headline becomes visually buried. Buried heads are unsightly and distracting to the reader.

Solutions include editing text or changing the size of graphics on the page.

## Box-itis & Rule-itis

*Don't overuse boxes and rules.*

Too many borders and lines make pages look compartmentalized and partitioned. Newsletters, in particular, often have this problem because of their highly modular designs. The result is a "busy" effect that interferes with reading.

Likewise, too many horizontal rules can break up the natural flow of the page.

Heavy rules next to headlines of approximately the same height can overwhelm the headlines.

# Loft Space Available

## Similar Typefaces

*Strive for obvious contrast between different typefaces used in a single publication.*

When using different typefaces for headlines and text, for example, go for contrast. Avoid typefaces that are similar.

When using different typefaces for headlines and text, go for contrast.

### This is Bookman.
Now is the time for all good men to come to the aid of their country. The history of the horse and buggy date back to a time when the modern car was not even a figment in

### This is Helvetica Bold.
Now is the time for all good men to come to the aid of their country. The history of the horse and buggy date back to a time when the modern car was not even a figment in

## Copy-filled Slides & Overheads

*Avoid cluttering presentation visuals with unnecessary copy.*

Slides and overheads are meant to support your oral presentation, not replace it. Using lots of words in slides, overheads, or Web pages means setting copy in small type. Stick to the main ideas, worded simply.

## The Planning Stage of Your Project

- Set all your objectives clearly and concisely
- Outline your main concepts in excruciating detail
- Brainstorm for ideas which might be usable later

## Planning Your Project

- Set objectives
- Outline concepts
- Brainstorm

## Irregularly Shaped Text Blocks

*Set type in novelty shapes only when doing so serves a purpose and the text retains its legibility.*

It might be fun to set text in the shape of a diamond, cloud, or reindeer, but chances are those special effects can diminish the overall effectiveness of your communication.

One
American's
Home
Thread...
Over a
decade ago, I
moved from the Midwest to
central North Carolina, a modern,
quickly developing region, a magnet of
high employmnet suburban sprawl in the
middle of a previously agricultural region
that contained farmsteads and vil-
lages among the oldest in the country.
Here, in the middle of this mag- net for
non- natives, most people I deal with
are from another state or na- tion; and
like most of them, I came for good
employment, better cli- mate and
for a change of scene, I guess.

Flush-left type is easiest to read. Lines without a consistent left margin take more time to read because readers lose track of each line's starting point.

# Rotated Type

*Rotated type works best in short banners or teasers. Don't make your readers strain to read it.*

Rotated, tilted, or angled type is difficult to read, especially if there's lots of copy or the type is set in a small point size. Readers are forced to tilt their heads, tilt the page, or even move on without reading.

## Underlining

*Underlining undermines readability.*

Use bold or italic type instead of underlining. More than a few underlined words cause visual clutter and confusion. Portions of the descenders often become lost in the underlining, making letters harder to identify and words harder to read.

---

**FURTHER READING**

Arnheim, Rudolf. <u>Visual Thinking.</u> Berkeley, CA: University of California Press, 1980.

Beaumont, Michael. <u>Type: Design, Color, Character & Use.</u> Cincinnati, OH: North Light Publishers, 1987.

Boom, Michael. <u>Music through MIDI.</u> Redmond, WA: Microsoft Press, 1987.

Busch, David D. <u>The Hand Scanner Handbook: Mac & PC Editions.</u> Homewood, IL: Business 1 Irwin, 1992.

---

**FURTHER READING**

Arnheim, Rudolf. *Visual Thinking.* Berkeley, CA: University of California Press, 1980.

Beaumont, Michael. *Type: Design, Color, Character & Use.* Cincinnati, OH: North Light Publishers, 1987.

Boom, Michael. *Music through MIDI.* Redmond, WA: Microsoft Press, 1987.

Busch, David D. *The Hand Scanner Handbook: Mac & PC Editions.* Homewood, IL: Business 1 Irwin, 1992.

---

## Widows & Orphans

*Watch for widows and orphans, which can cause unsightly gaps in text columns.*

An *orphan* is a syllable, word, or less than one-third of a line isolated at the bottom of a column, paragraph, or page.

---

The anchor is a means of securing, of holding fast, while the dolphin is capable of limitless movement. What adds to this tension is the way the dolphin is wrapped around the anchor. Is the dolphin lifting the anchor, or is the anchor holding down the dolphin?

A *widow* is a word or short phrase isolated at the top of a column or page.

better.

What makes this emblem so appropriate? It encapsulates the the mission of the Aldine Press: to sustain tradition while encouraging progress—in fact, to make them interdependent. As both a vehement classicist and an ardent innovator, Aldus used his creative resourcefulness in design and publishing technology to preserve the literature of the past.

You can banish widows and orphans from your layout by editing the text (the best solution), re-hyphenating line endings, or adjusting letter or word spacing.

## Unequal Spacing

*Strive for consistent spacing between the elements that make up an advertisement or publication.*

Readers notice even the smallest variations in spacing. Inconsistent spacing can brand your work as careless and unworthy of serious notice, giving the impression that your message isn't important.

Pay particular attention to the relative space between headlines, borders, and text:

# Fisherman's Review

Bringing You The Best Fish Tales Ever Told          Quarterly          $1.95

## The One That Got Away

To gaurd against their editions being counterfieted, Renaissance publishers customarily stamped a printer's mark, or colophon, on the title page of each book. With a unique colophon, each book could be clearly identified as the work of a particular publisher. For the Aldine Press, Aldus Manutius mulled over the range of classical and Christian icons and finally chose the dolphin and anchor.

### A Bloody Mess

In the early Christian era, the dolphin and anchor represented the soul being carried to salvation. Whether Aldus considered the Christian symbolism when he chose it, we can't be certain. But there may be a clue to his his intentions in the strange way the symbol contradicts itself.

The anchor is a means of securing, of holding fast, while the dolphin is capable of limitless movement.

### The Beast From the Deep

What adds to this tension is the way the dolphin is wrapped around the anchor. Is the dolphin lifting the anchor, or is the anchor holding down the dolphin? The ambiguity of the motto beneath it, "Festina lentes" ("Make haste slowly"), teases us further.

What makes this emblem so appropriate? It encapsulates the the mission of the Aldine Press: to sustain tradition while encouraging progress—in fact, to make them interdependent. As both a vehement classicist and an ardnt inovator, Aldus used his creative resourcefulness in design and publishing technology to preserve the literature of the past. The choice of colophon, however, could not be a casual one. It had to represent what was distinctive about the publishing house. For the Aldine Press, Aldus Manutius mulled over the range of classical and Christian icons and finally chose the dolphin and anchor.

### Fighting the Night Tide

In the early Christian era, the dolphin and anchor represented the soul being carried to salvation. Whether Aldus considered the Christian symbolism when he chose it, we can't be certain. But there may be a clue to his his intentions in the strange way the symbol contradicts itself.

The anchor is a means of securing, of holding fast, while the dolphin is capable of limitless movement. What adds to this tension is the dolphin.

## Sailing the Seven Seas for Salmon

It encapsulates the the mission of the Aldine Press: to sustain tradition while encouraging progress—in fact, to make them interdependent.

### The Chance to Cast

As both a vehement classicist and an ardnt inovator, Aldus used his creative resourcefulness in design and publishing technology to preserve the literature of the past. In turn, the need to preserve that literature gave him the opportunity to mold the future of publishing.

To gaurd against their editions being counterfieted, Renaissance publishers customarily stamped a printer's mark, or colophon, on the title page of each book. With a unique colophon, each book could be clearly identified as the work of a particular publisher.

### Fishing for Clues

The choice of colophon, however, could not be a casual one. It had to represent what was distinctive about the publishing house. For the Aldine Press, Aldus Manutius mulled over the range of classical and Christian icons and finally chose the dolphin and anchor.

Subheads and text:

title page of each book. With a unique colophon, each book could be clearly identified as the work of a particular publisher. For the Aldine Press, Aldus Manutius mulled over the range of classical and Christian icons and finally chose the dolphin and anchor.

### A Bloody Mess

In the early Christian era, the dolphin and anchor represented the soul being carried to salvation. Whether Aldus considered the Christian symbolism when he chose it, we can't be certain. But there may be a clue to his intentions in the strange way the symbol con-

tor, Aldus used his creative resourcefulness in design and publishing technology to preserve the literature of the past. The choice of colophon, however, could not be a casual one. It had to represent what was distinctive about the publishing house. For the Aldine Press, Aldus Manutius mulled over the range of classical and Christian icons and finally chose the dolphin and anchor.

### Fighting the Night Tide

In the early Christian era, the dolphin and anchor represented the soul being carried to salvation.

tain tradition while encouraging progress—in fact, to make them interdependent.

### The Chance to Cast

As both a vehement classicist and an innovator, Aldus used his creative resourcefulness in design and publishing technology to preserve the literature of the past. In turn, the need to preserve that literature gave him the opportunity to mold the future of publishing.

To gaurd against their editions being counterfieted, Renaissance publishers customarily stamped a printer's mark, or colophon, on the title page of each

## Captions and artwork:

A caption should be spaced the proper distance from the photo—this caption is too close.

A caption should be spaced the proper distance from the photo—this caption is not close enough.

A caption should be spaced the proper distance from the photo—this caption is correctly spaced.

## Artwork and text:

# Fisherman's Review

Bringing You The Best Fish Tales Ever Told          Quarterly          $1.95

## The One That Got Away

Captions should be spaced the proper distance from photos—neither too close nor too distant. This caption is poorly spaced.

To gaurd against their editions being counterfieted, Renaissance publishers customarily stamped a printer's mark, or colophon, on the title page of each book. With a unique colophon, each book could be clearly identified as the work of a particular publisher. For the Aldine Press, Aldus Manutius mulled over the range of classical and Christian icons and finally chose the dolphin and anchor.

In the early Christian era, the dolphin and anchor represented the soul being carried to salvation. Whether Aldus considered the Christian symbolism when he chose it, we can't be certain. But there may be a clue to his new intentions in the strange way the symbol seems to contradict itself.

The anchor is a means of securing, of holding fast, while the dolphin is capable of limitless movement.

A caption should be spaced the proper distance from the photo.

### Sailing the Seven Seas for Salmon

It encapsulates the the mission of the Aldine Press: to sustain tradition while encouraging progress—in fact, to make them interdependent.

**The Chance to Cast**

As both a vehement classicist and an ardent innovator, Aldus used his creative resourcefulness in design and publishing technology to preserve the literature of the past. In turn, the need to preserve that literature gave him the opportunity to mold the future of publishing.

**Fishing for Clues**

The choice of colophon, however, could not be a casual one. It had to represent what was distinctive about the publishing house. For the Aldine Press, Aldus Manutius mulled over the range of classical and Christian icons and finally chose the dolphin and anchor.

In the early Christian era, the dolphin and anchor represented the soul being carried to salvation. Aldus considered everything.

Column endings and bottom margins:

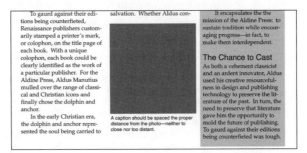

## Exaggerated Tabs & Indents

*Make your tabs and indents proportionate with the type size and column width of your pages.*

Default word processor and desktop publishing tab settings are often indented too deeply. Wide columns with large type usually require deeper tabs and indents than narrow columns with small type.

To guard against their editions being counterfeited, Renaissance publishers customarily put a printer's mark, or colophon, on the title page of each book. With a unique colophon, each book could be clearly identified as the work of a particular publisher or printer.

The choice of colophon, however, could not be a casual one. It had to represent what was distinctive about the publishing house. For the Aldine Press, Aldus Manutius mulled over the range of classical and Christian icons and finally chose the dolphin and anchor.

In the early Christian era, the dolphin and anchor represented the soul being

To guard against their editions being counterfeited, Renaissance publishers customarily put a printer's mark, or colophon, on the title page of each book. With a unique colophon, each book could be clearly identified as the work of a particular publisher or printer.

The choice of colophon, however, could not be a casual one. It had to represent what was distinctive about the publishing house. For the Aldine Press, Aldus Manutius mulled over the range of classical and Christian icons and finally chose the dolphin and anchor.

In the early Christian era, the dolphin and anchor represented the soul being

## Excessive Hyphenation

*Switch to manual hyphenation or adjust the hyphenation controls in your software when too many words are hyphenated.*

Five hundred years ago, Christopher Columbus was on his knees in throne rooms throughout Europe, scrambling to finance his first voyage to the New World. Meanwhile, his Venetian countryman Aldus Manutius—scholar, printer, and entrepreneur—was establishing what would become the greatest publishing house in Europe, the Aldine Press. Like Columbus, Aldus Manutius was driven by force of intellect and personality to realize a lifelong dream.

Aldus' greatest passion was Greek literature, which was rapidly gowing up in smoke in the wake of the marauding army. It seemed obvious to Aldus that the best way

Five hundred years ago, Christopher Columbus was on his knees in throne rooms throughout Europe, scrambling to finance his first voyage to the New World. Meanwhile, his Venetian countryman Aldus Manutius—scholar, printer, and entrepreneur—was establishing what would become the greatest publishing house in Europe, the Aldine Press. Like Columbus, Aldus Manutius was driven by force of intellect and personality to realize a lifelong dream.

Aldus' greatest passion was Greek literature, which was rapidly gowing up in smoke in the wake of the marauding army. It seemed obvious to Aldus that the best way

Excessive hyphenation occurs in narrow columns of type. Solutions include reducing type size, increasing column width, manually hyphenating lines of text, or choosing unjustified, flush-left alignment.

Increasing the hyphenation zone in your software allows longer words at the end of each line, but this may result in excessive word spacing.

Manual hyphenation gives you control over which words are hyphenated and which are moved intact to the next line.

## Cramped Logos & Addresses

*Design your advertisements from the bottom up.*

A firm's logo, address, phone number, and other identifying information are often difficult to read because they're treated as afterthoughts. To avoid that, build your documents around the logo and other vital information—or at least place those elements on the page first, instead of last.

## Having trouble establishing your corporate presence?

Owning a degree in business management doesn't always mean you have all the answers. You may have a great product, but without good name recognition, no one's going to notice it. And that means no one's going to buy it, either.

If your company's struggling to be noticed, you need to call Bright Ideas. We have fifty years' experience in improving corporate presence. Even the most obscure company name can become a household word after the Bright Ideas PR team works its magic.

John Q. Nobody, founder of Nobody Enterprises (and a satisfied Bright Ideas client), can vouch for the power of name recognition. "Before I went to Bright Ideas, we had no corporate presence at all. We couldn't even get a phone book listing. But BI retooled our image, and now everyone knows we're Nobody."

The power of Bright Ideas can work for you. Give us a call at 1-800-DIMBULB for a brighter future.

**BRIGHT IDEAS**

1012 Eureka Avenue, Suite #415
Brighton, CA  87526
1-800-DIMBULB

## Having trouble establishing your corporate presence?

Owning a degree in business management doesn't always mean you have all the answers. You may have a great product, but without good name recognition, no one's going to notice it. And that means no one's going to buy it, either.

If your company's struggling to be noticed, you need to call Bright Ideas. We have fifty years' experience in improving corporate presence. Even the most obscure company name can become a household word after the Bright Ideas PR team works its magic.

The power of Bright Ideas can work for you. Give us a call at 1-800-DIMBULB for a brighter future.

**BRIGHT IDEAS**

1012 Eureka Avenue, Suite #415
Brighton, CA  87526
1-800-DIMBULB

Many designers create a single graphic file consisting of a properly spaced logo, address, and other information. That file can then easily be added to any ad, flyer, or other document in a single step.

## Too Many Typefaces

*Avoid a potpourri of typefaces, sizes, and weights.*

Including too many typefaces on a single page—one of the most common desktop publishing mistakes—makes your pages look amateurish and confusing.

Use a few carefully-chosen typefaces, sizes, and weights to organize your information and create a hierarchy of importance. Each new typeface, size, or weight slows down the reader.

Avoid the "ransom note" school of typography.

### Ransom **Note** Review

Bringing You The *Best Fish Tales* Ever Told          Quarterly          $1.95

#### *The One* **That** *Got* **Away!**

To gaurd against their editions being counterfieted, Renaissance publishers customarily stamped a printer's mark, or colophon, on the title page of each book. With a unique colophon, each book could be clearly identified as the work of a particular publisher. For the Aldine Press, Aldus Manutius mulled over the range of classical and Christian icons and finally chose the dolphin and anchor.

**A Bloody Mess**

In the early Christian era, the dolphin and anchor represented the soul being carried to salvation. Whether Aldus considered the Christian symbolism when he chose it, we can't be certain. But there may be a clue to his his intentions in the strange way the symbol contradicts itself.

The anchor is a means of securing, of holding fast, while the dolphin is capable of limitless movement.

**The Beast From the Deep**

What adds to this tension is the way the dolphin is wrapped around the anchor. Is the dolphin lifting the anchor, or is the anchor holding down the dolphin? The ambiguity of the motto beneath it, "Festina lentes" ("Make haste slowly"), teases us further.

What makes this emblem so appropriate? It encapsulates the

the mission of the Aldine Press: to sustain tradition while encouraging progress—in fact, to make them interdependent. As both a vehement classicist and an ardnt inovator, Aldus used his creative resourcefulness in design and publishing technology to preserve the literature of the past. The choice of colophon, however, could not be a casual one. It had to represent what was distinctive about the publishing house. For the Aldine Press, Aldus Manutius mulled over the range of classical and Christian icons and finally chose the dolphin and anchor.

**Fighting Night Tide**

In the early Christian era, the dolphin and anchor represented the soul being carried to salvation. Whether Aldus considered the Christian symbolism when he chose it, we can't be certain. But there may be a clue to his his intentions in the strange way the symbol contradicts itself.

The anchor is a means of securing, of holding fast, while the dolphin is capable of limitless movement. What adds to this tension is the way the dolphin is wrapped around the anchor. Is the dolphin lifting the anchor, or is the anchor holding down the dolphin? The ambiguity of the motto beneath it, "Festina lentes" ("Make haste slowly"), teases us further. What makes

#### *Sailing* the Seas for **Salmon**

It encapsulates the the mission of the Aldine Press: to sustain tradition while encouraging progress—in fact, to make them interdependent.

*The Chance to Cast*

As both a vehement classicist and an ardnt inovator, Aldus used his creative resourcefulness in design and publishing technology to preserve the literature of the past. In turn, the need to preserve that literature gave him the opportunity to mold the future of publishing.

To gaurd against their editions being counterfieted, Renaissance publishers customarily stamped a printer's mark, or colophon, on the title page of each book. With a unique colophon, each book could be clearly identified as the work of a particular publisher.

**Fishing for Clues**

The choice of colophon, however, could not be a casual one. It had to represent what was distinctive about the publishing house. For the Aldine Press, Aldus Manutius mulled over the range of classical and Christian icons and finally chose the dolphin and anchor.

In the early Christian era, the dolphin and anchor represented

## Lack of Contrast Between Text & Other Elements

*Strive for as much contrast between type and background as possible for clear differentiation.*

Contrast is especially important when working on color documents, Web pages, or when designing color slides and overhead transparencies. Without sufficient contrast, it's hard to distinguish text from backgrounds or other elements overlapped by the text.

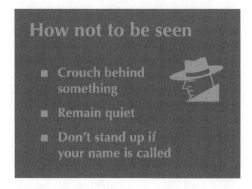

## Using Several Similar Visuals

*Establish a visual hierarchy by altering the size and shape of photos and illustrations.*

In an effort to use as many images as possible, designers sometimes run illustrations at the same size and shape. However, this can confuse readers who won't know which illustration to look at first.

After choosing the best images, run them in a variety of sizes and shapes, determined by their importance.

## Unnecessary Special Effects

*Overusing special type and graphic effects serves no effective purpose.*

There's no substitute for clean, concise design; using special effects for their own sake makes pages look frivolous and over-designed. Some computer-generated effects make information much more difficult to process and understand.

## Misaligned Elements

*Strive to keep all elements on separate pages aligned with each other.*

Consistency in aligning design elements, such as subheads, illustrations, and so on, can make the difference between a professional-looking document and a rag-tag disorderly one.

Align columns and graphics vertically; subheads, rules, boxes, bullets, and other items can rest along the same baseline as the text they accompany.

## Graphic Gimmickry

*Don't substitute or overshadow content with graphics and photos.*

Graphics and photos need to support the content and make complicated information easier to understand, not overshadow it. Access to a large library of art, whether it's clip art, photos, scans, or freehand illustrations doesn't mean that you should flood your document to show your artistic skill.

Too many elements simply clutter the page. This is particularly true for Web pages.

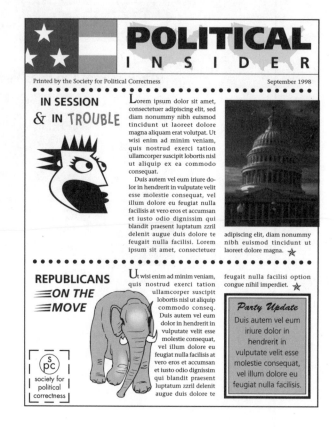

## Shoehorning

*Jam-packing every tidbit of information into the smallest available area will cause readers to fatigue.*

*Shoehorning* is tiresome for any reader since it forces them to strain as they visually attempt to separate what they're interested in from the rest of the page.

When designing Web pages, you'll find that conciseness is vital. On the average, reading from a computer screen is 25 percent slower than from the printed page. You should limit your writing to less than you'd usually write for a printed document.

## Too Much Gray

*Unless your reader is very devoted, a text-heavy page will discourage reading.*

Remember that gray pages send a visual signal that a page will be time-consuming. It won't matter how compelling your content is, readers will be discouraged from reading your document. However, a careful balance of text, graphics, and white space will keep your pages lively and generate reader interest.

A careful balance of text, graphics, and white space will keep your pages lively and generate reader interest.

On the Internet, readers who encounter a text-heavy Web page will quickly leave. Occasionally they will scan for buzzwords that interest them.

## Moving On

Next we'll explore redesign. Redesign is an important indicator of design maturity and creativity. It is a process that goes beyond known problems—what we call pitfalls.

# 15

# Redesign

## Overview

- Redesigning documents can highlight certain relationships or create new ones.

- Redesigning allows you to re-purpose documents for new readership, new information, or an updated profile.

- Reorganizing your information dramatically changes its meaning, impact, and value.

- A designer sets the pace or flow of information.

*Redesign transforms the elements of design.*

In redesign, the emphasis is shifted away from the rules of design for the production of good-looking documents. Instead, design rules are used as tools for informing designers or teaching about design (and other) relationships. Its outcome for good-looking materials is the same.

In each of the redesigns presented in this chapter we ask the question: How would reorganization of the information (a redesign) change its meaning and impact? Our redesign efforts are less about the facts and more about different points of view. You won't always find dramatic visual changes in all of the redesigns; some are quiet and subtle.

The better you know the product or service, processes, publishing task, and your audience, the more effectively you can design and redesign.

Redesign can mean re-purposing documents for new readership, new information, or a new updated profile. Through it, you can:

- Control the flow of information (set a pace).

- Elucidate what is most important (choose and establish a point of view).

- Change the context and tone (determine under which conditions which information applies).

- Simplify your message (increase the scale of information sent and received).

In the redesign process, traditional design rules do not stand on their own, rather they are combined and act jointly. Redesign disrupts old ways of thinking and doing things and provides the capabilities to do things differently. It suggests that some things may be done better if done differently. Redesign redraws the boundaries of what is appropriate and visually appealing.

The transforming effects of redesign disrupts old ways of thinking and provides the capabilities to do things differently.

## A Mismatch of Scales

*You'll find that design rules are sometimes too small for the big problems and too big for the small problems of today's communication needs.*

Your design goals and tasks are not always clear-cut or easy to understand. For example, should interest govern how your information gets organized, redesigned, and presented? Or should market, competition, or economy govern? And how do you determine which market, which economy, and which competitor should prevail?

Generally, the business of design doesn't leap all at once into the next generation of communication. All modes of communication still distinctly exist and their purposes are important. However, there are transition periods encumbered by an unavoidable mismatch of scales.

In the redesign process, you are not only creating better, good-looking design, you are also accommodating—little by little—some of what is new about information and communication today.

Skills for redesign can help make mismatched scales easier for you to understand and work with. Just being aware of them can help. Some of your publications are scaled to meet broadcast format (advertisements, newspapers), others are tailored to specific niche audiences (newsletters, reports). The next time you redesign them you may need to reverse or alter their scale. This increased flexibility will affect rules, making them mismatched to your redesign purposes and goals. (For more about varying your information to attract specific audiences see Chapter 13, "Advertising Materials: Response & Collection.")

Design rules lag behind today's need for flexibility. Keep in mind that rules are guidelines and unless you're willing to break, change, and redefine them you'll also lag behind. You may need to unlearn some design rules, redefine some, modify others, and invent some new ones.

## Redesign Gallery

The process of redesign can mean reorganizing an entire project or just one element within a project. In this gallery, you'll find both kinds in a variety of publication types.

## Advertisements (Original)

Make an effort to integrate text and visuals when designing advertisements. The photograph in the advertisement below may connote air travel, but it doesn't visibly tie in with the ad's "cheap airfare" theme.

The company's name never appears prominently—it only appears once in the body copy (hyphenated, no less), and the logo at the bottom of the ad is small and cramped.

A picture of a grounded airplane won't be a reassuring image to most people—it conjures up images of flight delays.

The disclaimer text at the end of the second paragraph interrupts the ad's positive message.

# WE OFFER THE CHEAPEST AIRFARE IN THE BUSINESS

For the remainder of the year, Sputter Airlines is offering the cheapest flight rates to be found anywhere! $69 to anywhere in the continental U.S., $99 to anywhere in North America (including Alaska and Hawaii), $149 to selected parts of Europe (England, France, Spain, Germany, and Scandinavia), and $219 for India and the Orient.

We're so sure that our fares are the lowest, we're willing to put money on it! If you can find cheaper airfare to the same location, we'll not only match the price, we'll beat it by $10! We call that our "Ten-Dollar Guarantee." (Written proof of the competing offer is required. Coupon specials and other forms of giveaways are not considered viable offers, and will not be honored with the Ten-Dollar Guarantee. Void where prohibited.)

So why take chances with some bargain airline? Come to the name you know, and get the lowest price available. We guarantee it!

**SPUTTER**

### Advertisements (Makeover)

A vague, humorous headline connects the photograph to the rest of the ad. The first paragraph of the body text has been enlarged to serve as a lead-in to the rest of the copy.

Bleeding the photo rather than boxing it makes the ad seem larger.

The company's logo has been enlarged and framed by white space.

The disclaimer text has been moved to the bottom of the page, set in smaller type. A discreet asterisk signals its existence without interrupting the flow of the copy.

Look who's nosing out the competition.

For the remainder of the year, Sputter Airlines is offering the cheapest flights to be found anywhere. Guaranteed.

$69 to anywhere in the continental U.S., $99 to anywhere in North America (including Alaska and Hawaii), $149 to selected parts of Europe (England, France, Spain, Germany, and Scandinavia), and $219 for India and the Orient.

We're so sure that our fares are the lowest, we're willing to put money on it!

If you can find cheaper airfare to the same location, we'll not only match the price, we'll beat it by $10. We call that our "Ten-Dollar Guarantee."*

So why take chances with some bargain airline? Come to the name you know, and get the absolute lowest price available. We guarantee it.

*Written proof of the competing offer is required. Coupon specials and other forms of giveaways are not considered viable offers, and will not be honored with the Ten-Dollar Guarantee. Void where prohibited.

SPUTTER

## Small Ads (Original)

All the text in this ad is treated with equal strength. As a result, no concept or benefit clearly emerges.

The beginning rhetorical question will probably turn off all but the most deter-mined reader.

The page border lacks definition and character.

> **WANT TO SAVE**
> # MONEY
> **ON YOUR LONG DISTANCE**
> ## PHONE BILL?
> ## 013/434-1278
> **North Central Communications**
> **Jack Winter**

## (Makeover)

Reducing the border and extending the keypad visual to break out of the box above and below make the ad appear larger.

The most important word has been significantly increased in size and given a drop shadow.

Important information, such as the phone number and the call to action, are significantly larger than subordinate information.

> # SAVE
> **ON LONG DISTANCE**
> For our low long distance phone rates, call
> ## 013/434–1278
> Jack Winter
> North Central Communications

### Recruitment Ads (Original)

Inappropriate graphics can be worse than no graphics at all. The clip art in the ad below suggests that the lab assistant will be performing chemical experiments and analyzing slides—but the duties listed in the job description are mostly clerical.

Relegating design elements to the corners of an ad can leave a discon-certing hole in the center.

Thin sans serif type with tight leading is difficult to read.

### (Makeover)

A simple stylized picture of a flask suggests a laboratory environment without misleading the applicant about the nature of the work.

Screening a small ad helps it stand out from adjacent ads.

The text of the ad reads more naturally without the ellipses.

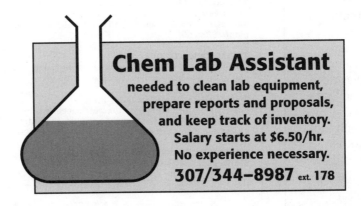

## Brochures (Original)

This brochure's informal tone is completely inappropriate for selling luxury items. Prominently displayed phrases like "On Sale" and "Get Ready to Save!!!" put emphasis on price—but buyers of gold pocketwatches are probably more interested in the quality of the merchandise.

Important ordering information is scattered all over the page—phone numbers at the top, restrictions at the bottom, and discount information near the right margin.

"Shoehorning" (using every available bit of space on the page) creates a claustrophobic feel.

The "Restrictions and Extra Charges" paragraph looks like another item in the list of merchandise.

# Fine Timepieces On Sale From Hannaford

To place orders, call toll-free 1-800-833-3328
For inquiries, call 1-617-535-5950
All prices are subject to change without notice.

**THE TRADITIONAL TIMEPIECE**
Features the classic look of days gone by. Black roman numerals on a white face, in a 24-karat gold case with gold chain attached. $395.00

Prices in effect from May 21, 1997 thru August 31, 1997

**THE MODERN TIMEPIECE**
Successfully blends the classic look with today's modern needs. Black arabic numerals on a white face, in a 24-karat gold case. Smaller dial inset on face displays seconds. $395.00

**THE SILVER TICKER**
Tastefully displays the elegance of silver. Silver numerals on a black face, in a sterling silver case with silver chain attached. $325.00

**THE MACHINERY-LOVERS' SPECIAL**
Lets the beauty of the watchmaker's craft show through. A transparent face allows the owner to watch the delicately-calibrated inner workings do their stuff. Comes in a 24-karat gold case with gold chain attached. $395.00

**THE MINIMALIST TIMEPIECE**
Features a daring blend of past and present style. The handsome 24-karat gold case and chain echo the look of the Traditional Timepiece, but the inner white face is blank. $385.00

**THE MYOPIC TIMEPIECE**
Adapts the Modern Timepiece for the visually impaired. Larger arabic numerals make reading easier. $395.00

**THE BRONZE BOMBSHELL**
Features the look and feel of the watches carried by American soldiers in World War I. Lovingly recrafted, the watch features a case and chain made from actual bombshells. $295.00

**Get ready to save!!!**
10% off orders of $500 or more
20% off orders of $1000 or more

**RESTRICTIONS AND EXTRA CHARGES**
Watches and cases not sold separately. C.O.D. only. There is a 10% shipping and handling charge for orders within the continental U.S. (15% for orders outside the U.S.) This charge does not count toward the price needed for a discount.

Hannaford Timepieces, P.O. Box 2241, 3 Bourbon Street, Peabody MA 97874

## **Brochures** (Makeover)

A typographic overhaul and a generous use of white space give the brochure a formal, refined tone.

Photographs of actual merchandise replace the frivolous clip-art graphic.

Precious space has been saved by combining the names and descriptions of the watches into single paragraphs.

All of the information needed to place an order has been moved to the bottom of the page.

# *Fine Timepieces from Hannaford*

*on sale from May 21–August 31, 1997*

The Modern Timepiece

The Myopic Timepiece

**The Traditional Timepiece** features the classic look of days gone by. Black roman numerals on a white face, in a 24-karat gold case with gold chain attached *(see above photo)*. $395.00

**The Modern Timepiece** successfully blends the classic look with today's modern needs. Black arabic numerals on a white face, in a 24-karat gold case. Smaller dial inset on face displays seconds *(see photo at right)*. $395.00

**The Silver Ticker** tastefully displays the elegance of silver. Silver numerals on a black face, in a sterling silver case with silver chain attached. $325.00

**The Machinery-Lovers' Special** lets the beauty of the watchmaker's craft show through. A transparent face allows the owner to watch the delicately-calibrated inner workings do their stuff. Comes in a 24-karat gold case with gold chain attached. $395.00

**The Minimalist Timepiece** features a daring blend of past and present style. The handsome 24-karat gold case and chain echo the look of the Traditional Timepiece, but the inner white face is blank. $385.00

**The Myopic Timepiece** adapts the Modern Timepiece for the visually impaired. Larger arabic numerals make reading easier *(see photo at right)*. $395.00

**The Bronze Bombshell** features the look and feel of the watches carried by American soldiers in World War I. Lovingly recrafted, the watch features a case and chain made from actual bombshells. $295.00

*Ordering Information*

To place orders, call toll-free **1-800-833-3328**

For inquiries, call **1-617-535-5950**

There is a *10% discount* on orders of $500 or more. There is a *20% discount* on orders of $1000 or more.

All prices are subject to change without notice. Watches and cases not sold separately. C.O.D. only. There is a 10% shipping and handling charge for orders within the continental U.S. (15% for orders outside the U.S.) This charge does not count toward the price needed for a discount.

Hannaford Timepieces
P.O. Box 2241
3 Bourbon Street
Peabody MA 97874

# Catalogs (Original)

Catalogs and price lists without illustrations present a unique set of design challenges. Type must be handled skillfully to avoid visual monotony.

Often, a symmetrical type treatment provides too little contrast to fully engage the reader.

Note how undifferentiated spacing creates a run-on effect, further discouraging readers.

---

**NORMAN ROCKWELL**
**323 MAGAZINE COVERS**
By Finch. 456 pages. Huge 12 X 15 1/4. This magnificent, large-format, full color volume spans the artist's long and prolific career, reproducing 323 of his cover paintings for the SATURDAY EVENING POST, LADIES HOME JOURNAL and other magazines. Published at $85.00. Only $45.00

**GREAT MAGAZINE COVERS OF THE WORLD**
By Kery. 184 pages. 9 1/4 X 12. A panorama of more than 500 great magazine covers (most reproduced in full color) from 20 countries, spanning a century and a half of magazine publishing around the world. Including examples from 200 19th and 20th century magazines. Published at $65. Only $$5.00

**VASARELY**
150 pages. 9 1/4 X 13. 180 illustrations, including 64 full color plates. Masterful reproductions and a text by the artist combine to form an authoritative yet personal study of one of the major figures of modern art. Published at $60,00. Only $35.00

**CHAGALL BY CHAGALL**
Sorlier. 262 pages. 11 1/4 X 12. 285 illustrations, including 83 full color plates. Illustrated autobiography. Published at $50.00. Only $40.00.

**MALFIELD PARRISH**
By Ludwig. 223 pages. 9 X 12. 184 illustrations, 64 in full color. Published at $25.00. Only $18.00.

**THE GREAT BOOK OF FRENCH IMPRESSIONISM**
By Kelder. 448 pages. 12 X 14 1/4. Over 200 illustrations, including 200 full color plates and 16 spectacular full color fold-outs. Huge, exquisitely produced treasury of French Impressionist art, packed with full-page reproductions. Examines the lives and works of all the major Impressionists and Post-Impressionists. Published at $100.00. Now $59.00

**CARL FABERGE: GOLDSMITH TO**
**THE IMPERIAL COURT OF RUSSIA**
By Snowman. 100 pages. 8 1/4 X 10 1/2. Over 185 photos, 111 in full color. Originally published at $35.00. Only $22.00

**CONTEMPORARY PAINTING**
By Vogt. 135 pages. 7 1/2 X 10 1/2. Over 50 in full color. Penetrating analysis of World War II European and American art. Including paintings by Jaspar Johns, Andy Warhol, Roy Lichtenstein, Jackson Pollock, others. $19.95. Now $14.95

**TWENTIETH CENTURY MASTERS**
**OF EROTIC ART**
By Smith. 212 pages. 9 X 12. 190 full color plates presents erotic works by such top-ranking artists as Picasso, Segal, Dali, Ernst, Rauschenberg, Rivers, Warhol, Schiele and others, many of which have never been displayed in public exhibitions. $30.00. Now $20.00

**LEONARDO DA VINCI**
538 pages. 11 X 14 1/2. Huge. 1,635 illustrations, including many large full color plates. Originally published in Italy by the Instituto Geografico De Agostini, this new edition is the most lavish, authoritative ever produced. Published at $60. Now $50.00.

**REMBRANT PAINTINGS**
By Gerson. 527 pages. 11 X 14 1/2. Huge. Over 730 illustrations, including many large full color plates. Complete, authoritative and beautiful presentation of the great master's work. Written by one of the world's foremost Rembrandt authorities. The book was thirty years in the making in Amsterdam, and is lavishly illustrated with spectacular reproductions. Published at $60.00. Only $50.00

**ENGLISH CAMEO GLASS**
By Grover. 480 pages. 8 X 11. A wealth of rare firsthand material and over 1,000 color and black and white plates makes this book an invaluable reference. Published at $50.00. Now $25.00.

**20,000 YEARS OF WORLD PAINTING**
By Jaffe. 416 pages. 9 X 13. Historical survey from early to modern art. 1,000 reproductions in full color. Was $50.00. Now $20.00.

**STAINED GLASS**
By Seddon & Stephens. 205 pages. 473 full color photos. 11 X 14. Covers stained glass from the beginning to the present. Was $39.95. Now $19.95.

**THE COMPLETE BOOK OF EROTIC ART**
By Kronhausen. 781 black and white plates. Extraordinary collection of the world's erotic art from Japan, China, India, Renaissance masters and modern greats. Originally published in 2 Volumes at $50.00. New, Complete 1 Volume Edition only $25.00.

**COLLECTING POLITICAL AMERICANA**
By Sullivan 1980. 250 pages. 8 X 11. 400 illustrations. Packed with reading. Out of print. $15.95. Now $10.00.

**DIAMONDS**
Myth, magic and reality. Revised edition. Over 420 full color illustrations. Beautiful and informative look at the worlds most magnificent and mysterious stone. Tells how to recognize and appreciate quality stones, more. 288 pages. Large. 10 1/4 X 12/ Originally published at $50.00. Only $29.00.

**THE GREAT BOOK OF JEWELS**
By Heninger. 206 full color plates. 94 black and white photos. The most spectacular, lavishly illustrated, comprehensive volume ever published on jewels and jewelry. Nearly 300 photos specially made for this volume, many gems neve available for public inspection before. Includes bibliography, table of gemstones: much more. Huge. 11 1/4 X 13 3/4. Published at $69.50. Now $29.95.

10

# Catalogs (Makeover)

Subtle changes in spacing and typeface create contrast and promote readability.

The two-columned format is retained, but body copy is set ragged-right (instead of justified) to add contrast and break up type.

Titles now appear in sans serif type, which provides more contrast to body copy.

The "Reference Art Books" logo (taken from the front cover) has been reversed and repeated on each page, along with the firm's toll-free phone number.

**NORMAN ROCKWELL**
323 Magazine Covers
By Finch. 456 pages. Huge 12 X 15 1/4. This magnificent, large-format, full color volume spans the artist's long and prolific career, reproducing 323 of his cover paintings for the SATURDAY EVENING POST, LADIES HOME JOURNAL and other magazines. Published at $85.00. Only $45.00

**GREAT MAGAZINE COVERS OF THE WORLD**
By Kery. 184 pages. 9 1/4 X 12. A panorama of more than 500 great magazine covers (most reproduced in full color) from 20 countries, spanning a century and a half of magazine publishing around the world. Including examples from 200 19th and 20th century magazines. Published at $65. Only $$5.00

**VASARELY**
150 pages. 9 1/4 X 13. 180 illustrations, including 64 full color plates. Masterful reproductions and a text by the artist combine to form an authoritative yet personal study of one of the major figures of modern art. Published at $60,00. Only $35.00

**CHAGALL BY CHAGALL**
Sorlier. 262 pages. 11 1/4 X 12. 285 illustrations, including 83 full color plates. Illustrated autobiography. Published at $50.00. Only $40.00.

**MALFIELD PARRISH**
By Ludwig. 223 pages. 9 X 12. 184 illustrations, 64 in full color. Published at $25.00. Only $18.00.

**THE GREAT BOOK OF FRENCH IMPRESSIONISM**
By Kelder. 448 pages. 12 X 14 1/4. Over 200 illustrations, including 200 full color plates and 16 spectacular full color foldouts. Huge, exquisitely produced treasury of French Impressionist art, packed with full-page reproductions. Examines the lives and works of all the major Impressionists and Post-Impressionists. Published at $100.00. Now $59.00

**CARL FABERGE: GOLDSMITH TO THE IMPERIAL COURT OF RUSSIA**
By Snowman. 100 pages. 8 1/4 X 10 1/2. Over 185 photos, 111 in full color. Originally published at $35.00. Only $22.00

**CONTEMPORARY PAINTING**
By Vogt. 135 pages. 7 1/2 X 10 1/2. Over 50 in full color. Penetrating analysis of World War II European and American art. Including paintings by Jaspar Johns, Andy Warhol, Roy Lichtenstein, Jackson Pollock, others. $19.95. Now $14.95

**TWENTIETH CENTURY MASTERS OF EROTIC ART**
By Smith. 212 pages. 9 X 12. 190 full color plates presents erotic works by such top-ranking artists as Picasso, Segal, Dali, Ernst, Rauschenberg, Rivers, Warhol, Schiele and others, many of which have never been displayed in public exhibitions. $30.00. Now $20.00

**LEONARDO DA VINCI**
538 pages. 11 X 14 1/2. Huge. 1,635 illustrations, including many large full color plates. Originally published in Italy by the Instituto Geografico De Agostini, this new edition is the most lavish, authoritative ever produced. Published at $60. Now $50.00.

**REMBRANT PAINTINGS**
By Gerson. 527 pages. 11 X 14 1/2. Huge. Over 730 illustrations, including many large full color plates. Complete, authoritative and beautiful presentation of the great master's work. Written by one of the world's foremost Rembrandt authorities. The book was thirty years in the making in Amsterdam, and is lavishly illustrated with spectacular reproductions. Published at $60.00. Only $50.00

**ENGLISH CAMEO GLASS**
By Grover. 480 pages. 8 X 11. A wealth of rare firsthand material and over 1,000 color and black and white plates makes this book an invaluable reference. Published at $50.00. Now $25.00.

**20,000 YEARS OF WORLD PAINTING**
By Jaffe. 416 pages. 9 X 13. Historical survey from early to modern art. 1,000 reproductions in full color. Was $50.00. Now $20.00.

**STAINED GLASS**
By Seddon & Stephens. 205 pages. 473 full color photos. 11 X 14. Covers stained glass from the beginning to the present. Was $39.95. Now $19.95.

**THE COMPLETE BOOK OF EROTIC ART**
By Kronhausen. 781 black and white plates. Extraordinary collection of the world's erotic art from Japan, China, India, Renaissance masters and modern greats. Originally published in 2 Volumes at $50.00. New, Complete 1 Volume Edition only $25.00.

**COLLECTING POLITICAL AMERICANA**
By Sullivan 1980. 250 pages. 8 X 11. 400 illustrations. Packed with reading. Out of print. $15.95. Now $10.00.

**DIAMONDS**
Myth, magic and reality. Revised edition. Over 420 full color illustrations. Beautiful and informative look at the worlds most magnificent and mysterious stone. Tells how to recognize and appreciate quality stones, more. 288 pages. Large. 10 1/4 X 12/ Originally published at $50.00. Only $29.00.

**THE GREAT BOOK OF JEWELS**
By Heninger. 206 full color plates. 94 black and white photos. The most spectacular, lavishly illustrated, comprehensive volume ever published on jewels and jewelry. Nearly 300 photos specially made for this volume, many gems neve available for public inspection before. Includes bibliography, table of gemstones: much more. Huge. 11 1/4 X 13 3/4. Published at $69.50. Now $29.95.

**Reference Art Books** PHONE TOLL-FREE / 1-800-238-8288

### Flyers (Original)

Announcement-style flyers should be brief and eye-catching. Readers are likely to ignore large amounts of text.

The centered, all-caps text is difficult to read.

The most important words on the flyer, "CLASSIC CAR SHOW," are no larger than the rest of the body copy.

Exclamation points at the end of each line of copy make it seem as if the document is shouting at the reader.

The graphics seem to have been added as an afterthought. The noticeable difference in the cars' sizes is jarring.

# COME ONE COME ALL
## TO THE
## CLASSIC CAR SHOW!!!!

**ALL MAKES - ALL MODELS
FROM THE ROARING 20'S
TO THE NIFTY 50'S!**

**AUTO BUFFS WON'T WANT
TO MISS THIS EXTRAVAGANZA!**

**TO BE HELD AT MCMILLAN PARK
SATURDAY, AUGUST 23
FROM 2:00 PM
TO 6:00 PM**

**IT'LL DRIVE YOU BUGGY!**

### Flyers (Makeover)

Deleting all but the most relevant text—what, where, when—increases the flyer's readability. A catchy lead-in completes the makeover.

A decorative typeface serves as an attention-getter.

A light gray screen makes the graphics stand out.

The title of the event is now prominently featured in the center of the flyer.

## **Flyers** (Original)

When working with text-heavy documents, readability should be your primary concern. In the question-and-answer flyer below, small text in a wide text column makes reading difficult.

The question marks are redundant because the headline and the content clearly communicate the Q&A format.

The text and visuals are crowded.

Answers beginning with a single, bold-face word (e.g., "Yes!") look as if they might belong with the preceding bold-face question.

**Answers to Questions Frequently Asked About Tri-Steel Homes**

**1. What is the Tri-Steel concept and why is it different from conventional wood frame construction?**
The Tri-Steel concept is based upon the utilization and superior quality and strength of steel to form the frame or shell of the home. This allows the home to be stick built on site, but with steel instead of wood and bolts and fasteners instead of nails and staples.

The superior strength of steel means that the frame spacing can be on 6-foot and 8-foot centers instead of 16-inch and 24-inch centers. Plus, we can utilize 9 inches of insulation on the sides and also provide consistent quality, less maintenance, and much greater strength than is possible with conventional construction. In addition, this gives you much greater flexibility inside the home since none of the walls need to be load bearing. **Also important, the entire shell can often be dried-in within 4 to 5 days by an inexperienced crew.**

**2. How are Tri-Steel homes unique?**
Our homes utilize an engineered and computer designed steel structural system. You can choose from a wide selection of contemporary slant wall designs which stand out among conventional wooded structures or numerous conventional-looking straight wall designs ranging from conservatively gabled roof lines to ultra-modern units allowing clerestory window placement.

**3. What are some of the advantages of Tri-Steel homes?**
Tri-Steel homes can cost less to erect and can go up much faster. They are exceptionally energy efficient, require almost no exterior maintenance, and are tremendously flexible in their design. In addition to these areas of savings, they offer the strength and durability of steel to withstand extreme weather conditions, termites and fire. The quality of steel is consistently high. Pre-engineered framing components ensure your home goes up one way - the right way! Special snow or wind loads are possible with very little extra cost. The also meet Seismic 4 earthquake specifications - the highest rating required.

**4. Have these homes been tried and proven?**
**Absolutely!** In terms of the history of home building, Tri-Steel homes are a new and unique concept; however, these homes have been in use throughout the South for over ten years. Tri-Steel has thousands of structures all across the nation and we are constantly receiving letters from satisfied homeowners attesting to the beauty, strength and energy savings of Tri-Steel structures.

**5. Can I put up one of these homes myself and is construction assistance available?**
**Yes!** The home is actually designed to be constructed independently by the buyer. No heavy lifting equipment or special tools are required. The steel beams are designed to bolt together - A to B, B to C - with prepunched holes so you are basically working with a giant erector set. No cutting or welding is required on the job site and complete instructions and drawings are included with the package. Tri-Steel can provide your choice of construction assistance. As part of the assistance available, we can consult with you over the phone, have your shell erected, or provide on-site supervision on a daily or weekly basis.

**6. How much flexibility do I have choosing a home size?**
**Infinite!** A virtually unlimited variety of home sizes are offered from 800 square feet on up. Our homes come in one, two of three level designs with slant of straight walls. We have hundreds of plans drawn and available for immediate mailing and we can also draw custom designs to meet virtually any floor plan or size requirements.

**7. Can I add to the home at a later date?**
**Yes!** Additional space may be added in the future at low cost and relative ease allowing you to enlarge your home economically

Tri-Steel Structures
5800 Campus Circle, Irving, TX 75063
Telephone (214) 580-3400
© 1987, All Rights Reserved

## Flyers (Makeover)

A two-column format is more inviting for the reader. Using a different typeface for the questions makes scanning for specific information easier.

Illustrations have been omitted to allow larger type and more white space.

Oversized Q's and A's with drop-shadow blocks mirror the title design.

The Tri-Steel logo feature is now larger and more readable.

---

Building a Tri-Steel home:

Tri-Steel
Structures
5800 Campus Circle, Irving, TX 75063
Telephone (214) 580-9400
© 1987, All Rights Reserved

# *Q*uestions

# *& A*nswers

**Q** What is the Tri-Steel concept and why is it different from conventional wood frame construction?

**A** The Tri-Steel concept is based upon the utilization and superior quality and strength of steel to form the frame or shell of the home. This allows the home to be stick built on site, but with steel instead of wood and bolts and fasteners instead of nails and staples.

The superior strength of steel means that the frame spacing can be on 6-foot and 8-foot centers instead of 16-inch and 24-inch centers. Plus, we can utilize 9 inches of insulation on the sides and also provide consistent quality, less maintenance, and much greater strength than is possible with conventional construction. In addition, this gives you much greater flexibility inside the home since none of the walls need to be load bearing. Also important, the entire shell can often be dried-in within 4 to 5 days by an inexperienced crew.

**Q** How are Tri-Steel homes unique?

**A** Our homes utilize an engineered and computer designed steel structural system. You can choose from a wide selection of contemporary slant wall designs which stand out among conventional wooded structures or numerous conventional-looking straight wall designs ranging from conservatively gabled roof lines to ultra-modern units allowing clerestory window placement.

**Q** What are some of the advantages of Tri-Steel homes?

**A** Tri-Steel homes can cost less to erect and can go up much faster. They are exceptionally energy efficient, require almost no exterior maintenance, and are tremendously flexible in their design. In addition to these areas of savings, they offer the strength and durability of steel to withstand extreme weather conditions, termites and fire. The quality of steel is consistently high. Pre-engineered framing components ensure your home goes up one way—the right way! Special snow or wind loads are possible with very little extra cost. The also meet Seismic 4 earthquake specifications—the highest rating required.

**Q** Have these homes been tried and proven?

**A** Absolutely! In terms of the history of home building, Tri-Steel homes are a new and unique concept; however, these homes have been in use throughout the South for over ten years. Tri-Steel has thousands of structures all across the nation and we are constantly receiving letters from satisfied homeowners attesting to the beauty, strength and energy savings of Tri-Steel structures.

**Q** Can I put up one of these homes myself and is construction assistance available?

**A** Yes! The home is actually designed to be constructed independently by the buyer. No heavy lifting equipment or special tools are required. The steel beams are designed to bolt together—A to B, B to C—with prepunched holes so you are basically working with a giant erector set. No cutting or welding is required on the job site and complete instructions and drawings are included with the package. Tri-Steel can provide your choice of construction assistance. As part of the assistance available, we can consult with you over the phone, have your shell erected, or provide on-site supervision on a daily or weekly basis.

**Q** How much flexibility do I have choosing a home size?

**A** Infinite! A virtually unlimited variety of home sizes are offered from 800 square feet on up. Our homes come in one, two of three level designs with slant of straight walls. We have hundreds of plans drawn and available for immediate mailing and we can also draw custom designs to meet virtually any floor plan or size requirements.

**Q** Can I add to the home at a later date?

**A** Yes! Additional space may be added in the future at low cost and relative ease allowing you to enlarge your home economically as your needs and income requires.

## Business Cards & Logos (Original)

An excessive amount of detail can be a hindrance when designing a pictorial logo; the eye is much better at processing and remembering simple images. The skull logo below may be anatomically correct, but it's not very memorable—and its detail will invariably be lost if the logo is faxed or shrunk.

The company's name is set in the same drab font as the rest of the text on the card.

The company motto is too small, and contains a bad text break.

## (Makeover)

A simpler, more exaggerated skull is easier to remember and will reproduce well at small sizes. Using a distinctive font for the company name also aids recognition.

Enlarging and reversing the motto helps it stand out. The ragged edge of the reversed area is evocative of blood on a horror-movie poster.

## Nameplates (Original)

Creating a good nameplate is often the best way to improve the look of a newsletter or tabloid.

Excessively heavy type set against thin horizontal lines is distracting.

The subhead is far too large and contributes little to the message.

## (Makeover)

Simple nameplates are best; slender, condensed, lowercase type creates valuable white space, punctuated by rules above and below.

The subhead has been eliminated and replaced by the less obtrusive "Restaurant Technology" slugline.

## Newsletters (Original)

Make sure the design of your newsletter matches the tone of its content. In the newsletter below, the comical dinosaur graphic and the article titles seem to be striving for a sense of fun—but the design is extremely conservative.

The scattered nameplate is difficult to read—is it "The Fossil Record" or "Fossil The Record"?

The words "In This Issue" are too big—except for the nameplate, they're the largest words on the page.

The museum's logo is overpowered by the larger dinosaur above it.

The Official Newsletter of the ● LITHICUS MUSEUM                    July 1995

### DEM BONES, DEM BONES...

Lorem ipsum dolor sit amet, consectetuer adipiscing elit, sed diam nonummy nibh euismod tincidunt ut laoreet dolore magna aliquam erat volutpat. Ut wisi enim ad minim veniam, quis nostrud exerci tation ullamcorp suscipit lobortis nisl ut aliquip ex ea commodo consequatvelit esse molestie consequat. Duis autem vel eum iriure dolor in hendrerit in vulputate velit esse molestie consequat, vel illum dolore eu feugiat nulla facilisis at vero eros et accumsan et iusto odio dignissim qui blandit praesent luptatum zzril delenit augue duis dolore te feugait nulla facilisi. Lorem ipsum dolor sit amet, consectet adipiscing elit, sed diam nonummy nibh euismod tincidunt ut laoreet dolore magna aliquam erat volutpat.

Ut wisi enim ad minim veniam, quis nostrud exerci tation ullamcorper suscipit lobortis nisl ut aliquip ex ea commodo consequat. Duis autem vel eum iriure dolor in hendrerit in vulputate velit esse molestie consequat, vel illum dolore eu feugiat nulla facilisis at vero eros et accumsan et iusto odio dignissim qui blandit praesent luptatum zzril delenit augue duis dolore nulla facilisi.

Nam liber tempor cum soluta nobis eleifend option congue nihil imperdiet doming id quod mazim placerat facer possim assum. Lorem ipsum dolor sit amet, consectetuer adipiscing elit, sed diam nonummy nibh euismod tincidunt ut laoreet dolore magna aliquam erat volutpat. Ut wisi enim ad minim veniam, quis nostrud exerci tation ullamcorper suscipit lobortis nisl ut aliquip

### IN THIS ISSUE

ex ea commodo consequat. Duis autem vel eum iriure dolor in hendrerit in vulputate velit esse molestie consequat.

Duis autem vel eum dolor in hendrerit in vulputate velit esse molestie consequat, vel illum dolore eu feugiat nulla facilisis.

### COELACANTH MAKES QUITE A COMEBACK

Lorem ipsum dolor sit amet, consectetuer adipiscing elit, sed diam nonummy nibh euismod tincidunt ut laoreet dolore magna aliquam erat volutpat. Ut wisi enim ad minim veniam, quis nostrud exerci tation ullamcorp suscipit lobortis nisl ut aliquip ex ea commodo consequatvelit esse molestie consequat. Duis autem vel eum iriure dolor in hendrerit in vulputate velit esse molestie consequat, vel illum dolore eu feugiat nulla facilisis at vero eros et accumsan et iusto odio dignissim qui blandit praesent luptatum zzril delenit augue duis dolore te feugait nulla facilisi. suscipit lobortis. Lorem ipsum dolor sit amet, consectet adipiscing elit, sed diam nonummy nibh euismod tincidunt ut laoreet dolore magna minim veniam, quis aliquam erat volutpateu feugiat.

Ut wisi enim ad minim veniam, quis nostrud exerci tation ullamcorper suscipit lobortis nisl ut aliquip ex ea commodo consequat. Duis autem vel eum iriure dolor in hendrerit in vulputate velit esse molestie consequat, vel illum dolore eu feugiat nulla facilisis at vero eros et accumsan et iusto odio dignissim qui blandit praesent luptatum zzril delenit augue duis dolore nulla facilisi.

Nam liber tempor cum soluta nobis eleifend option congue nihil imperdiet doming id quod mazim placerat facer possim assum. Lorem ipsum dolor sit amet, consectetuer adipiscing elit, sed diam nonummy nibh euismod tincidunt ut laoreet dolore magna aliquam erat volutpat. Ut wisi enim ad minim veniam, quis nostrud exerci tation ullamcorper suscipit lobortis nisl ut aliquip consequat. Nam liber tempor cum soluta nobis congue nihil imperdiet.

## **Newsletters** (Makeover)

A looser, more unconventional design makes the newsletter's informality explicit.

Headlines are now half-buried in their corresponding stories—a visual pun on the newsletter's content, perhaps?

The table of contents has been integrated into the nameplate.

The empty column on the far left opens up the page, and provides a good place for the museum's logo.

IN THIS ISSUE

**2** Plaster of Paris–
Paleontology Pal

**4** Interview with
Winston Shovel

**3** Strange Reports
from Costa Rica

**6** Truths About
Triceratops

# THE FOSSIL RECORD

*Official Newsletter of the Lithicus Museum / July 1996*

### Dem bones, dem bones...

Lorem ipsum dolor sit amet, consectetuer adipiscing elit, sed diam nonummy nibh euismod tincidunt ut laoreet dolore magna aliquam erat volutpat. Ut wisi enim ad minim veniam, quis nostrud exerci tation ullamcorp suscipit lobortis nisl ut aliquip ex ea commodo consequatvelit esse molestie consequat. Duis autem vel eum iriure dolor in hendrerit in vulputate velit esse molestie consequat, vel illum dolore eu feugiat nulla facilisis at vero eros et accumsan et iusto odio dignissim qui blandit praesent luptatum zzril delenit augue duis dolore te feugait nulla facilisi. Lorem ipsum dolor sit amet, consectet adipiscing elit, sed diam nonummy nibh euismod tincidunt ut laoreet dolore magna aliquam erat volutpat.

Ut wisi enim ad minim veniam, quis nostrud exerci tation ullamcorper suscipit lobortis nisl ut aliquip ex ea commodo

consequat. Duis autem vel eum iriure dolor in hendrerit in vulputate velit esse molestie consequat, vel illum dolore eu feugiat nulla facilisis at vero eros et accumsan et iusto odio dignissim qui blandit praesent luptatum zzril delenit augue duis dolore nulla facili.

Nam liber tempor cum soluta nobis eleifend option congue nihil imperdiet doming id quod mazim placerat facer possim assum. Lorem ipsum dolor sit amet, consectetuer adipiscing elit, sed diam nonummy nibh euismod tincidunt ut laoreet dolore magna aliquam erat volutpat. Ut wisi enim ad minim veniam, quis nostrud exerci tation ullamcorper suscipit lobortis nisl ut aliquip ex ea commodo consequat. Duis autem vel eum iriure dolor in hendrerit in vulputate velit esse molestie consequat.

Duis autem vel eum dolor in hendrerit in vulputate velit esse molestie consequat, vel illum dolore eu feugiat nulla facilisis.

### Coelacanth makes quite a comeback

Lorem ipsum dolor sit amet, consectetuer adipiscing elit, sed diam nonummy nibh euismod tincidunt ut laoreet dolore magna aliquam erat volutpat. Ut wisi enim ad minim veniam, quis nostrud exerci tation ullamcorp suscipit lobortis nisl ut aliquip ex ea commodo consequatvelit esse molestie consequat. Duis autem vel eum iriure dolor in hendrerit in vulputate velit esse molestie consequat, vel illum dolore eu feugiat nulla facilisis at vero eros et accumsan et iusto odio dignissim qui blandit praesent luptatum zzril delenit augue duis dolore te feugait nulla facilisi. suscipit lobortis. Lorem ipsum dolor sit amet, consectet adipiscing elit, sed diam nonummy nibh euismod tincidunt ut laoreet dolore magna minim veniam, quis aliquam erat volutpateu feugiat.

LITHICUS
MUSEUM

Ut wisi enim ad minim veniam, quis nostrud exerci tation ullamcorper suscipit lobortis nisl ut aliquip ex ea commodo consequat. Duis autem vel eum iriure dolor in hendrerit in vulputate velit esse molestie consequat, vel illum dolore eu feugiat nulla facilisis at vero eros et accumsan et iusto odio dignissim qui blandit praesent luptatum zzril delenit augue duis dolore nulla facili.

Nam liber tempor cum soluta nobis eleifend option congue nihil imperdiet doming id quod mazim placerat facer possim assum. Lorem ipsum dolor sit amet, consectetuer adipiscing elit, sed diam nonummy nibh euismod tincidunt ut laoreet dolore magna aliquam erat volutpat. Ut wisi enim ad minim veniam, quis nostrud exerci tation ullamcorper suscipit lobortis nisl ut aliquip consequat. Nam liber tempor cum soluta nobis congue nihil imperdiet.

## Business Reports (Original)

The low-contrast, "gray" tone of business reports and memos often neutralizes the positive effects of good writing, persuasive argument, and strong evidence.

Typewritten text in a wide text column doesn't lend itself to speed-reading—an important consideration for a busy manager.

Although critical to the report, long blocks of supporting evidence tend to discourage readers.

Awkward spacing of data interrupts the flow of reading.

---

CURRENT SNOOZE ALARM SALES

As stated previously, we believe that a high number of present users of snooze alarm technology will want to own TardiSnooz. Current sales of snooze alarms have never been higher, as the figures below show:

| YEAR | # UNITS SOLD | $ RETAIL |
|------|-------------|----------|
| 1965 | 1,000 | $ 12,000 |
| 1970 | 65,000 | 430,000 |
| 1975 | 220,000 | 2,800,000 |
| 1980 | 673,000 | 5,900,000 |
| 1985 | 1,220,000 | 11,760,000 |

A corresponding trend of employee tardiness has become evident, particularly in the last ten years. In fact, some researchers believe that snooze alarms have indeed played a large part in causing employee tardiness. According to Real Life Information in Palo Alto, California, "Snooze alarm technology is largely responsible for the dramatic rise in employee tardiness and late calls. Further, the admonishment thrust upon the average employee, compounded by the guilt, feelings of inadequacy and consequent resentment, creates an unresolved <u>authority-figure conflict</u>, resulting in sharply decreased productivity.... One solution to this problem is a mechanism whereby the employee can at least call in late with a feeling of efficiency and accomplishment, instead of languishing in a <u>commuter-frustrated dissonance</u> on his or her way to work."

Clearly, the above findings indicate the need for added features to snooze technology. This, coupled with the fall in wholesale modem chip prices, could make TardiSnooz our sale item of the decade.

PROJECTED TARDISNOOZ SALES

Based on a 1,000-piece consumer survey mailed last month (see attached data), we found consumers receptive, and indeed eager, to pay the slightly higher price that TardiSnooze would command. Below are projected sales figures, based on out survey:

PROJECTED TARDISNOOZ SALES

| YEAR | # UNITS PROJECTED | $ RETAIL |
|------|-------------------|----------|
| 1990 | 34,000 | $ 430,000 |
| 1991 | 81,000 | 970,000 |
| 1992 | 239,000 | 2,400,000 |
| 1993 | 310,000 | 3,700,000 |
| 1994 | 228,000 (Break-even) | 2,200,000 |
| 1995 | 426,000 (Recession Projected) | 4,450,000 |

When you examine the above figures, and consider that all we have to do is add a $.93 modem chip to our present alarms, the conclusion is inescapable to all but the most ardent critics that our company should move forward with plans to implement our new "Tardi-Snooz" line of products. Accordingly, our current line of products should be gradually and unobtrusively discontinued, with the intention of disavowing any knowledge of these offerings at the beginning of the next fiscal year.

## **Business Reports** (Makeover)

Even the most basic layout software allows you to substitute informative charts, diagrams, and other visuals for text-based data.

A narrower text column makes for easy reading. Charts can be placed in the empty column, alongside the accompanying text.

Separating the research information from the rest of the body copy by thin rules underscores its importance.

Using indents rather than full line spaces to indicate new paragraphs can save space.

Snooze Alarm Sales 1965 — 1985

### Current Snooze Alarm Sales

As stated previously, we believe that a high number of present users of snooze alarm technology will want to own TardiSnooz. Current sales of snooze alarms have never been higher, as the figures at left show.

A corresponding trend of employee tardiness has become evident, particularly in the last ten years. In fact, some researchers believe that snooze alarms indeed played a large part in causing employee tardiness. Real Life Information, a statistical analysis firm located in Palo Alto, California, has this to say about snooze alarm technology:

*"Snooze alarm technology is largely responsible for the dramatic rise in employee tardiness and late calls. Further, the admonishment thrust upon the average by the guilt, feelings of inadequacy and consequent resentment, creates an unresolved authority figure conflict resulting in sharply decreased productivity.... One solution to this problem is a mechanism whereby the employee can at least call in late with feeling of efficiency and accomplishment, instead of languishing in commuter frustrated dissonance on his or her way to work."*

Clearly, the above findings indicate the need for added features to snooze technology. This, coupled with the fall in wholesale modem chip prices, could make TardiSnooz our sale item of the decade.

Based on a 1000- piece consumer survey mailed last month (see attached data), we found consumers receptive, and indeed eager to pay the slightly higher price that TardiSnooz would command. The graph at right shows the projected sales figures, based on our informal survey.

When you examine these figures, and consider that all we have to do is add a $.93 modem chip to our present alarms, the conclusion is inescapable to all but the most ardent critics that our company should move forward with implementing the new "Tardi-Snooz" line of products. Accordingly, our current line of products should be gradually and unobtrusively discontinued, with the intention of disavowing any knowledge of these offerings at the beginning of the next fiscal year.

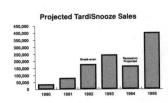

Projected TardiSnooze Sales

# SECTION FOUR

# Appendices

# Appendix A
# About the Companion CD-ROM

The CD-ROM included with your copy of *Looking Good In Print* contains valuable software programs. To view the CD-ROM:

- **Macintosh:** Double click on the LAUNCHME icon after opening the CD on your desktop. You'll see a menu screen offering several choices. See the "Navigating the CD-ROM" section below for your options.

- **Windows 3.1/Windows 95/Windows NT:** Double click on the LAUNCHME.EXE file from your Window Explorer or File Manager.

## Navigating the CD-ROM

Your choices for navigating the CD-ROM appear on the opening screen. You can quit the CD, view the software, browse the Hot Picks, or learn more about Ventana.

The software, textures, and icons are listed in the Install folder on the CD. You can install the items one at a time to your hard drive by dragging them from the folder onto your desktop.

- **For Macintosh users:** If the Ventana Viewer does not run properly on your machine, you may install the software using their individual folders.

- **For Windows users:** If you have trouble running the CD, copy LAUNCHME.EXE to your hard drive and execute it from Windows Explorer or File Manager.

## Software on the Companion CD-ROM

| Software | Descriptions |
| --- | --- |
| Adobe Acrobat 2.1 | a portable document viewer |
| BBEdit Lite 3.5.1 | a text editor for the Macintosh |
| BBEdit 4.0 Demo | a powerful text editor for the Macintosh |
| Catalog | Curtis Catalog demo |
| DeBabelizer Lite LE | reads and writes BMP, PICT, TIFF, and GIF formats |
| DeBabelizer Toolbox Demo | demo of DeBabelizer's tools |
| GifBuilder 0.4 | creates animated GIF files |
| GIF Converter | an image conversion utility |
| Graphic Converter | a graphic conversion utility |
| HTML Editor | an HTML editing tool |
| JPEGView | an image editor |
| Lview Pro | a shareware image editor |
| Mapserve | a Macintosh image mapping utility |
| PaintShop Pro | an image editing and creation package |
| Page Draw | a Web page creation tool |
| PhotoGIF 1.1.4 | plug-in for Adobe Photoshop |
| PM2HTML | converts PageMaker file to HTML |
| RTF2HTML | converts RFT to HTML |
| SpeedBook | SpeedBook demo |
| ThumbsPlus | graphics file viewer, browser and cataloger |
| Transparency 1.04b | a freeware that makes images transparent |
| WebForms 2.1b | creates Web forms |
| WebImage 1.72 16-bit | an image utility for the Web |
| WebImage 1.72 | 32-bit an image utility for the Web |
| XL2HTML | converts Microsoft Excel spreadsheets to HTML |

*LView Pro software Copyright © 1993-1996 by Leonardo Haddad Loureiro.*

*In the Images folder, the 54 images from Adobe and Image Club are used with express permission. Adobe® and Image Club Graphics™ are trademarks of Adobe Systems Incorporated.*

## Technical Support

Technical support is available for installation-related problems only. The technical support office is open from 8:00 AM to 6:00 PM Monday through Friday and can be reached via the following methods:

Phone: (919) 544-9404, extension 81
Faxback Answer System: (919) 544-9404, extension 85
E-mail: help@vmedia.com
Fax: (919) 544-9472
World Wide Web: http://www.vmedia.com/support
America Online: keyword Ventana

## Limits of Liability & Disclaimer of Warranty

The author and publisher of this book have used their best efforts in preparing the CD-ROM and the programs contained in it. These efforts include the development, research, and testing of the theories and programs to determine their effectiveness. The author and publisher make no warranty of any kind expressed or implied, with regard to these programs or the documentation contained in this book.

The author and publisher shall not be liable in the event of incidental or consequential damages in connection with, or arising out of, the furnishing, performance, or use of the programs, associated instructions, and/or claims of productivity gains.

Some of the software on this CD-ROM is shareware; there may be additional charges (owed to the software authors/ makers) incurred for their registration and continued use. See individual program's README or VREADME.TXT files for more information.

## Appendix B
# Clip Art, Photographs & Font Resources

As a desktop designer, you may be interested in incorporating photographs and clip art into your documents or using new fonts. But where do you start? Where do you find clip art? Where do you go for photographs? How about fonts?

This appendix offers some guidance on locating clip art, photos, and fonts. Professional-quality electronic clip art is widely available for any kind of desktop publishing platform. As with fonts and photos, clip art can be bought through mail-order vendors, in retail outlets, direct from the manufacturer, and via the Internet. The following are some good resources.

- 3G Services
  114 Second Ave. South, Suite 104
  Edmonds, WA 98020
  (800) 456-0234

  Provides a huge CD-ROM collection of excellent images and color line drawings ranging from cartoons to realistic. Images from this extensive and impressive collection can be edited easily using Adobe Illustrator. Files are stored in several formats, including black-and-white and color EPS and PICT file formats.

- Cliptures by Dream Maker Software
  925 West Kenyon Ave., Suite 16
  Englewood, CO 80110
  (800) 876-5665
     Provides a collection of EPS images, including business and sports graphics. Cliptures also features an extensive collection of flags. Look for their Web site soon.

- Comstock Photos
  30 Irving Place
  New York, NY 10003
  (800) 225-2727
     Comstock is one of the larger stock photo agencies. CDs contain images related to business, health and fitness, travel and vacations, and people. The images vary in size and resolution.

- Husom & Rose Photographics
  1988 Stanford Ave.
  St. Paul, MN 55105
  (612) 699-1858
     Husom & Rose's Photographics disk contains a wide variety of general photos, including people, places, backgrounds, clouds, trees, water, and other nature images. The files are available in both high-resolution 24-bit color TIFF and screen-resolution PICT formats.

- Photodisc
  2013 Fourth Avenue
  Seattle, WA 98121
  (800) 528-3472
  http://www.photodisc.com
     A long time favorite, Photodisc sells contemporary images by the volumes. You'll find lifestyle shots, vignettes, and something from nearly every theme you can imagine.

## News Services & Historical Archives

Similar to stock photo companies, some news organizations license secondary use of photos originally taken for and printed in newspapers, magazines, and other publications. News services may offer their images as prints, slides, or on disk. Some even upload photos to online services, where you can pay to download and use them.

Many universities, public libraries, historical societies, and other organizations maintain massive collections of photographs related to a specific field of study or local interest. If you're working on a specific project, many organizations will lend you photos from their archives free of charge.

- Image Club Graphics & Fonts
  (800) 387-9193
  http://www.imageclub.com/
      Order an Image Club catalog to browse their collections of fonts and other graphics. You'll also find desktop publishing tips and the latest offerings in software.

- T/Maker ClickArt
  1390 Villa Street
  Mountain View, CA 94041
  (415) 962-0195
      Collections of fonts, cartoons, photos, and clip art that you can order from their catalog.

## Appendix C
# Resources for Desktop Publishers

Mastering design and desktop publishing can't be done in a day, or in a week or month for that matter. Methods, styles, and trends are constantly evolving and like all disciplines, these require a long-term commitment to keep looking, reading, asking, and experimenting.

The resources listed here can help you locate everything from high-quality design seminars to great books that help you look good in print.

## Books

- The Afga Prepress Series:
  - *An Introduction to Digital Color Prepress*
  - *Working With Prepress and Printing Suppliers*
  - *An Introduction to Digital Scanning*
  - *An Introduction to Digital Photo Imaging*
  - *Postscript Process Color Guide*

  Afga Prepress Education Resources, P.O. Box 7917, Mt. Prospect, IL, 60056, (800) 395-7007.

- American Press Institute. *Newspaper Design: 2000 and Beyond*. Reston, VA: American Press Institute, 1989.

  Contains "before" and "after" versions of some of the country's most famous newspapers, showing how they are adapting to changing reader tastes in the television age. The use of full color throughout this publication adds to its visual impact.

- Baker, Kim and Sunny Baker. *Color Publishing on the Macintosh: From Desktop to Print Shop*. New York: Random House, 1992.

- Beach, Mark. *Graphically Speaking: An Illustrated Guide to the Working Language of Design & Printing*. Manzanita, OR: Coast to Coast Books, 1992.

- Beaumont, Michael. *Type: Design, Color, Character & Use*. Cincinnati: North Light Books, 1991.

- Berry, Susan and Judy Martin. *Designing With Color*. Cincinnati: North Light Books, 1991.

- Binns, Betty. *Better Type: Learn to see subtle distinctions in the faces and spaces of text type*. New York: Watson-Guptill, 1989.

  Concise text with numerous illustrations showing how the slightest changes in letter, line, and word spacing can have a major effect on a publication's appearance and readability.

- Binns, Betty. *Designing With Two Colors*. New York: Watson-Guptill Publications, 1991.

- Bly, Robert W. *The Copywriter's Handbook*. New York: Henry Holt & Co., 1990.

  An entertaining but thorough review of the tools of effective copywriting that can restore vigor to tired copy.

- Bly, Robert W. *Secrets of a Freelance Writer*. New York: Henry Holt & Co., 1990.

    Although focused on surviving as a freelance writer, many of the ideas in this book can be used by freelance graphic designers and desktop publishers too.

- Brown, Alex. *In Print: Text and Type in the Age of Desktop Publishing*. New York: Watson-Guptill, 1989.

    Combines concise, highly readable descriptions of the aesthetic qualities of different typefaces and techniques to make effective use of any typeface.

- Burke, Clifford. *Type From the Desktop: Designing With Type and Your Computer*. RTP, NC: Ventana, 1990.

    A thought-provoking exploration into the world of typography and design. Filled with type examples, this book explores the functions and aesthetics of type.

- Cook, Alton, ed. *Type and Color: A Handbook of Creative Combinations*. Rockport, MA: Rockport Publications, 1989.

    Previews more than 800,000 possible type/background combinations. Contains more than 100 pages of color samples and removable acetate overlays to let you experiment with black, colored, or reversed type on a variety of background colors.

- Dayton, Linnea and Jack Davis. *The Photoshop 3 Wow! Book*. Berkeley, CA: Peachpit Press, 1995.

- Finberg, Howard I., and Bruce D Itule. *Visual Editing: A Graphic Guide for Journalists*. Belmont, CA: Wadsworth, 1990.

    More than just guidelines for the effective use of photographs, charts and information graphics, *Visual Editing* thoroughly investigates how computerized publishing is revolutionizing newspaper production.

- Floyd, Elaine. *Advertising From the Desktop, Second Edition: The Desktop Publisher's Guide to Designing Ads That Work.* RTP, NC: Ventana, 1994.

  Put Madison Avenue in your mouse! *Advertising From the Desktop* provides readers with savvy design advice and helpful how-to instructions for creating persuasive ads on the computer. For use with any hardware or software, the book is a unique, idea-packed resource for improving the look and effect of desktop-produced ads.

- Floyd, Elaine. *Marketing With Newsletters: How to Boost Sales, Add Members and Raise Funds With a Printed, Faxed or Web Site Newsletter, Second Edition.* New Orleans: Newsletter Resources, 1997.

  Shows for-profit and non-profit organizations how to promote themselves with a newsletter. Includes information on newsletter content, writing, and design. Also: information on setting a budget, saving money, developing a readership base, surveying readers, coordinating the newsletter with other marketing projects, and finding subcontractors. Over 200 illustrations and sidebars emphasize text discussions.

- Gosney, Michael, John Odam, and Jim Schmal. *The Gray Book, Second Edition: Designing in Black & White on Your Computer.* RTP, NC: Ventana, 1993.

  This "idea gallery" offers a lavish variety of the most interesting black, white, and gray graphic effects from laser printers, scanners, and high-resolution output devices.

- Grossmann, Joe. *The Makeover Book: 101 Design Solutions for Online & Desktop Publishers.* RTP, NC: Ventana, 1996.

  Hundreds of examples, tips, and techniques that let you compare original documents with their makeovers.

- Grossmann, Joe, with David Doty. *Newsletters From the Desktop, Second Edition: Designing Effective Publications With Your Computer.* RTP, NC: Ventana, 1994.

- Lichty, Tom. *Desktop Publishing With Word for Windows for 2.0*. RTP, NC: Ventana, 1993.

    Provides Word users with the design know-how necessary for creating successful, appealing documents. Contains chapters on the use of typography, style sheets, graphic placement, and more.

- Mansfield, Richard. *Desktop Publishing With WordPerfect 6.0*. RTP, NC: Ventana, 1993.

    Offers a wealth of advice and examples for creating documents, working with graphics, and creating style sheets. Addresses new tools and techniques available in WordPerfect 6.0, including the GUI, customizable button bar, WYSIWYG editing, dialog boxes, and more.

- Moen, Daryl R. *Newspaper Layout and Design*. 2nd ed. Ames, IA: Iowa State University Press, 1989.

    Detailed analysis of the component parts of a modern newspaper, including observations on current trends.

- Monroy, Bert, and David Biedny. *Adobe Photoshop: A Visual Guide for the Mac*. Addison-Wesley Publishing Company, 1996.

- DiNucci, Darcy, ed. *The Macintosh Bible*. 5th ed. Berkeley, CA: Peachpit Press, 1994.

    An invaluable aid for both experienced and first-time Macintosh users. Contains capsule reviews of hardware and software plus software-specific practical tips on the most popular programs.

- Nelson, Roy Paul. *The Design of Advertising*. 6th ed. Dubuque, IA: William C. Brown, 1989.

    A no-nonsense favorite, focusing on effective use of color, space, and typography when designing magazine and newspaper ads.

- Nelson, Roy Paul. *Publication Design*. 5th ed. Dubuque, IA: William C. Brown, 1989.

  This large-format volume focuses on the challenges presented by the various types of publications.

- Nemoy, Sheldon, and C.J. Aiken. *Looking Good With CorelDRAW for Version 4.0*. 2nd ed. RTP, NC: Ventana, 1993.

  Guidelines and suggestions are offered for taking advantage of CorelDRAW's newest features. Two galleries of annotated artwork feature a stunning array of award-winning black-and-white and four-color illustrations.

- One Club for Art and Copy, Inc. *The One Show: Judged to Be Advertising's Best in Print, Radio and TV*. Vol. 14. New York: One Club for Art & Copy, 1992.

  The annually published *The One Show* is a lavishly illustrated, large-format book containing full-color reproductions of award-winning advertisements of all types. *The One Show* often provides fresh insight into solutions for your current design problems.

- Parker, Roger C. *Desktop Publishing With WordPerfect for 5.0 & 5.1*. 2nd ed. RTP, NC: Ventana, 1990.

  *Desktop Publishing With WordPerfect* includes invaluable information on organizing your documents into attractive layouts, working with graphics, and creating style sheets for consistency and speed.

- Parker, Roger C. *Newsletters From the Desktop: Designing Effective Publications With Your Computer*. RTP, NC: Ventana, 1990.

  This desktop design guide offers a wealth of desktop publishing techniques and design advice for producing your newsletter, including layout suggestions, creating the nameplate, and selecting typefaces.

- Pattison, Polly, Mary Pretzer, and Mark Beach. *Outstanding Newsletter Designs*. Available from: Polly Pattison, 5092 Kingscross Rd., Westminster, CA 92683.

  A potpourri of inspirational ideas for newspaper publishers. Any one of its ideas is well worth the cost of this fully illustrated, large-format book.

- Rabb, Margaret Y. *The Presentation Design Book: Tips Techniques & Advice for Creating Effective, Attractive Slides, Overheads, Screen Shows, Multimedia & More*. 2nd ed. RTP, NC: Ventana, 1993.

  This general design guide reviews the essentials of creating good-looking slides, overheads, charts, diagrams, and handouts. Alerts you to basic pitfalls of producing presentation graphics, and provides examples of how to choose and tailor the best medium for your audience.

- Shushan, Ronnie, and Don Wright with Laura Lewis. *Desktop Publishing by Design: Everyone's Guide to PageMaker 6, Fourth Edition*. Microsoft Press, 1996.

- Sitarz, Daniel. *The Desktop Publisher's Legal Handbook: A Comprehensive Guide to Computer Publishing Law*. Carbondale, IL: Nova Publishing, 1989.

  A new set of challenges faces writers who become publishers. This concise volume provides copyright information essential to today's computer-based publishers.

- Strunk, William, Jr., and E. B White. *The Elements of Style*. 3rd ed. New York: Macmillan, 1979.

  Required reading for all desktop publishers, writers, and editors. Provides an entertaining review of the basics of effective writing, as well as a quick reference for grammar and usage issues.

- Swann, Alan. *How to Understand and Use Design and Layout*. Cincinnati, OH: North Light Books, 1991.

  This handsomely illustrated volume does an excellent job of balancing theory and practical example. Numerous rough layouts illustrate various formats and ways of placing type on a page.

- Ueland, Brenda. *If You Want to Write: A Book About Art and Spirit, Second Edition*. St. Paul, MN: Graywolf Press, 1987.

- Wallace, Rick. *Special Edition: Using PageMaker 6 for the Mac.* Macmillan Publishing, 1996.

- Weinman, Lynn. *Designing Web Graphics*. Macmillan Publishing, 1995.

- White, Alex. *Type in Use*. New York: Design Press, 1992.
  Further explores the seemingly infinite number of ways type can be placed and manipulated on a page. Contains hundreds of thought-provoking examples.

- White, Jan. *Color for the Electronic Age*. New York: Watson-Guptill, 1990.
  Demonstrates, in dozens of examples, many shown in three stages (no color, badly used color, cleverly used color), how color can be used to enhance text, charts, and graphs.

- Zinsser, William. *On Writing Well: An Informal Guide to Writing Nonfiction*. 4th ed. New York: Harper & Row, 1990.
  This is a book you'll want to use over and over again, long after you've read it the first time. Emphasizes the importance of clarity and simplicity.

## Periodicals

- *Adobe Magazine*, Adobe Systems Incorporated, 1585 Charleston Rd., P.O. Box 7900, Mountain View, CA 94039, (206) 628-2321.

- *Aldus Magazine*, Aldus Corp., 411 First Ave. South, Seattle, WA 98104. Bimonthly, with special issues throughout the year.
  Helpful hints and general information for all registered users of Aldus PageMaker and Freehand, by request. One idea can save you dozens of hours of work.

- *Before & After: How to Design Cool Stuff on Your Computer*, PageLab, 1830 Sierra Gardens Dr., #30, Roseville, CA 95661-2912, (916) 784-3880. Bimonthly.

  This exciting, full-color, bimonthly publication is full of tips and techniques for advanced desktop publishers and those who want to become advanced desktop publishers. Concisely written and profusely illustrated, not an inch of wasted space.

- *Communication Arts*, Coyne & Blanchard, 410 Sherman Ave., Palo Alto, CA 94306, (415) 326-6040. Eight issues/year.

  Traditional required reading for art directors and graphic designers, now devoting increased space to desktop publishing concerns. Special focus issues showcase samples of the year's best designs in advertising, illustration, and photography.

- *Design Tools Monthly*, The Nelson Group, 2111 30th Street, Suite H, Boulder, CO 80301, (303) 444-6876. Classes: (303) 589-2932.

- *Digital Chicago*, Peregrine Marketing Associates, 515 E. Golf Road, Suite 201, Arlington Heights, IL 60005, (847) 439-6575. Bimonthly.

- *Font & Function: The Adobe Type Catalog*, Adobe Systems, P.O. Box 7900, Mountain View, CA 94039-7900. Three times a year.

  This free publication includes articles on new typeface designs, gives samples of Adobe typefaces in use, and shows specimens of all available Adobe fonts.

- *In-House Graphics*, United Communications, 11300 Rockville Pike, Ste. 1100, Rockville, MD 20852-3030, (301) 816-8950, (800) 929-4824. Monthly.

  Practical advice for results-oriented graphic designers. Previous articles have ranged from the use of metallic inks and software-specific design techniques to compensation trends for designers and desktop publishers.

- *International Typeface*, 866 Second Ave., New York, NY 10017. Bimonthly.

    This free large-format tabloid contains features written by many of the world's leading typeface designers. It balances a historical perspective with down-to-earth treatment of contemporary publishing issues.

- *Newsletter Design*, Newsletter Clearinghouse, 44 West Market St., P.O. Box 311, Rhinebeck, NY 12572. Monthly.

    A visual treat, each month's issue contains illustrations on the front cover and inside spreads of over 20 newsletters, along with detailed commentary on their strengths and weaknesses. Provides numerous ideas that can be incorporated into your newsletter.

- *Newsletter News: Ideas & Inspiration for Promoters & Editors*, Newsletter Resources, 6614 Pernod Ave., St. Louis MO 63139, (314) 647-6788. Quarterly.

- *Newsletter on Newsletters*, Newsletter Clearinghouse, 44 West Market St., P.O. Box 311, Rhinebeck, NY 12572. Biweekly.

    Want to know what's going on in the newsletter business? This concise publication contains a capsule look, along with features focusing on graphic, economic, postal, and promotional issues.

- *The Page*, The Cobb Group, 9420 Bunsen Pkwy, Suite 300, Louisville, KY 40220, (800) 223-8720.

- *The Page*, P.O. Box 14493, Chicago, IL 60614. Ten issues/year.

    A delightful publication written for Macintosh desktop publishers. *The Page* is an impartial, informed, and reader-friendly look at Macintosh desktop publishing from a hands-on perspective.

- *Print*: *America's Graphic Design Magazine*, RC Publications, Inc., 3200 Tower Oaks Blvd., Rockville, MD 20852, (800) 222-2654. Bimonthly.

    The techniques and economics of professional graphic design, with an eye on advances in desktop publishing. Its yearly regional design and advertising design issues by themselves justify its subscription price.

- *Publish!* Integrated Media, Inc., P.O. Box 5039, Brentwood, TN 37024, (800) 685-3435.

    In-depth critiques of the latest hardware and software, along with design and technique oriented articles. Of special interest is its monthly typography column.

- *Step-By-Step Electronic Design: The How-to Newsletter for Desktop Designers*, Dynamic Graphics, 6000 N. Forest Park Dr., P.O. Box 1901, Peoria, IL 61614-3592, (800) 255-8800. Monthly.

    Advertising-free, technique oriented advice for advanced desktop publishers and others who aspire to greater expertise in layout and design.

- *X-Ray Magazine*, P.O. Box 200068, Denver, CO 80220, (415) 861-9258. Bimonthly.

## Seminars & Training

- Career Track, 3085 Center Green Dr., M/S 2, Boulder, CO 80301-5408, (303) 447-2323 or (800) 334-6780

    Offers seminars, audios, and videos on a wide range of desktop publishing and newsletter-related subjects as well as management communication and personal development subjects.

- Dynamic Graphics & Education Foundation, 6000 N. Forest Park Dr., Peoria, IL 61614-3592, (309) 688-8800 or (800) 255-8800

  Sponsors both generic and software-specific workshops throughout the world focusing on desktop publishing design issues.

- Cowles Business Media, 11 River Bend Dr. S., Box 4949, Stamford, CT 06907, (800) 927-5007

  Each year *Folio: The Magazine for Magazine Management* presents a series of two- and three-day conferences around the country, featuring presentations by leading designers and other professionals.

- Image Inc., 45 E. 30th (15th floor), New York, NY 10016, (800) 513-3011.

- National Association of Desktop Publishers, 462 Boston St., Topsfield, MA 01983, (508) 887-7900

  Professional organization for desktop publishers. Publishes *The Journal* (hardware and software reviews, how-to articles, job, show, and equipment directories).

- Newsletter Publishers Association, 1501 Wilson Blvd., Ste. 500, Arlington, VA 22209, (703) 527-2333, (800) 356-9302

  Sponsors seminars and publishes periodicals for newsletter editors.

- Newsletter Clearinghouse, P.O. Box 311, Rhinebeck, NY 12572, (914) 876-2081, (800) 572-3451.

  Publishes books and newsletters, membership listings, and special reports. Sponsors conferences, seminars, and design competition. Monthly newsletter: *Newsletter Design*. Seminar: "How to Start a Newsletter." Bimonthly newsletter: *Newsletters on Newsletters*.

- Onsite Advertisers, 1828 Westgate Ave., Royal Oak, MI 48073, (810) 542-6230

  Offers seminars on design for desktop publishers including newsletter design, custom database programming, Web pages, and more.

- Padgett-Thompson, 11221 Roe Ave., Leawood, KS 66211, (913) 491-2700 or (800) 255-4141

  A division of American Management Association, the nation's oldest not-for-profit business training organization; offers one- and two-day seminars on desktop publishing, newsletters, copywriting, editing, and proofreading.

- Promotional Perspectives, 1829 W. Stadium Blvd., Ste. 101, Ann Arbor, MI 48103, (313) 994-0007.

# Index

# VENTANA

## Macromedia Director 5 Power Toolkit

*$49.95, 552 pages, illustrated, part #: 1-56604-289-5*

Macromedia Director 5 Power Toolkit views the industry's hottest multimedia authoring environment from the inside out. Features tools, tips and professional tricks for producing power-packed projects for CD-ROM and Internet distribution. Dozens of exercises detail the principles behind successful multimedia presentations and the steps to achieve professional results. The companion CD-ROM includes utilities, sample presentations, animations, scripts and files.

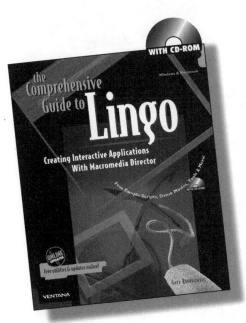

## The Comprehensive Guide to Lingo

*$49.99, 700 pages, illustrated, part #: 1-56604-463-4*

Master the Lingo of Macromedia Director's scripting language for adding interactivity to presentations. Covers beginning scripts to advanced techniques, including creating movies for the Web and problem solving. The companion CD-ROM features demo movies of all scripts in the book, plus numerous examples, a searchable database of problems and solutions, and much more!

## Shockwave!

*$49.95, 400 pages, illustrated, part #: 1-56604-441-3*

Breathe new life into your web pages with Macromedia Shockwave. *Shockwave!* teaches you how to enliven and animate your Web sites with online movies. Beginning with step-by-step exercises and examples, and ending with in-depth excursions into the use of Shockwave Lingo extensions, *Shockwave!* is a must-buy for both novices and experienced Director developers. Plus, tap into current Macromedia resources on the Internet with Ventana's Online Companion. The companion CD-ROM includes the Shockwave plug-in, sample Director movies and tutorials, and much more!

# VENTANA

## Official Online Marketing With Netscape Book

*$34.99, 544 pages, illustrated, part #: 1-56604-453-7*

The perfect marketing tool for the Internet! Learn how innovative marketers create powerful, effective electronic newsletters and promotional materials. Step-by-step instructions show you how to plan, design and distribute professional-quality pieces. With this easy-to-follow guide, you'll soon be flexing Netscape Navigator's marketing muscle to eliminate paper and printing costs, automate market research and customer service, and much more.

## Official Netscape Guide to Online Investments

*$24.99, 528 pages, illustrated, part #: 1-56604-452-9*

Gain the Internet investment edge! Here's everything you need to make the Internet a full financial partner. Features an overview of the Net and Navigator; in-depth reviews of stock and bond quote services, analysts, brokerage houses, and mutual fund reports. Plus a full listing of related financial services such as loans, appraisals, low-interest credit cards, venture capital, entrepreneurship, insurance, tax counseling, and more.

## Official Netscape Guide to Internet Research

*$29.99, 480 pages, illustrated, part #: 1-56604-604-1*

Turn the Internet into your primary research tool. More than just a listing of resources, this official guide provides everything you need to know to access, organize, cite and post information on the Net. Includes research strategies, search engines and information management. Plus timesaving techniques for finding the best, most up-to-date data.

# VENTANA

## Official Netscape Messenger & Collabra Book

*$39.99, 352 pages, part #: 1-56604-685-8*

Windows, Macintosh • Intermediate to Advanced

**The Power of Web-based Communications—Without a Web Site!**
Stay in touch with customers; promote products and services visually; share the latest market trends—with simple Internet dial-up access! This step-by-step guide helps you harness Netscape Communicator's e-mail, newsreader, HTML authoring and real-time conference tools to achieve faster, more powerful business communications—without the effort or expense of a Web site. Learn how to:
- Integrate Messenger, Collabra, Conference and Composer for efficient business communications.
- Distribute eye-catching, HTML-based marketing materials without a Web site.
- Use the Net to gather, organize and share information efficiently.

## Official Netscape Composer Book

*$39.99, 600 pages, part #: 1-56604-674-2*

Windows • Beginning to Intermediate

Forget about tedious tags and cumbersome code! Now you can create sophisticated, interactive Web pages using simple, drag-and-drop techniques. Whether you want to create your personal home page, promote your hobby, or launch your business on the Web, here's everything you need to know to get started:
- Step-by-step instructions for designing sophisticated Web sites with no previous experience.
- JavaScript basics and techniques for adding multimedia, including animation and interactivity.
- Tips for businesses on the Web, including creating forms, ensuring security and promoting a Web site.

The CD-ROM features a wide selection of Web tools for designing Web pages, adding multimedia, creating forms and building image maps.

## Official Netscape Plug-in Book, Second Edition

*$39.99, 700 pages, part #: 1-56604-612-2*

Windows, Macintosh • All Users

**Your One-Stop Plug-in Resource & Desktop Reference!**
Why waste expensive online time searching the Net for the plug-ins you want? This handy one-stop reference includes in-depth reviews, easy-to-understand instructions and step-by-step tutorials. And you avoid costly download time—the hottest plug-ins are included! Features:
- In-depth reviews & tutorials for most Netscape plug-ins.
- Professional tips on designing pages with plug-ins.
- Fundamentals of developing your own plug-ins.

The CD-ROM includes all the featured plug-ins available at press time.

# VENTANA

## The Director 6 Book

*$49.99, 560 pages, part #: 1-56604-658-0*

Macintosh, Windows 95/NT
Intermediate to Advanced

Raise your standards—and your stock—as a multimedia specialist by harnessing what's new in Macromedia Director 6. This professional-level guide focuses on key techniques for creating, manipulating and optimizing files. Your projects will look, sound and play back better and more consistently than ever.
Provides:
• Undocumented tricks for Director 6.
• Tips for moving from Director 5 to 6.
• Issues and answers for cross-platform presentations.
• Techniques for integrating Director 6 with JavaScript, CGI and Shockwave audio.

The CD-ROM includes more than 50 sample Director movies with code included, plus Macromedia and gmatter Xtras, shareware and more.

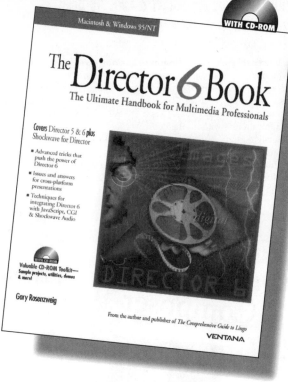

## The Lingo Programmer's Reference

*$39.99, 672 pages, part #: 1-56604-695-5*

Windows 95/NT, Macintosh
Intermediate to Advanced

The Ultimate Resource for Director Professionals! High-level mastery of Lingo is the only route to real Director expertise. This comprehensive reference goes beyond tutorials and simple listings to provide thorough explanations of every aspect of Lingo, supported by practical examples, professional tips and undocumented tricks. Includes:
• What's new in Director 6, property lists for sprites and other objects, and a JavaScript reference for Lingo programmers.
• In-depth discussions, including types of parameters to pass to properties, commands, functions and type of data returned.
• Encyclopedic listing, extensively cross-referenced for easy access to information.

The CD-ROM features a searchable, hyperlinked version of the book.

# VENTANA

## FreeHand 7 Graphics Studio
## The Comprehensive Guide

*R. Shamms Mortier*
*$49.99, 800 pages, illustrated, part #: 679-3*

**A master class in cutting-edge graphics!** Express
your creative powers to the fullest in print, on the
Web, on CD-ROM—anywhere sophisticated imagery
is in demand. Step-by-step exercises help you master
each component—Freehand 7, xRes, Fontographer
and Extreme3D—with professional guidelines for
using them separately, together, and in partnership
with third-party products.
**CD-ROM:** Sample files, sample web pages, free
Xtras, plug-ins & more!

*For Windows, Macintosh • Intermediate to Advanced*

## Web Publishing With Macromedia Backstage
## Internet Studio 2

*R. Shamms Mortier, Winston Steward*
*$49.99, 448 pages, illustrated, part #: 598-3*

Farewell to HTML! This overview of all four tiers of
Backstage Internet Studio 2 lets users jump in at
their own level. With the focus on processes as well
as techniques, readers learn everything they need to
create center-stage pages.

**CD-ROM:** Plug-ins, applets, animations, audio files,
Director xTras and demos.

*For Windows, Macintosh • Intermediate to Advanced*

# VENTANA

## Web Publishing With Adobe PageMill 2

*$34.99, 480 pages, illustrated, part #: 1-56604-458-8*

Now, creating and designing professional pages on the Web is a simple, drag-and-drop function. Learn to pump up PageMill with tips, tricks and troubleshooting strategies in this step-by-step tutorial for designing professional pages. The CD-ROM features Netscape plug-ins, original textures, graphical and text-editing tools, sample backgrounds, icons, buttons, bars, GIF and JPEG images, Shockwave animations.

## Web Publishing With QuarkImmedia

*$39.99, 552 pages, illustrated, part #: 1-56604-525-8*

Use multimedia to learn multimedia, building on the power of QuarkXPress. Step-by-step instructions introduce basic features and techniques, moving quickly to delivering dynamic documents for the Web and other electronic media. The CD-ROM features an interactive manual and sample movie gallery with displays showing settings and steps. Both are written in QuarkImmedia.

# VENTANA

## TO ORDER ANY VENTANA TITLE, COMPLETE THIS ORDER FORM AND MAIL OR FAX IT TO US, WITH PAYMENT, FOR QUICK SHIPMENT.

| TITLE | PART # | QTY | PRICE | TOTAL |
|-------|--------|-----|-------|-------|
|       |        |     |       |       |
|       |        |     |       |       |
|       |        |     |       |       |
|       |        |     |       |       |
|       |        |     |       |       |
|       |        |     |       |       |
|       |        |     |       |       |
|       |        |     |       |       |
|       |        |     |       |       |

## SHIPPING

For orders shipping within the United States, please add $4.95 for the first book, $1.50 for each additional book.
For "two-day air," add $7.95 for the first book, $3.00 for each additional book.
Email: vorders@kdc.com for exact shipping charges.
Note: Please include your local sales tax.

SUBTOTAL = $ _____

SHIPPING = $ _____

TAX = $ _____

TOTAL = $ _____

**Mail to: International Thomson Publishing • 7625 Empire Drive • Florence, KY 41042**
☎ **US orders 800/332-7450 • fax 606/283-0718**
☎ **International orders 606/282-5786 • Canadian orders 800/268-2222**

Name _____

E-mail _____ Daytime phone _____

Company _____

Address (No PO Box) _____

City _____ State _____ Zip _____

Payment enclosed ____VISA ____MC ____ Acc't # _____ Exp. date _____

Signature _____ Exact name on card _____

Check your local bookstore or software retailer for these and other bestselling titles, or call toll free:

# 800/332-7450

8:00 am - 6:00 pm EST